Speaking and Writing Spanish

SPEAKING AND WRITING
Spanish

FREDERICK B. AGARD

ANGELA PARATORE

RAYMOND S. WILLIS, JR.

London

DAILY EXPRESS LANGUAGE COURSES
FLEET STREET · LONDON · E.C.4

*First published in Great Britain
in 1956*

Reprinted 1958

© *Oldbourne Press*

PRINTED IN GREAT BRITAIN
BY JARROLD AND SONS LIMITED, NORWICH

PREFACE

The aim of this course is, first to teach you to speak everyday Spanish and understand it when you hear it spoken; second, to read and write the Spanish that you learn to talk. Although it is a course for beginners, it is designed so that you will be able to put what you learn to practical use immediately.

We, the authors, believe that control of the spoken language is the first requisite, whatever ultimate use — reading, writing, understanding, or speaking — you make of Spanish. If you are primarily interested in a reading knowledge, you should supplement the course with additional reading texts.

The language is presented through real conversations which are to be heard and imitated, rather than through lists of words and grammatical "rules" for putting the words together into sentences. In these conversations (called *Basic Dialogues*), all the words and the grammatical patterns you are expected to acquire appear for the first time. The conversations will be presented orally by the native speaker on the records. You are to imitate the words of the speaker phrase by phrase, model and mimic them repeatedly until you have "overlearned" them.

As you listen to the *Basic Dialogues*, it is intended that you follow with your eye the column entitled "Aids to Listening." You will also find it helpful to refer to this column when you speak the dialogues by yourself. Each symbol of the transcription given in the Aids to Listening consistently represents one and the same sound of spoken Spanish.

Once you have mastered the words and phrases of the *Basic Dialogues* you will be able to understand and reproduce the related conversations from real life found in the *Listening In* section of each unit. These words and phrases, too, will be your model upon which to build new conversations varying the content to include words, expressions, and constructions you learned in earlier units.

In the *Grammatical Analyses* of each unit, the essential patterns of the spoken language are systematized and described in terms of forms and expressions that you have already learned. The *Grammatical Drills* give practice in applying and extending these principles. In this way grammar becomes, as you proceed, an aid to flexibility of expression, but never an end in itself.

Every fifth unit in the course is devoted to review, primarily of the four immediately preceding units. Features peculiar to the review units include a series of question-and-answer exercises, a series of sentences for translation from English into Spanish, and a reference vocabulary of the new words first introduced in the units under review.

We have tried to make the subject-matter of the dialogues as practical as possible and have concentrated on normal, everyday conversations in which you would naturally take part when you first try out your Spanish.

PREFACE

The vocabulary of the course is small enough and practical enough to be mastered in its entirety. It comprises approximately 1200 basic entries of highest frequency in spoken and written Spanish.

Every word of Spanish in the course has been carefully considered by native Spanish speakers from many different regions in order that the language (syntax, vocabulary, and pronunciation) may represent a broad standard acceptable to all.

In syntax, there is only one noteworthy deviation from standard Madrid Spanish: the second-person verb and pronoun forms (vos- otros, sois, etc.) have been replaced by those of the third person (ustedes, son, etc.) even in familiar address. It is, of course, widely recognized that this is current standard usage in all of Spanish America.

For invaluable suggestions and assistance given during the preparation of this course, we express particular thanks to Lola Amador, Ilda Carriazo, Cleland Harris, Alicia Huber, Víctor López, Fresia Marull, José Marull, and Amada Segarra.

F. B. Agard
R. S. Willis, Jr.
A. Paratore

SPECIAL NOTE

Only the first twelve Dialogues are recorded. The vocabulary and pronunciation of these units contain all words used in the two remaining Dialogues.

CONTENTS

[v]

CONTENTS

Greetings. Names. Families.

Nouns and Adjectives: Number, Gender. Definite and Indefinite
Articles. Number Words; One, Two or More. Verbs: Person and
Number.

A. BASIC DIALOGUES

1. "Where are you going?"

ENGLISH MEANING	AIDS TO LISTENING	SPANISH SPELLING

Record Side 1, beginning.

STUDENT:

good days	buénoş días	buenos días
madam	señóra	señora
Good morning, madam.	buénoş días señóra.*	Buenos días, señora.*

TEACHER:

Mr. López	señór lópeθ	señor López
how are	kómo está	cómo está
you	ustéd	usted
Good morning, Mr. López, how are you?	buénoş días señór lópeθ. ¿ kómo está ustéd?	Buenos días, señor López; ¿ cómo está usted?

STUDENT:

(I) am well	estói ƀién	estoy bien
thanks, thank you	gráθias	gracias
and you	i-ustéd	y usted
I'm well, thanks; and (how are) you?	estói ƀién gráθias. ¿ i-ustéd?	Estoy bien, gracias; ¿ y usted?

TEACHER:

very well	múi ƀién	muy bien
Very well, thank you.	múi ƀién gráθias.	Muy bien, gracias.
to where	a-dónde	a dónde
go you	ƀá ustéd	va usted
Where are you going?	¿ a-dónde ƀá ustéd?	¿ A dónde va usted?

STUDENT:

to the corner	a-la-eskína	a la esquina
to take	a-tomár	a tomar
the bus	el-autobús	el autobús

* A full treatment of Spanish pronunciation is given in eight instalments placed immediately after BASIC DIALOGUES
in UNITS 1, 2, 3, 4, 6, 7, 8, and 9.

ENGLISH MEANING	AIDS TO LISTENING	SPANISH SPELLING
To the corner, to take the bus.	a-la-eskína, a-tomár el-autoƀús.	A la esquina, a tomar el auto-bús.

TEACHER:

there comes	aƚá ƀiéne	allá viene
good-bye	adiós	adiós
There comes the bus; good-bye.	aƚá ƀiéne el-autoƀús. adiós.	Allá viene el autobús; adiós.

STUDENT:

Good-bye, madam.	adiós señóra.	Adiós, señora.

2. "What's *your* name?"

MAN:

is this	es-ésta	es ésta
the room	la-sála	la sala
number four	número kuátro	número cuatro
Miss	señoríta	señorita
Is this Room Four?	¿ es-ésta la-sála número kuátro, señoríta ?	¿ Es ésta la sala número cuatro, señorita ?

GIRL:

yes	sí	sí
Yes, this is it.	sí, es-ésta.	Sí, es ésta.

MAN:

where is	dónde está	dónde está
the teacher, the professor	el-profesór	el profesor
Where's the teacher?	¿ dónde está el-profesór ?	¿ Dónde está el profesor ?

GIRL:

There he comes.	aƚá ƀiéne.	Allá viene.

MAN:

who	kién	quién
Who is he?	¿ kién és ?	¿ Quién es ?

GIRL:

[the] Mr. González	el-señór gonθáleθ	el señor González
It's Mr. González.	es-el-señór gonθáleθ.	Es el señor González.

MAN:

is nice	es-simpátiko	es simpático
Is Mr. González nice?	¿ es-simpátiko el-señór gonθáleθ ?	¿ Es simpático el señor Gon-zález ?

GIRL:

(he) is very nice	es-múi simpátiko	es muy simpático
but	péro	pero
(he does) not speak	no-áƀla	no habla
English	inglés	inglés

ENGLISH MEANING	AIDS TO LISTENING	SPANISH SPELLING
Yes, he's very nice, but he doesn't speak English.	sí, es-múi simpátiko, pero-no--ábla inglés.	Sí, es muy simpático, pero no habla inglés.
MAN:		
I	yó	yo
call myself	me-Ĭámo	me llamo
My name's Richard Ross.	yó me-Ĭámo rrikárdo rrós.	Yo me llamo Ricardo Ross.
GIRL:		
And mine's Silvia Evans.	i-yó me-Ĭámo sílbia ébans.	Y yo me llamo Silvia Evans.
MAN:		
much	múcho	mucho
pleasure	gústo	gusto
How do you do?	múcho gústo señoríta.	Mucho gusto, señorita.
GIRL:		
How do you do?	múcho gústo señór.	Mucho gusto, señor.

3. "Where are you from?"

LUISA:		
from where	de-dónde	de dónde
Where are you from?	¿ de-dónde es-ustéd señór ?	¿ De dónde es usted, señor ?
MIGUEL:		
I am	yó sói	yo soy
from Saint Louis	de-san-luís	de San Luis
I'm from Saint Louis.	yó soi-de-san-luís.	Yo soy de San Luis.
And (where are) you (from)?	¿ i-ustéd ?	¿ Y usted ?
LUISA:		
from London	de-lóndres	de Londres
I'm from London.	yó soi-de-lóndres.	Yo soy de Londres.
(we) have	tenémos	tenemos
house, home	kása	casa
here	akí	aquí
my parents	mis-padres	mis padres
are in Spain	están en-espáña	están en España
now	aóra	ahora
We have (a) home here, but my parents are in Spain now.	tenémos kása akí, pero-mis--padres están en-espáña aóra.	Tenemos casa aquí, pero mis padres están en España ahora.
MIGUEL:		
have you not	no-tiéne ustéd	no tiene usted
brothers (and sisters)	ermános	hermanos
Don't you have (any) brothers and sisters?	¿ no-tiéne ustéd ermános ?	¿ No tiene usted hermanos ?

[3]

ENGLISH MEANING	AIDS TO LISTENING	SPANISH SPELLING
LUISA:		
how not	kómo nó	cómo no
(we) are five sons (and daughters)	sómos θínko íjos	somos cinco hijos
three men	trés ómbres	tres hombres
two women	dóṣ mujéres	dos mujeres
Yes indeed! There are five of us: three boys and two girls.	kómo nó. somos-θínko íjos. trés ómbres i-dóṣ mujéres.	¡ Cómo no! Somos cinco hijos: tres hombres y dos mujeres.
MIGUEL:		
are nice	son-simpátikos	son simpáticos
your brothers (and sisters)	sus-ermános	sus hermanos
Are your brothers and sisters nice?	¿ son simpátikos sus-ermános ?	¿ Son simpáticos sus hermanos ?
LUISA:		
Yes, they're very nice.	sí, son-múi simpátikos.	Sí, son muy simpáticos.
MIGUEL:		
I have one	yó téngo úno	yo tengo uno
that is much	éso eṣ-múcho	eso es mucho
I have one, and that's a lot.	yó téngo úno, i-éso eṣ-múcho.	Yo tengo uno, y eso es **mucho**.
LUISA:		
a brother	un-ermáno	un hermano
or a sister	o-una-ermána	o una hermana
A brother or a sister?	¿ un-ermano o-una-ermana.	¿ Un hermano o una hermana ?
MIGUEL:		
A brother.	un-ermáno.	Un hermano.
LUISA:		
you speak	ustéd ábla	usted habla
Spanish	español	español
You speak Spanish very well.	ustéd ábla mui-bién el-español señór.	Usted habla muy bien el **español**, señor.
MIGUEL:		
many thanks	múchaṣ gráθias	muchas gracias
(I) am Mexican	soi-mejikáno	soy mexicano
Thank you very much. I'm Mexican.	múchaṣ gráθias señoríta. soi-mejikáno.	Muchas gracias, señorita. Soy mexicano.
LUISA:		
How's that?	¡ kómo es-éso !	¿ Cómo es eso ?
You're from Saint Louis and you're Mexican?	¿ ustéd eṣ-de-san-luís i-eṣ-mejikáno ?	Usted es de San Luis ¿ y es mexicano ?
MIGUEL:		
Yes. I'm from Saint Louis Potosí in Mexico.	sí señoríta. soi-de-san-luís potosí en-méjiko.	Sí, señorita. Soy de San Luis Potosí en México.

ENGLISH MEANING	AIDS TO LISTENING	SPANISH SPELLING
LUISA:		
you call yourself	se-ĺáma ustéd	se llama usted
What's your name?	¿ kómo se-ĺáma ustéd.	¿ Cómo se llama usted?
MIGUEL:		
My name's Miguel Centeno.	yó me-ĺámo migél θenténo.	Yo me llamo Miguel Centeno.
And what's yours?	¿ i-ustéd kómo se-ĺáma?	Y usted, ¿ cómo se llama?
LUISA:		
My name's Luisa Quiroga.	yó me-ĺámo luísa kiróga.	Yo me llamo Luisa Quiroga.
MIGUEL:		
Are you Mexican?	¿ eṣ-mejikána ustéd?	¿ Es mexicana usted?
LUISA:		
my father	mi-pádre	mi padre
My father's Mexican.	mi-pádre eṣ-mejikáno.	Mi padre es mexicano.
there-are	ái	hay
in England	en-inglatérra	en Inglaterra
There aren't many Mexicans in England.	no-ái múchoṣ mejikános en--inglatérra.	No hay muchos mexicanos en Inglaterra.

NOTES ON PRONUNCIATION AND SPELLING

All the sounds of the Spanish language are present in the dialogues of this first unit, but it is not practical to describe and discuss all of them in a single treatment at the beginning. Analysis of all the sounds, and of the way they are spelled in written Spanish, will be completed in the first ten units. Meanwhile, imitate as best you can each sound you hear, and try to relate it in your mind with the symbol used for it in the column of phonetic transcription headed "Aids to Listening."

CONSONANTS

Spanish has nineteen basic consonant sounds, which appear in the transcription column as: b ch d f g j k l ĺ m n ñ p r rr s θ t y. In this unit we comment on four of these consonants: s θ y ĺ.

1. THE s-SOUND

Spanish has no important difference between the "hissed" and "buzzed" sounds of English *hiSS* vs. *hiS*. The Spanish s is normally a hissed sound, like that in English *SiSter*. It is always spelled s (never ss). Examples:

TRANSCRIPTION

señóra, ustéd, es-ésta, inglés, ermános, kása, el-profesór, luísa.

WRITTEN SPANISH

señora, usted, es ésta, inglés, hermanos, casa, el profesor, Luisa.

A slightly "buzzed" sound, approaching that of English *wiSdom*, does occur when a word with a final s-sound is followed by a word beginning with b, d, g, l, ĺ, m, n, or y. We transcribe this variety as ṣ, though it is not distinguished in Spanish spelling. Examples:

TRANSCRIPTION

buénoṣ días, múchaṣ gráθias, eṣ-múcho, dóṣ mujéres

WRITTEN SPANISH

buenos días, muchas gracias, es mucho, dos mujeres

[5]

NOTE: When the s-sound occurs before any consonant (español, ustéd, la-eskína), many speakers of Spanish pronounce it so lightly that it is heard as a kind of h-sound. If you hear this kind of s before another consonant, you may safely imitate it, as it will be understood by Spanish speakers anywhere.

2. THE θ-SOUND.

This closely resembles the sound of English *THick, THin*. It is spelled c before i or e, and z elsewhere. Examples:

TRANSCRIPTION

gráθias, θínko, θenténo; lópeθ, gonθáleθ

WRITTEN SPANISH

gracias, cinco, Centeno; López, González

NOTE: Speakers throughout Spanish America, as well as in some parts of Spain, do not have the θ-sound; they use the s-sound in its place. If you hear s where the transcription has either s or θ, you may safely imitate it. And if you do adopt this pronunciation, it will be easy enough for you to read both s and θ as s in the transcription.

3. THE y-SOUND.

This is like the sound in English *Yet*, but rather more strongly pronounced. In Spanish spelling it is always y, as in the one example in this unit:

TRANSCRIPTION

yó

WRITTEN SPANISH

yo

4. THE ĺ-SOUND.

This is a combination of l and y pronounced together, quite similar to the sound in English *miLLIon, vaLue*. In Spanish it is always spelled ll. Examples:

TRANSCRIPTION

aĺá, me-ĺámo, se-ĺáma

WRITTEN SPANISH

allá, me llamo, se llama

NOTE: Many speakers of Spanish, especially in Spanish America, do not have the ĺ-sound; they use the y-sound in its place. If you hear y where the transcription has either y or ĺ, you may safely imitate it. And in that case read both y and ĺ as y in the transcription.

In some sections, particularly Argentina, speakers having only the y-sound pronounce it like the sound in English *viSIon, meaSure*. This pronunciation is understood anywhere, and may be safely imitated.

B. STUDY

Review SECTION A, *following these steps:*

(*1*) Run through each dialogue: (*a*) reading silently a complete English utterance in order to fix the meaning of the Spanish in your mind; (*b*) reading silently the Spanish equivalent; (*c*) reading the Spanish aloud, trying hard to imitate the pronunciation you have heard.

(*2*) Now cover the English, so that you can see only the Spanish. Read the Spanish aloud. As you do so, be sure you know what you're saying.

Note the words or phrases you don't remember; check on their meaning AFTER, not DURING, your reading of each dialogue.

(*3*) With the English covered up, repeat STEP 2 until you can say the whole section with full awareness of what everything in it means. DON'T INTERRUPT YOUR READING to check on elusive meanings; as you read, note your weaknesses and CHECK ON THEM AFTER you have finished reading the entire section.

[6]

C. LISTENING IN

1. *Review* SECTION A, *repeating the Spanish and giving the English.*

2. *With book closed, listen in as Señor López and Señorita Quiroga converse about the González family.*

Record Side 1, first spiral.

SEÑOR: Buenos días, señorita Quiroga.

SEÑORITA: Buenos días, señor López.

SEÑOR: ¿ Cómo está usted ?

SEÑORITA: Muy bien, gracias, ¿ y usted ?

SEÑOR: Bien, gracias.

SEÑORITA: ¿ Quién es el señor González ?

SEÑOR: El señor González es un profesor.

SEÑORITA: ¿ Un profesor de inglés ?

SEÑOR: No, es un profesor de español, pero habla inglés.

SEÑORITA: ¿ Habla bien el inglés ?

SEÑOR: Sí, habla muy bien el inglés.

SEÑORITA: ¿ Es simpática la señora González ?

SEÑOR: Sí, la señora es muy simpática.

SEÑORITA: ¿ Tienen hijos el señor y la señora González ?

SEÑOR: Sí, tienen cuatro hijos: tres hombres y una mujer.

SEÑORITA: ¿ Cómo se llama la hija ?

SEÑOR: La hija se llama Silvia.

SEÑORITA: ¿ Dónde están los hijos del profesor González ? ¿ Están en España ?

SEÑOR: No, están en Londres.

SEÑORITA: ¿ Los hijos hablan español ?

SEÑOR: Sí, hablan muy bien el español.

SEÑORITA: ¿ De dónde es usted, señor López ?

SEÑOR: Yo soy de aquí.

SEÑORITA: ¿ Tiene usted hermanos ?

SEÑOR: Sí, tengo cinco hermanos.

SEÑORITA: Yo no tengo hermanos.

SEÑOR: ¿ Es usted mexicana, señorita ?

SEÑORITA: Mis padres son mexicanos.

SEÑOR: Usted habla muy bien el inglés.

SEÑORITA: Gracias. Muchos mexicanos hablan inglés.

SEÑOR: Allá viene mi autobús, señorita. Adiós.

SEÑORITA: Adiós, señor López.

D. GRAMMATICAL ANALYSIS

I. NOUNS AND ADJECTIVES

(1) Number: Singular and Plural. Some Spanish nouns and adjectives have a singular form ending in a vowel-sound:

Mucho gusto.
Mi padre es mexicano.

In the plural form, the sound -s is added to the singular:

Buenos días.
Mis padres son mexicanos.

Unlike English adjectives, which do not vary in form (*good morning; good times*), Spanish adjectives do vary their endings in "agreement" with the nouns they accompany. Thus, in the last two examples above, the adjective **buenos** has the plural form in agreement with the noun **días**; the adjective **mexicanos** is plural to agree with the noun **padres**.

(2) Gender: Masculine and Feminine. Many Spanish adjectives sometimes have -a as their final vowel (**muchas gracias**) and sometimes -o as their final vowel (**mucho gusto**).

These vowel-variations mark agreement with the grammatical feature called "gender" inherent in every Spanish noun, whether it refers to a living being or not. There are two gender-classes, the MASCULINE and the FEMININE. It happens that most nouns with final vowel -o are masculine (**gusto, número**), and that most nouns with final vowel -a are feminine (**esquina, gracias;** but **día** is masculine). In the same way, many adjectives have the vowel -o when in agreement with a masculine noun, and -a when agreeing with a feminine noun.

With very few exceptions, person-nouns designating males are masculine, and person-nouns designating females are feminine. Some person-nouns which designate EITHER males or females

[7]

belong to *both* gender-classes and vary their endings accordingly: **hermano,** *brother,* **hermana,** *sister.* In the case of such nouns the masculine plural often denotes a group of males and females, as in **hermanos,** *brothers-and-sisters;* also **mis padres,** *my father-and-mother, my parents,* which is simply the plural of **mi padre,** *my father.*

Summing up, we find that many Spanish adjectives, and some person-nouns, have four possible forms in accordance with the grammar of number and gender:

	SINGULAR	PLURAL
MASC.	mucho	muchos
FEM.	mucha	muchas
MASC.	hijo	hijos
FEM.	hija	hijas

(*3*) **Definite and Indefinite Articles.** The Spanish "definite article" (English *the*) and the Spanish "indefinite article" (English *a, an*) are like adjectives in the way they show the number and gender of their nouns. Both of them have, however, special forms without final **-o** when they go with MASCULINE nouns IN THE SINGULAR: **los hermanos, la esquina, las salas,** but **el profesor; una hermana** but **un hermano.**

II. NUMBER WORDS

(*1*) **One.** The Spanish indefinite article also serves as the numeral *one,* and when in this sense it stands by itself (that is, not directly before a noun), it shows the full form **uno** when referring to a masculine noun: **yo tengo uno** (referring to **hermano**).

The "context" of a phrase automatically tells you whether this word is acting as the article or the numeral. Also, as a numeral it is apt to be somewhat stressed in speech.

(*2*) **Two or more.** The Spanish numerals for *two* and on up don't have variable endings. Some happen to end in **-s** (**dos, tres**) and some don't (**cuatro, cinco**). Of course they are by nature plural, but they show no gender agreement: **cinco hombres** or **cinco mujeres.**

III. VERBS

(*1*) **Person and Number.** The Spanish verb forms in the DIALOGUES of this unit are all in the "present tense."

Spanish verbs vary in form not only according to tense, but also according to both the person (first, second, or third) and the number (singular or plural) of their subject. For example, in the sentence

¿ Son simpáticos sus hermanos?

the verb-form is **son** because the subject (**sus hermanos**) is both THIRD PERSON and PLURAL. Of course a NOUN subject like this one shows its own person-number; but in any language there are many utterances which have no noun subject. In such utterances, English makes wide use of "pronoun" substitutes (*I, we; you; he, she, it, they*) to indicate the person-number, because the verb itself doesn't do it (except for the third-person singular *-s* of the present tense: *say, says*). In Spanish, however, the verb-form itself in nearly all cases indicates the person-number of its subject with precision; therefore Spanish makes much less use of subject pronouns than English. Thus for example, in the answer

Sí, **son** muy simpáticos.

the form **son** can only mean that *they* are nice and hence no pronoun is needed. Similarly in the sentences

Estoy bien, gracias.
Tenemos casa aquí.

the form **estoy** can only mean that *I am . . .,* the form **tenemos** only that *We have;* hence the pronouns corresponding to English *I* and *we* need not be expressed.

There follows a tabular summary of the present tense forms of three very common Spanish verbs which you can now use. We label them the verbs **ser, estar,** and **tener** (by forms you will identify later).

ser

	SINGULAR	PLURAL
1ST PERSON:	soy	somos
3RD PERSON:	es	son

estar

	SINGULAR	PLURAL
1ST PERSON:	estoy	estamos
3RD PERSON:	está	están

tener

	SINGULAR	PLURAL
1ST PERSON:	tengo	tenemos
3RD PERSON:	tiene	tienen

These verbs also have second-person forms, but you don't need them at this stage because when you call someone **usted** you are using a pronoun derived from a "courtesy title" which once meant "*your grace*" rather than just "*you*," and is therefore third-person.

Comparative Usage

Being. Where English uses the verb *be*, Spanish sometimes uses **ser** and sometimes **estar**.

The true Spanish verb of "*being*" is **ser**, but its range of meanings and usages is more limited than the English verb, so that often other Spanish verbs appear where English uses "*be*." One which occurs in many kinds of expression is **estar**, which literally means "*stand*." For example, (*a*) **estar** is used in expressing WHERE the subject is:

Where is the teacher?
¿ Dónde **está** el profesor?

My parents are in Spain.
Mis padres **están** en España.

(*b*) **estar** is also used in expressing HOW — in the sense of "*in what condition*" — the subject is:

How are you?
¿ Cómo **está** usted?

I'm well, thanks.
Estoy bien, gracias.

E. GRAMMATICAL DRILLS

1. THE.

Say each of the following words aloud, with the proper form of the Spanish DEFINITE ARTICLE (*English* "*the*") *before it:*

EXAMPLE:

esquina

MODEL:

la esquina

1. hermano	10. padre
2. casa	11. hombres
3. señorita	12. mujeres
4. profesor	13. número
5. señora	14. hijas
6. esquinas	15. hermanos
7. hijo	16. señoritas
8. salas	17. hija
9. señor	18. autobús

19. mexicanos	24. hermanas
20. hijos	25. mexicana
21. mexicano	26. números
22. señoras	27. hermana
23. padres	28. mexicanas

2. ADJECTIVE ENDINGS.

Make noun + adjective phrases out of the items that follow, by filling the blank with the adjective **simpático** *and giving it the appropriate gender-number ending* (-o, -a, -os, -as).

EXAMPLE:

una señora ——

MODEL:

una señora simpática

1. un hijo muy ——	3. un profesor ——
2. una casa ——	4. dos señoritas ——

5. cinco hermanos ——   9. cuatro señoras ——
6. un padre muy ——   10. tres mujeres ——
7. un hermano ——   11. dos hombres ——
8. una sala ——   12. una hija muy ——

3. BEING: ser.

A. *Take each of the words or phrases that follow and make a sentence ending with . . .* **de Londres,** *selecting the proper person-number form of the verb* **ser** *from among the forms:* **soy, es, somos, son.**

EXAMPLE:

Miguel

MODEL:

Miguel **es** de Londres.

1. mi hermano   5. usted
2. yo   6. usted y yo
3. mis padres   7. mis hermanos y yo
4. Ricardo y Silvia   8. el señor López

B. *Do the same thing again, this time ending the sentence with the proper gender-number form of the word* **mexicano.**

4. BEING: estar.

As you say the following sentences, telling WHERE *someone or something is, fill the blank with the proper person-number form of the verb* **estar** *by selecting from among the forms* **estoy, está, estamos, están.**

EXAMPLE:

Mis hijos —— en San Luis.

MODEL:

Mis hijos **están** en San Luis.

1. El autobús no —— en la esquina.
2. Yo —— en México.
3. Usted —— en la casa.
4. ¿ —— aquí la señorita Evans?
5. Mis padres —— en San Luis ahora.
6. ¿ —— allá el autobús?
7. Las mujeres —— en la esquina.
8. Miguel y Luisa no —— en Inglaterra.
9. Muchos mexicanos —— en California.
10. Usted y yo no —— en el autobús.
11. ¿ Quién —— en la casa ahora?
12. La señora González —— en España.

5. HAVING: tener.

As you say the following sentences, fill the blank with the proper person-number form of the verb **tener** *by selecting from among the forms* **tengo, tiene, tenemos, tienen.**

EXAMPLE:

La señora Quiroga —— tres hijos.

MODEL:

La señora Quiroga **tiene** tres hijos.

1. Yo —— un hermano y una hermana.
2. ¿ —— muchos hijos el señor y la señora López?
3. Usted y yo no —— casa.
4. ¿ —— dos casas el profesor González?
5. ¿ Quién —— cinco hijos?
6. Yo no —— hermanos.
7. Silvia no —— hermanos.
8. Mis padres —— casa en San Luis.

F. STUDY

1. *Review* SECTION A, *following these steps:*
(*a*) Cover the Spanish, so that you can see only the English. Using the English as a guide, say the Spanish aloud as perfectly as you can. Note the words or phrases you don't remember how to say, and check them AFTER, not DURING, the first time through.

(*b*) Work through repeatedly this way with the Spanish covered, checking AFTERWARD for elusive phrases until you've succeeded in saying the whole section in Spanish.

2. *Prepare the* CONVERSATIONS *of Section* G.

G. CONVERSATIONS

1. *Reproduce the* BASIC DIALOGUES *in Spanish.*

2. *Using the* BASIC DIALOGUES *as your model, develop conversations of your own, such as:*

(*a*) Greeting a friend.

(*b*) Introducing yourself to somebody.

(*c*) Talking about Mr. López, Mrs. López, Miss López, Professor González, Silvia Evans, Ricardo Ross, Miguel Centeno, Luisa Quiroga, your parents, your brothers and sisters, telling for example:

Where they're from.

Whether they speak English or Spanish, and how well they speak.

Where they are now, or where they're going.

What your parents' and brothers' and sisters' names are.

Houses and People.   Weather.   Eating and Drinking.   Buying.
Telephoning.

UNIT
2

Nouns and Adjectives: Number and Gender.   Demonstrative Words.
Noun Compounds.   Comparative Usage: Expressions of Sensation;
Weather;   "There is";   "There are."

A. BASIC DIALOGUES

1. "This and that."

ENGLISH MEANING	AIDS TO LISTENING	SPANISH SPELLING

Record Side 1, after first spiral.

STUDENT: (*gesticulating*)

this house	ésta kása	esta casa
of Peter	de-pédro	de Pedro
that house	ésa kása	esa casa
of you	de-ustédes	de ustedes
"This house is Peter's . . ."	ésta kása eṣ-de-pédro.	« Esta casa es de Pedro . . . »
"That house is yours. . . ."	ésa kása eṣ-de-ustédes.	« Esa casa es de ustedes . . . »

LADY:

How's that?	¿ kómo es-éso ?	¿ Cómo es eso ?

STUDENT:

these gentlemen	éstos señóres	estos señores
those young ladies	ésas señorítas	esas señoritas
"These gentleman are brothers . . ."	éstos señóres son-ermános.	« Estos señores son hermanos . . . »
"Those young ladies are sisters . . ."	ésas señorítas son-ermánas.	« Esas señoritas son hermanas . . . »

LADY:

what	ké	qué
say you	díθe ustéd	dice usted
What are you saying, Miss?	¿ ké díθe ustéd señoríta ?	¿ Qué dice usted, señorita ?

STUDENT:

those	akéĺos	aquéllos
"Those are the teacher's children . . ."	akéĺos son-los-íjoṣ del-profesór.	« Aquéllos son los hijos del profesor . . . »
that	akéĺa	aquélla
"That is the teacher's wife . . ."	akéĺa eṣ-la señóra del-profesór.	« Aquélla es la señora del profesor . . . »

ENGLISH MEANING	AIDS TO LISTENING	SPANISH SPELLING
LADY:		
Young lady, are you all right?	señoríta, ¿ está ustéd bién?	Señorita, ¿ está usted bien?
STUDENT:		
(I) have to learn	téngo ke-aprendér	tengo que aprender
for tomorrow	para-mañána	para mañana
Yes, but I have to learn this for tomorrow.	sí, pero-téngo ke-aprendér ésto para-mañána.	Sí, pero tengo que aprender esto para mañana.
You speak Spanish very well.	ustéd ábla mui-bién el-español.	Usted habla muy bien el español.
Are you Spanish?	¿ es-ustéd españóla?	¿ Es usted española?
LADY:		
(I) am English	soi-inglésa	soy inglesa
No, I'm English.	nó señoríta soi-inglésa.	No, señorita, soy inglesa.
Spanish friends	amígos españóles	amigos españoles
But I have Spanish friends.	pero-téngo amígos españóles.	Pero tengo amigos españoles.

2. "What kind of weather do you have?"

PEDRO:		
what weather	ké tiémpo	qué tiempo
(it) makes	áθe	hace
the country	el-país	el país
What's the weather like in your country?	¿ ké tiémpo áθe en-el-país de--ustéd?	¿ Qué tiempo hace en el país de usted?
DICK:		
my country	mi-país	mi país
large, big	gránde	grande
Man (alive)! My country's very big!	¡ ombre! mi-país es-mui--gránde.	¡ Hombre! ¡ Mi país es muy grande!
PEDRO:		
how is	kómo és	cómo es
the climate	el-klíma	el clima
in general	en-jenerál	en general
Well, what's the climate like in general?	buéno, ¿ kómo es-el-klíma en--jenerál?	Bueno, ¿ cómo es el clima en general?
DICK:		
(it) makes cold	áθe frío	hace frío
in the winter	en-el-imbiérno	en el invierno
and in the summer	i-en-el-beráno	y en el verano
(it) makes heat	áθe kalór	hace calor

ENGLISH MEANING	AIDS TO LISTENING	SPANISH SPELLING
In general it's cold in the winter, and in the summer it's hot.	en-jenerál áθe frío en-el-imbiérno — i-en-el-beráno áθe kalór.	En general hace frío en el invierno, y en el verano hace calor.
in the south	en-el-súr	en el sur
there is not snow	no-ái niébe	no hay nieve
In the south there isn't (any) snow in the winter.	en-el-súr no-ái niébe en-el-imbiérno.	En el sur no hay nieve en el invierno.

PEDRO:

then	entónθes	entonces
like the climate	komo-el-klíma	como el clima
of here	de-akí	de aquí
Then it's like the climate here.	entónθes es-komo-el-klíma de--akí.	Entonces es como el clima de aquí.

DICK:

more or less	más o-ménos	más o menos
Yes, more or less.	sí, más o-ménos.	Sí, más o menos.

PEDRO:

the spring	la-primabéra	la primavera
What's the spring like?	¿ kómo es-la-primabéra.	¿ Cómo es la primavera ?

DICK:

beautiful	ermósa	hermosa
pleasant, agreeable	agradáble	agradable
It's beautiful and pleasant.	es-ermósa i-agradáble.	Es hermosa y agradable.
too, also	también	también
(it) rains much	luébe múcho	llueve mucho
But it rains a lot in the spring, too.	pero-también luébe múcho en--la-primabéra.	Pero también llueve mucho en la primavera.

PEDRO:

(they) say	díθen	dicen
that (it) makes much wind	ke-áθe múcho biénto	que hace mucho viento
They say it's very windy, too.	díθen ke-áθe múcho biénto también.	Dicen que hace mucho viento también.

DICK:

the autumn	el-otóño	el otoño
dry	séko	seco
fresh, cool	fréskos	frescos
The autumn is dry and the days are cool.	el-otóño es-séko, i-los-días son--fréskos.	El otoño es seco, y los días son frescos.

PEDRO:

(I) have thirst	téngo séd	tengo sed
I'm hot and I'm thirsty.	téngo kalór i-téngo séd.	Tengo calor y tengo sed.

ENGLISH MEANING	AIDS TO LISTENING	SPANISH SPELLING
(let's) go	bámos	vamos
to take something	a-tomár álgo	a tomar algo
Let's go (and) get something (to drink).	¡ bámos a-tomár álgo.	Vamos a tomar algo.

DICK:

(I) have more hunger	téngo más ámbre	tengo más hambre
than thirst	ke-séd	que sed
I'm more hungry than thirsty, but let's go . . .	yó téngo más ámbre ke-séd, pero-bámos . . .	Yo tengo más hambre que sed, pero vamos . . .

(*Later*)

PEDRO:

What are you going to have, Dick?	¿ ké bá ustéd a-tomár, rrikárdo ?	¿ Qué va usted a tomar, Ricardo ?

DICK :

a lemonade	una-limonada	una limonada
a sandwich of cheese	un-sánuich de-késo	un sándwich de queso
A lemonade and a cheese sandwich.	una-limonada i-un-sánuich de-késo.	Una limonada y un sándwich de queso.
the shop	la-tiénda	la tienda
of clothing, of clothes	de-rrópa	de ropa
which is there	ke-está aĺá	que está allá
Pedro, is that clothing shop over there (any) good ?	pedro, ¿ eş-buéna la-tiéda de--rrópa k'está aĺá ?	Pedro, ¿ es buena la tienda de ropa que está allá ?

PEDRO:

that (one)	akéĺa	aquélla
very bad	múi mála	muy mala
No, that (one)'s no good.	nó, akéĺa eş-múi mála.	No, aquélla es muy mala.
some large shops	unas-tiéndaş grándes	unas tiendas grandes
in the centre	en-el-θéntro	en el centro
But there are some large shops in town that are very good.	pero-ái unas-tiéndaş grándes en--el-θéntro ke-son-múi buénas.	Pero hay unas tiendas grandes en el centro que son muy buenas.
(do) you want	kiére ustéd	quiere usted
to buy	komprár	comprar
What do you want to buy ?	¿ ké kiére ustéd komprár.	¿ Qué quiere usted comprar ?

DICK:

(I) want	kiéro	quiero
a hat	un-sombréro	un sombrero
I want to buy a hat.	kiéro komprár un-sombréro.	Quiero comprar un sombrero.
of my brother	de-mi-ermáno	de mi hermano
This is my brother's hat.	éste es-el-sombréro de-mi--ermáno.	Éste es el sombrero de mi hermano.

ENGLISH MEANING	AIDS TO LISTENING	SPANISH SPELLING
PEDRO:		
(I) have sleepiness	téngo sueño	tengo sueño
Well, Dick, I'm sleepy.	buéno rrikárdo. yó téngo sueño.	Bueno, Ricardo. Yo tengo sueño.
(I) go home	bói a-kása	voy a casa
to rest	a-deskansár	a descansar
I'm going home (and) rest.	bói a-kasa a-deskansár.	Voy a casa a descansar.
DICK:		
Very good, Pedro.	múi biém pédro.	Muy bien, Pedro.
(I) call you	lo-łámo	lo llamo
by telephone	por-teléfono	por teléfono
I('ll) call you up tomorrow.	lo-łámo por-teléfono mañána.	Lo llamo por teléfono mañana.
PEDRO:		
my phone number	mi-número de-teléfono	mi número de teléfono
My phone number's two-four-three-five.	mi-número de-teléfono eş-dós kuátro trés θínko.	Mi número de teléfono es dos-cuatro-tres-cinco.
DICK:		
Thanks, Pedro.	gráθias pédro.	Gracias, Pedro.
until	ásta	hasta
See you tomorrow.	asta-mañána.	Hasta mañana.

NOTES ON PRONUNCIATION AND SPELLING

CONSONANTS

1. THE SPANISH b-SOUND.

This sound has two varieties, which appear in the transcription column as b and ƀ. There is no great difference between these two varieties, which simply alternate in accordance with the sounds surrounding them. The difference in quality is not recognized in Spanish writing, which spells EITHER variety as **b** in some words and as **v** in other words.

(*1*) At the very beginning of a word-group, or after **m**, the b-sound is as in English *BamBoo*, formed with the lips fully closed. We transcribe this variety as b. Examples:

TRANSCRIPTION

buéno, bámos, bói a-kása, ómbre, tamb…én, ámbre, un-sombréro, en-el-imbiérno

WRITTEN SPANISH

bueno, vamos, voy a casa, hombre, también, hambre, un sombrero, en el invierno

(*2*) In any other surroundings, the b-sound is formed with the lips brought toward each other but not quite closed, so that the breath continues to pass between them. We transcribe this variety as ƀ. Examples:

TRANSCRIPTION

el-autobús, mui-ƀién, áƀla, eş-ƀuéna, ałá ƀiéne, pero-ƀámos, en-el-ƀeráno, łuéƀe, la-primaƀéra

WRITTEN SPANISH

el autobús, muy bien, habla, es buena, allá viene, pero vamos, en el verano, llueve, la primavera

For a good Spanish accent, it is very important for you to imitate and practise this variety of the b-sound until you can make it the way a Spanish speaker does.

STRESS

In most Spanish words one of the syllables is "stressed" — that is, spoken more loudly than the others. In our transcription, the stressed syllable of a word is shown by an accent-mark (′) over the vowel of that syllable. Spanish spelling also indicates stress, through a system of use and non-use of the accent-mark which we will analyse in a later unit.

B. STUDY

Review SECTION A. *Follow the same procedure that was prescribed in* SECTION B *of* UNIT 1, *by covering the English and learning to say the whole section with knowledge of what it means.*

C. LISTENING IN

1. *Review* SECTION A, *repeating the Spanish and giving the English.*

2. *With book closed, listen in as Miguel and Harry talk about weather.*

Record Side 1, after first spiral.

MIGUEL: ¿ Qué tiempo hace aquí en el invierno?

HARRY: Hace frío en el invierno. También hay nieve y hace mucho viento.

MIGUEL: Entonces no es agradable el invierno.

HARRY: Sí, es agradable, pero hace mucho frío.

MIGUEL: ¿ Llueve mucho en el otoño?

HARRY: Llueve más en la primavera que en el otoño.

MIGUEL: Entonces hace frío y calor en este país.

HARRY: En general hace calor en el verano.

MIGUEL: En mi país no hay nieve en el invierno y no hace mucho frío.

HARRY: Eso es muy bueno.

MIGUEL: ¿ No tiene usted hambre?

HARRY: No. Yo tengo sed. Quiero tomar una limonada.

MIGUEL: Yo también. Vamos a esa tienda.

HARRY: No hay limonada en esa tienda.

MIGUEL: Entonces vamos al centro. También quiero comprar algo.

HARRY: ¿ Qué quiere usted comprar?

MIGUEL: Quiero comprar un sombrero.

HARRY: ¿ No tiene sombrero usted?

MIGUEL: Sí, tengo uno, pero es grande y no es muy bueno.

HARRY: ¿ Quiere tomar el autobús, Miguel?

MIGUEL: No, no quiero tomar el autobús. Es muy malo . . .

HARRY: Allá está la tienda, Miguel.

MIGUEL: ¿ Dónde está?

HARRY: Es esa que está en la esquina. Es de unos españoles.

MIGUEL: ¿ Tengo que hablar español?

HARRY: No. También hablan inglés en la tienda . . .

MIGUEL: Bueno, Harry, tengo sueño. Voy a casa a descansar. Lo llamo por teléfono mañana.

HARRY: ¿ Tiene usted mi número?

MIGUEL: Sí, lo tengo. Es cuatro-dos-cinco-uno.

HARRY: Hasta mañana, entonces.

MIGUEL: Hasta mañana, Harry.

D. GRAMMATICAL ANALYSIS

I. NOUNS AND ADJECTIVES

(*1*) **Number.** Some Spanish nouns and adjectives have a singular form ending in a consonant-sound: señoR, autobúS, españoL. The plural form of all such words has the ending -es: señoRES, autobuSES, españoLES. Similarly, **usted** has the plural form usteDES, *you* (*all*).

(*2*) **Gender.** Some Spanish adjectives have the same ending whether the noun they accompany is masculine or feminine. Many of these have final vowel -e:

MASC.:	un verano agradable	sombreros grandes
FEM.:	una primavera agradable	tiendas grandes

Some adjectives have the normal final -a when accompanying feminine nouns, but with masculines have NO final vowel instead of the usual -o. With the plural for each gender formed directly on the singular, we get the following four forms for such adjectives as the ones meaning 'Spanish' and 'English':

	SING.	PLU.
MASC.	español	españoles
FEM.	española	españolas
MASC.	inglés	ingleses
FEM.	inglesa	inglesas

(*3*) **This AND that.** The Spanish "demonstrative" words corresponding to *this, these* and *that, those* show gender-number agreement with their nouns as follows:

	SING.	PLU.
MASC.	este	estos
FEM.	esta	estas
MASC.	ese	esos
FEM.	esa	esas
MASC.	aquel	aquellos
FEM.	aquella	aquellas

Note that for all three demonstratives the masculine SINGULAR form does not end in -o, but that the masculine PLURAL form, as well as the feminine forms, fit the usual pattern.

Nevertheless all three demonstratives do occur with final -o, as two of them do in the following sentences:

¿ Cómo es eso?
Tengo que aprender esto para mañana.

These are "abstract" forms, designating a previous statement, or some unidentified thing, or a fact, or a situation. As in the above examples, these forms neither accompany nor refer to any noun, and are therefore GENDERLESS.

Comparative Usage

(*1*) *that:* **ese** VS. **aquel.** Spanish has two demonstratives corresponding to English *that* (plural *those*).

(*A*) In referring to a person or thing near to or associated with the person addressed, **ese** and not **aquel** is used:

That house is yours.
Esa casa es de ustedes.

How's that (that you just said)?
¿ Cómo es **eso**?

(*B*) In referring to someone or something equally remote from both the speaker and the person addressed, it is common though not necessary to use **aquel**:

Is that shop (over there) any good?
¿ Es buena **aquella** tienda?

That is the teacher's wife.
Aquélla es la señora del profesor.

(*2*) ENGLISH: *that one.* English frequently uses the word *one* after a demonstrative in the singular, as a substitute for an unexpressed noun (*this one, that one*). Spanish uses no such substitute:

No, that one's no good.
No, **aquélla** es muy mala.

(*3*) NOUN COMPOUNDS. English puts two nouns together to make "compounds" such as *cheese sandwich, telephone number, teacher's wife.*

Such noun compounds are not found in Spanish, which instead uses phrases linking the two nouns with **de**, *of*, corresponding literally to "sandwich of cheese," "number of telephone," etc.

a cheese sandwich
un sándwich **de** queso

the teacher's wife
la señora **del** profesor

my telephone number
mi número **de** teléfono

the teacher's children
los hijos **del** profesor

Thus also the Spanish equivalent of the English possessive *'s* (plural *s'*) is **de** before the noun. If the sense requires it, the definite article appears before BOTH Spanish nouns where the English compound has only the initial article. (Note that the combination **de** + **el** is written as the single word **del**.)

II. VERBS

Comparative Usage: BEING

We learned in UNIT 1 that the range of meaning and usage of Spanish **ser** is more limited than that of English *be*. Here are some further situations in which Spanish uses some verb other than **ser** where English has *be:*

(*1*) **Expressions of sensation.** When conveying the idea that a living subject has a "sensation" of hunger, cold, or the like, English uses *be* with an adjective ("*I'm hungry*") and Spanish uses **tener**, *have*, with a noun denoting the sensation (literally "*I have hunger*"):

I'm hot and I'm thirsty.
Tengo calor y **tengo sed.**

Are you cold?
¿ **Tiene** usted **frío** ?

I'm more hungry than thirsty.
Yo **tengo** más **hambre** que **sed.**

I'm very sleepy.
Yo **tengo mucho sueño.**

The last example shows that where English has *very* before the adjective *sleepy*, Spanish has **mucho** before the noun **sueño** ("*much sleepiness*").

(*2*) **Expressions of weather.** In "impersonal" expressions describing the weather, English uses *be* with an adjective ("*It's cold*") and Spanish uses the verb **hacer**, *make*, with a noun (literally "*It makes cold*"):

It's cold in the winter.
Hace frío en el invierno.

It's cool in the autumn.
Hace fresco en el otoño.

In the summer it's hot.
En el verano **hace calor.**

It's very windy, too.
Hace mucho viento también.

In these expressions, where the subject of the English verb *be* is *it*, the Spanish verb **hace** is SUBJECTLESS. Even in describing weather, if the expression does have a subject, **hace** is not used.

The spring is beautiful.
La primavera es hermosa.

The days are cool.
Los días son frescos.

(*3*) **There is, There are.** The Spanish equivalent of English *there is*, *there are* is the subjectless **hay**, a form of the verb **haber**, *have*.

There aren't many Mexicans in England.
No **hay** muchos mexicanos en Inglaterra.

There isn't (any) snow in the south.
No **hay** nieve en el sur.

There are some large shops in town.
Hay unas tiendas grandes en el centro.

English *there* in these expressions is not the DEMONSTRATIVE adverb of "*There's Bill*" or "*There's the bus*," which is Spanish **allá**. (What verb would you use after **allá** to say "*There's the bus*" in Spanish?)

E. GRAMMATICAL DRILLS

1. this AND that.

A. *Go through the following list of nouns and make "demonstrative" phrases by substituting the proper gender-number form of* **este** *for the definite article. Then go through the list again, changing each singular to the plural and each plural to the singular. Also give the English for each phrase.*

EXAMPLE:

la casa

MODEL:

First round: **esta** casa.
Second round: **estas** casas.

1. el país
2. la esquina
3. el queso
4. los sombreros
5. la tienda
6. el profesor
7. la sala
8. los hombres
9. las mujeres
10. el hermano
11. la señora
12. las señoritas
13. los autobuses
14. las hijas
15. los mexicanos
16. los señores
17. el padre
18. las hermanas

B. *Go through the above list again, doing the same thing with* **ese**.

C. *Do the same thing again, with* **aquel**.

2. ADJECTIVES.

Take each numbered expression and match it with each item in the list which follows, being sure you put the adjective in the right person-number form. (In the first series **sed**, **nieve** *and* **hambre** *are feminine,* **calor** *is masculine.) Also remember that all the adjectives except* **mucho** *come after their noun.*

EXAMPLE:

mucho

—— hermanos, sombreros, sed

MODEL:

muchos hermanos, **muchos** sombreros, **mucha** sed

1. **mucho**

hermanos, hijas, sed, viento, nieve, hombres, calor, profesores, frío, hambre, mexicanos.

2. **grande**

una tienda, este sombrero, esas casas, dos salas, aquellos países.

3. **español.** 4. **inglés**

una señora, los profesores, estas mujeres, un padre, la sala.

5. **un clima.** 6. **esa primavera**

frío, hermoso, malo, fresco, seco, agradable, bueno.

3. BEING.

The English equivalents of the Spanish sentences that follow would all have a form of "be" as the verb. As you say the Spanish sentences aloud, supply the proper person-number form of the missing Spanish verb. Then give the English.

EXAMPLE:

¿ Cómo —— usted?

MODEL:

¿ Cómo **está** usted?
How are you?

1. Las primaveras —— frescas.
2. ¿ Dónde —— la señora González?
3. Este sombrero —— muy grande.
4. ¡ No —— queso en este sándwich!
5. Cuando —— calor, yo —— calor.
6. Mis padres no —— aquí.
7. Allá —— los padres de Ricardo.
8. Aquí el invierno —— muy frío.
9. Silvia —— sed y quiere tomar algo.
10. La nieve —— fría.
11. Esa señorita —— muy hermosa.
12. —— muy bien, gracias, ¿ y usted?
13. Aquellas casas —— muy grandes.
14. El clima de aquí no —— muy agradable.

15. Cuando no —— sueño, no quiero descansar.
16. ¿ —— muchas tiendas en el centro.
17. En general el otoño —— seco.
18. ¿ —— españoles esos señores?
19. ¿ —— usted mucha hambre, Luisa?
20. Esa tienda de ropa no —— muy buena.
21. ¿ —— mexicana la señora López?
22. ¿ —— en México el profesor Castro?
23. Luisa y yo —— españoles.
24. ¿ —— bueno el profesor?
25. Este —— un país frío.
26. Aquí —— mucha nieve en el invierno.
27. No —— mucho viento en el verano.
28. Yo —— el profesor de Miguel.
29. Pedro y Carlos —— hambre.
30. En general yo —— frío en el invierno.

4. NOUN COMPOUNDS.

Give the Spanish equivalents for the following English noun compounds:

EXAMPLE: the clothing shop

MODEL: **la tienda de ropa**

1. a summer hat
2. the professor's wife
3. Peter's parents
4. my sister's clothes
5. summer days
6. a spring day
7. this cheese sandwich
8. my father's hat
9. the house number
10. the winter weather
11. the London climate
12. my brother's house
13. the summer heat
14. Mr. López's number
15. spring clothes
16. that hat shop

F. STUDY

1. *Review* SECTION A *again. Follow the same procedure that was prescribed in* SECTION F *of* UNIT 1, *aiming at being able to say the whole section with the Spanish covered.*

2. *Prepare the* CONVERSATIONS *of* SECTION G.

G. CONVERSATIONS

1. *Reproduce the* BASIC DIALOGUE *in Spanish.*

2. *Using the* BASIC DIALOGUES *as your model, develop conversations of your own, such as:*

(*a*) Discussing the weather: how it is here today; how it generally is in your country (or section of the country) in the summer, in the autumn, in the winter, in the spring.

(*b*) Are you hungry or thirsty? What do you want to eat or drink? Where do you want to get it?

(*c*) Do you need to buy anything in that shop over there?

(*d*) Pointing out people and asking, or telling, who they are.

Learning. Spanish for Fun and Money. Going to the Cinema. Holiday.

Verbs: Infinitive; Present Tense; Participle; Gerund.

UNIT

3

A. BASIC DIALOGUES

1. "We have a Spanish lesson to do, but let's go to the cinema."

ENGLISH MEANING	AIDS TO LISTENING	SPANISH SPELLING

Record Side 1, after second spiral.

TOM:

have you learned	a-aprendído ustéd	ha aprendido usted
the lesson	la-lekθión	la lección
of today	de-ói	de hoy
Have you learned today's lesson?	¿ 'aprendído ustéd la-lekθión de-ói?	¿ Ha aprendido usted la lección de hoy?

GEORGE:

What lesson?	¿ ké lekθión.	¿ Qué lección?

TOM:

the third lesson	la-terθéra lekθión	la tercera lección
The third Spanish lesson.	la-terθéra lekθión d'españól.	La tercera lección de español.

GEORGE:

(I) have learned	e-aprendído	he aprendido
the two first pages	laṣ-dós priméras pájinas	las dos primeras páginas
I've learned the first two pages.	e-aprendído laṣ-dós priméras pájinas.	He aprendido las dos primeras páginas.
finished	terminádo	terminado
Have you finished?	¿ ustéd a-terminádo?	¿ Usted ha terminado?

TOM:

I yes	yó sí	yo sí
my mother	mi-mamá	mi mamá
I have, thanks to my mother.	yó sí, gráθias a-mi-mamá.	Yo sí, gracias a mi mamá.

GEORGE:

How's that?	¿ kómo es-éso?	¿ Cómo es eso?

TOM:

she	éḷa	ella
helps me	me-ayúda	me ayuda
She helps me.	éḷa me-ayúda.	Ella me ayuda.

GEORGE:

how good	ké ƀuéno	qué bueno

[22]

ENGLISH MEANING	AIDS TO LISTENING	SPANISH SPELLING
Man, that's good!	¡ ómbre, ké buéno!	¡ Hombre, qué bueno!
for what	por-ké	por qué
(does she) help you	lo-ayúda	lo ayuda
Why does she help you?	¿ por-ké lo-ayúda?	¿ Por qué lo ayuda?

TOM:

(I) believe, think, suppose	kréo	creo
(in order) to make me study	para-aθér-me estudiár	para hacerme estudiar
I suppose it's to make me study.	kréo k'es-par'aθér-me estudiár.	Creo que es para hacerme estudiar.

GEORGE:

(I) am tired	estói kansádo	estoy cansado
I'm tired of this lesson.	estói kansádo de-ésta lekθión.	Estoy cansado de esta lección.
to give a walk	dár una-buélta	dar una vuelta
Let's take a walk.	¡ bámos a-dár una-buélta.	Vamos a dar una vuelta.

TOM:

(they) are giving	están dándo	están dando
the film, the picture	la-pelíkula	la película
you and me	tú i-yó	tú y yo
They're showing the film *You and Me* at the Regis.	están dándo la-pelíkula tú i-yó en-el-rréjis.	Están dando la película *Tu y Yo* en el Regis.

GEORGE:

(do) not please me	no-me-gústan	no me gustan
the romantic films	las-pelíkulas rromántikas	las películas románticas
I don't like romantic films.	¡ no-me-gústan las-pelíkulas rromántikas.	No me gustan las películas románticas.
other	ótra	otra
What other film is there?	¿ ké ótra pelíkula ái?	¿ Qué otra película hay?

TOM:

The Bandits of the Rio Grande.	los-bandídos del-rrío gránde.	*Los Bandidos del Río Grande.*

GEORGE:

to see it	bér-la	verla
Let's go (and) see it.	¡ bámos a-bér-la.	Vamos a verla.
In those pictures they speak Spanish.	en-ésas pelíkulas áblan español.	En esas películas hablan español.

2. "How I'm learning Spanish and why."

JIM:

(do) you study	estúdia ustéd	estudia usted
Why are you studying Spanish?	¿ por-ké estúdia ustéd el-español?	¿ Por qué estudia usted el español?

ENGLISH MEANING	AIDS TO LISTENING	SPANISH SPELLING

BOB:

| because (I) like it | por-ke-me-gústa | porque me gusta |
| Because I like it (very) much. | por-ke-me gústa múcho. | Porque me gusta mucho. |

JIM:

to work	trabajár	trabajar
in Latin America	en la-amérika latína	en la América Latina
I want to work in Latin America.	yố kiéro trabajár en-l'amérika latína.	Yo quiero trabajar en la América Latina.

BOB:

how much time	kuánto tiémpo	cuánto tiempo
(does) one need	neθesíta úno	necesita uno
in order to learn	para-aprender	para aprender
How long do you need to learn Spanish?	¿ kuánto tiémpo neθesíta úno par'aprendér el-español ?	¿ Cuánto tiempo necesita uno para aprender el español ?

JIM:

hard to say it	difíθil deθír-lo	aifícil decirlo
It's hard to say.	eş-difíθil deθír-lo.	Es difícil decirlo.
my third year	mi-terθér áño	mi tercer año
already	yá	ya
This is my third year and I've already learned a lot.	éste eş-mi-terθér áño i-yá e--aprendído múcho.	Éste es mi tercer año, y ya he aprendido mucho.

BOB:

| an intelligent boy | un-muchácho intelijénte | un muchacho inteligente |
| Yes, but you're an intelligent fellow. | sí, pero-ustéd es-un-muchácho intelijénte. | Sí, pero usted es un muchacho inteligente. |

JIM:

so much	tánto	tanto
Not so very.	nó tánto:	No tanto.
you are speaking, talking	ustéd está ablándo	usted está hablando
after fifteen days	despuéş de-kínθe días	después de quince días
You're already talking after two weeks.	ustéd yá está ablándo despuéş de-kínθe días.	Usted ya está hablando después de quince días.

BOB:

It's not hard.	nó-eş difíθil.	No es difícil.
the teacher	la-profesóra	la profesora
says a thing	díθe una-kósa	dice una cosa
(we) all say it	lo-deθímos tódos	lo decimos todos
The teacher says something and then we all say it.	la-profesóra díθe una-kósa i-despuéş lo-deθímos tódos.	La profesora dice una cosa y después lo decimos todos.

[24]

ENGLISH MEANING	AIDS TO LISTENING	SPANISH SPELLING

JIM:

That's all right ! ¡ está mui-ƀién éso ! ¡ Está muy bien eso !
    you are learning ustédes están aprendiéndo ustedes están aprendiendo
    as the children learn komo-aprénden loş-níños como aprenden los niños
You're learning the way children ustédes están aprendiéndo komo- Ustedes están aprendiendo como
    learn. -aprénden loş-níños. aprenden los niños.

BOB:

    easy fáƀil fácil
    to imitate imitár imitar
Yes, it's easy to imitate the sí, es-fáƀil imitár a-la-profesóra. Sí, es fácil imitar a la profesora.
    teacher.
    (we) have learned emos-aprendído hemos aprendido
We've already learned a lot. yá emos-aprendído múcho. Ya hemos aprendido mucho.

JIM:

    are you tired están kansádos ustédes están cansados ustedes
    after the class despuéş de-la-klásc después de la clase
Aren't you tired after class ? ¿ no-están kansádos ustédeş des- ¿ No están cansados ustedes des-
    puéş de-la-kláse ? pués de la clase ?

BOB:

    (we) are tired estámos kansádos estamos cansados
Yes, we're all tired. sí, tódos estámos kansádos. Sí, todos estamos cansados.
The teacher's tired too. la-profesóra también está kan- La profesora también está can-
    sáda. sada.

JIM:

    (do) you know sábe ustéd sabe usted
    (we) are going to have ƀámos a-tenér vamos a tener
    eight days ócho días ocho días
    of holiday de-ƀakaθiónes de vacaciones
Do you know we're going to have ¿ sábe ustéd ke-ƀámos a-tenér ¿ Sabe usted que vamos a tener
    a week's holiday ? ócho díaş de-ƀakaθiónes ? ocho días de vacaciones ?

BOB:

    are you going to do ƀá a-aθér ustéd va a hacer usted
    during those days duránte éşoş días durante esos días
What are you going to do during ¿ ké ƀá 'aθér ustéd duránte éşoş ¿ Qué va a hacer usted durante
    those days ? días ? esos días ?

JIM:

    the first day el-primér día el primer día
    (I) raise myself me-leƀánto me levanto
    from the bed de-la-káma de la cama
The first day I'm not getting out el-primér día no-me-leƀánto de- El primer día no me levanto de
    of bed. -la-káma. la cama.

[25]

ENGLISH MEANING	AIDS TO LISTENING	SPANISH SPELLING
second	segúndo	segundo
only to eat	sólo para-komér	sólo para comer
The second day I'm only getting up to eat.	el-segúndo día me-lebánto sólo para-komér.	El segundo día me levanto sólo para comer.

Bob:

the third day	el-terθér día	el tercer día
the fourth	el-kuárto	el cuarto
The third day you're resting, and the fourth (day) too.	el-terθér día deskánsa, i-el--kuárto tamb ién.	El tercer día descansa, y el cuarto también.

Jim:

That's it.	éso és.	Eso es.
some friends	unos-amígos	unos amigos
Then I'm going to see some Spanish friends.	despueş bói a-bér a-unos--amígos españóles.	Después voy a ver a unos amigos españoles.

Bob:

(in order) to speak	para-ablár	para hablar
To speak Spanish?	¿ par'ablár español ?	¿ Para hablar español ?

Jim:

No! To speak English!	¡ nó, ómbre ! ¡ par'ablár inglés !	¡ No, hombre ! Para hablar inglés.
A holiday's a holiday.	laş-bakaθiónes som-bakaθiónes.	Las vacaciones son vacaciones.

NOTES ON PRONUNCIATION AND SPELLING

CONSONANTS

1. THE SPANISH d-SOUND.

Like the Spanish b-sound, this consonant has two varieties, which appear in the transcription as d and d. There is no great difference between these two varieties, which simply alternate in accordance with the sounds surrounding them. The difference is not recognized in Spanish writing, which spells both varieties as d.

(*1*) At the very beginning of a word-group, or after n or l, the d-sound is formed with the tongue-tip tightly pressed AGAINST the teeth; this is somewhat different from the English sound in *DanDy*, in which the tongue is pressed ABOVE the teeth. We transcribe this variety as d. Examples:

TRANSCRIPTION

dónde, díθen, tiéndaş grándes, están dándo, ablándo, aprendiéndo, difíθil deθír-lo

WRITTEN SPANISH

dónde, dicen, tiendas grandes, están dando, hablando, aprendiendo, difícil decirlo

(*2*) In any other surroundings, the d-sound is formed with the tongue-tip held loosely BETWEEN the upper and lower teeth, so that the breath continues to pass through. This variety approximates the sound spelled *th* in English *faTHer*, *moTHer*. We transcribe it as d.   Examples:

TRANSCRIPTION

adiós, mi-pádre, ustéd, ustédes, limonáda, agradáble, kansáda, tódos, rrikárdo, es-de-pédro, a-deskansar, a-terminádo, me-ayúda, el-primér día, ócho días, las-dós, estudiár, téngo séd.

WRITTEN SPANISH

adiós, mi padre, usted, ustedes, limonada, agradable, cansada, todos, Ricardo, es de Pedro, a descansar, ha terminado, me ayuda, el primer día, ocho días, las dos, estudiar, tengo sed

NOTE: When the d-sound is the final sound in a word (*as in* ustéd, séd), some speakers pronounce it very lightly. Many other speakers of Spanish have no d-sound at all at the end of a word, and therefore pronounce « ustéd » as « usté, » « téngo séd » as « téngo sé, » etc. If you hear this pronunciation without final d, you may safely imitate it.

2. THE SPANISH t-SOUND.

This sound is always formed with the tongue-tip pressed AGAINST the teeth, rather than ABOVE the teeth as with the English sound in *ToTal*. It is always spelled t, and we so transcribe it. Examples:

TRANSCRIPTION

está ustéd, tenémos, trés, a-tomár, el-autobús, kuátro, kuárto, señoríta, gústo, simpátiko, rromántikas, kuánto tiémpo, por-teléfono, tra-bajár, me-lebánto

WRITTEN SPANISH

está usted, tenemos, tres, a tomar, el autobús, cuatro, cuarto, señorita, gusto, simpático, románticas, cuánto tiempo, por teléfono, trabajar, me levanto

VOWELS

Spanish has just five basic vowel-sounds, which appear in our transcription as i e a o u. We comment on three of them in this unit, and the remaining two in the next unit.

3. THE VOWEL-SOUNDS e, a, AND o.

These vowel sounds have no important variations. Either stressed or unstressed they approximate, respectively, the first vowel-sounds of English *baker, father, water*. They are always e, a, o in Spanish spelling. Examples:

TRANSCRIPTION

ésta, tenémos, téngo, séd, θenténo, de-pédro, akélos, ke-aprendér, séko, fréskos, késo, en-el-θéntro, por-teléfono, el-sombréro, inglés

WRITTEN SPANISH

ésta, tenemos, tengo sed, Centeno, de Pedro, aquellos, que aprender, seco, frescos, queso, en el centro, por teléfono, el sombrero, inglés

TRANSCRIPTION

están dándo, a-tomár, la-sála, gonθáleθ, me-lámo, kása, limonáda, ermános, para-mañána, en-jenerál, en-el-beráno, agradáble, trabajár

WRITTEN SPANISH

están dando, a tomar, la sala, González, me llamo, casa, limonada, hermanos, para mañana, en general, en el verano, agradable, trabajar

TRANSCRIPTION

señóra, señóres, lópeθ, kómo, a-dónde, el-profesór, aóra, español, entónθes, ermósa, el-otóño, lóndres

WRITTEN SPANISH

señora, señores, López, cómo, a dónde, el profesor, ahora, español, entonces, hermosa, el otoño, Londres

B. STUDY

Review SECTION A *as in* UNITS 1 *and 2, covering up the English.*

C. LISTENING IN

1. *Review* SECTION A, *repeating the Spanish and giving the English.*

2. *With book closed, listen in as Manuel tells Jorge why he isn't studying his English lesson.*

Record Side 1, after second spiral.

JORGE: ¿ Qué está haciendo usted ?

MANUEL: Estoy descansando.

JORGE: ¿ Por qué no estudia usted la lección de inglés ?

MANUEL: No necesito estudiar. Soy un muchacho inteligente.

JORGE: No lo creo.

MANUEL: Estoy cansado de estudiar. La lección es difícil.

JORGE: ¡ Es fácil, hombre! Yo he terminado las tres primeras páginas.

MANUEL: ¿ Cuánto tiempo necesita usted para aprender una lección de inglés ?

JORGE: Necesito uno o dos días.

MANUEL: Yo necesito tres o cuatro días.

JORGE: Creo que a usted no le gusta trabajar.

MANUEL: La segunda lección es más difícil que la primera.

JORGE: Y la tercera es más difícil que la segunda.

MANUEL: No quiero ver la cuarta lección.

JORGE: ¿ Por qué no se levanta usted de la cama ? Es difícil estudiar en la cama.

MANUEL: Me levanto de la cama sólo para comer.

JORGE: Ya hemos aprendido mucho inglés en quince días. Es agradable imitar a la profesora.

MANUEL: Sí, es simpática la profesora. Pero no es agradable estudiar en casa.

JORGE: Yo creo que usted no está muy bien.

MANUEL: ¿ Quién ? ¿ Yo ? ¿ Por qué ?

JORGE: Porque no quiere trabajar . . . está cansado . . .

MANUEL: Yo estoy muy bien, gracias, pero necesito vacaciones.

JORGE: ¿ Cuántos días de vacaciones necesita usted ?

MANUEL: Quince días, más o menos. ¿ Qué tiempo hace hoy ?

JORGE: Hace fresco. Es un día muy agradable.

MANUEL: Vamos a dar una vuelta.

JORGE: ¿ No está cansado usted ?

MANUEL: Para dar una vuelta no estoy cansado.

D. GRAMMATICAL ANALYSIS

VERBS

1. THE GENERAL FORM (**Infinitive**).

You have by now handled several verb-forms ending in **-r: ser, hablar, tener, tomar,** etc. This is the "general" form or "infinitive," corresponding to that form in English which is often preceded by *to* (*to be, to have, to take,* etc.). Observe it in the following sentences:

Vamos a **tomar** algo.
Me levanto sólo para **comer**.
Es fácil **imitar** a la profesora.

Like a verb preceded by *to* in English, the Spanish general form is never the verbal core of a sentence; it is free from matters of tense, person-number, etc., and is therefore invariable.

As we said in UNIT 1, this general form is convenient for IDENTIFYING a Spanish verb. It is also the best starting-point for classifying and studying TYPES of verbs.

We may begin this study by stating that there are two main types of Spanish verb, distinguishable by the general form:

TYPE I

VOWEL **-a-**: hablar, estudiar, trabajar, *etc.*

TYPE II

VOWEL **-e-** or **-i-**: tener, comer, decir, *etc.*

2. THE PRESENT TENSE

The SIGN of the present tense in a Spanish verb is simply the same type-vowel which appears in its general form. The following are present-tense forms of the verbs **hablar**, *speak* and **aprender**, *learn*, which are REGULAR verbs. (Verbs are called REGULAR when it is possible to predict ALL their various forms on the basis of their general form alone.)

TYPE I: **hablar**

	SING.	PLU.
IST PER.	hablo	hablamos
3RD PER.	habla	hablan

TYPE II: **aprender**

	SING.	PLU.
IST PER.	aprendo	aprendemos
3RD PER.	aprende	aprenden

In the first and third singular there are no person-number endings, but in BOTH TYPES the type-vowel is replaced by **-o** in the first singular.

In the plural the type-vowel is followed by the person-number endings: **-mos** for the first person, and **-n** for the third person.

The stress, in the present-tense forms of regular verbs, is always on the NEXT-TO-LAST VOWEL. This means that it falls on the TYPE-VOWEL where the ending **-mos** occurs, but on the ROOT-VOWEL in the other forms.

Deviations from this regular pattern for the present tense, including TYPE II verbs with vowel **-i-**, will be studied in later units.

3. THE COMPLETIVE FORM (**Participle**).

What we will call the "completive" form or "participle" of the Spanish verb has the same relationship to the general form as English *learned*, *finished*, *spoken*, *been*, etc. have to *learn*, *finish*, *speak*, *be*, etc. In most verbs it has the following shape:

TYPE I: **-ado**

terminar: termin**ado**
hablar: habl**ado**
dar: d**ado**

TYPE II: **-ido**

aprender: aprend**ido**
tener: ten**ido**
ser: s**ido**

(*1*) **The Completive Form as an Adjective.** In both English and Spanish the completive form of the verb is often used as an adjective. The completive form of **cansar**, *tire* is so used in the following two sentences:

¿ No están **cansados** ustedes ?
La profesora también está **cansada.**

In this pattern the completive form varies its endings in AGREEMENT just like **simpático, mucho,** etc.

(*2*) **The Completive Form in Phrases.** Likewise both English and Spanish make phrases denoting that an action HAS BEEN COMPLETED:

¿ **Ha aprendido** usted la lección ?
Ya **hemos aprendido** mucho.

In these phrases the completive form is not an adjective and it ends invariably in **-o.**

Here the "pre-verb" or "auxiliary," corresponding to English *have*, is not the familiar **tener,** but rather one which is used with this meaning ONLY in completive phrases. Its general form is **haber,** and its present-tense forms are irregular (except for the plural endings), being as follows:

	SING.	PLU.
IST PER.	**he**	**hemos**
3RD PER.	**ha**	**han**

4. THE PROGRESSIVE FORM (Gerund).

What we will call the "progressive" form or "gerund" of the Spanish verb has the same relationship to the general form as English *learning*, *speaking*, etc. have to *learn*, *speak*, etc. In all verbs it has the following shape:

TYPE I: -ando

hablar: hablando
tomar: tomando
dar: dando

TYPE II: -iendo

aprender: aprendiendo
comer: comiendo
ser: siendo

The Progressive Form in Progressive Phrases.
Both English and Spanish make phrases denoting
that an action IS IN PROGRESS:

Usted ya **está hablando.**
Están dando la película.

Like the completive form in completive
phrases, the progressive form invariably ends in **-o.**
The pre-verb used in progressive phrases,
where English uses *be*, is always **estar.**

Comparative Usage in Verb Phrases

(*1*) The English pre-verb *do* — used in verb
phrases expressing negations or questions — has
no equivalent in Spanish. In making negative
statements, Spanish simply places **no** before the
verb:

He doesn't speak English.
No habla inglés.

I don't study much.
Yo **no** estudio mucho.

In asking questions, Spanish simply reverses
subject and verb — ALWAYS after a question-word:

How much time does one need?
¿ Cuánto tiempo **necesita** uno ?

What do you want to buy?
¿ Qué **quiere usted** comprar ?

— and usually in a "yes-or-no" question:

Do you know we're going to have eight days?
¿ **Sabe usted** que vamos a tener ocho días ?

(*2*) In completive phrases, English often puts
another word between *have* and the completive
form, but in Spanish **haber** and the completive
form are strictly inseparable:

We've already learned a lot.
Ya **hemos aprendido** mucho.

They haven't eaten.
No **han comido.**

Have you finished?
¿ Usted **ha terminado** ?

(The last example shows that non-reversal
of subject and verb is possible in a yes-or-no question. This order — instead of ¿ **Ha terminado
usted** ? — gives a little extra emphasis to the
subject **usted.**)

(*3*) English uses the progressive phrase more
freely than Spanish, where its use tends to denote
that the subject literally "stands (**estar**) engaged"
in an action. When this is not literally the case,
Spanish is likely to use a simple verb where English
has a progressive phrase:

Why are you studying Spanish?
¿ Por qué **estudia** usted el español ?

The first day I'm not getting up.
El primer día no me **levanto.**

Spanish also avoids the progressive phrase
in expressions of "going":

Where are you going?
¿ A dónde **va** usted ?

Then I'm going to see some Spanish friends.
Después **voy** a ver a unos amigos españoles.

E. GRAMMATICAL DRILLS

1. PRESENT TENSE

*As you say the following sentences aloud, supply
the proper person-number form of the present tense
of the verb identified in parentheses. Then give the
English.*

EXAMPLE:

¿ (hablar) usted español ?

MODEL:

¿ **Habla** usted español ?
Do you speak Spanish?

1. ¿ Dónde (comer) ustedes?
2. ¿ Cómo se (llamar) la hermana de Luisa?
3. ¿ Qué (aprender) ustedes en la clase de español?
4. Las mujeres (comprar) muchos sombreros.
5. Los niños no (descansar) durante el día.
6. Pedro me (ayudar) a aprender la lección.
7. José y yo (estudiar) en mi casa.
8. La clase (imitar) a la profesora.
9. Yo (necesitar) hablar con usted.
10. Yo me (levantar) de la cama sólo para comer.
11. Esa película no (terminar) bien.
12. ¿ Dónde (trabajar) el hermano de Miguel?
13. Yo (descansar) durante las vacaciones.
14. Manuel no (creer) eso.
15. Yo (comer) en el centro.
16. ¿ Qué (hacer) ustedes?
17. Miguel y yo (tomar) el autobús.
18. No me (gustar) esta clase.
19. Los muchachos no (saber) la lección.
20. Luisa y yo no (hablar) inglés.

2. COMPLETIVE PHRASES.

As you say the following sentences, fill the blank with the proper person-number form of **haber,** *and put the verb in parentheses in the completive form. Then give the English.*

EXAMPLE:

Yo no —— (trabajar) hoy.

MODEL:

Yo no **he trabajado** hoy.
I haven't worked today.

1. Jorge y yo —— (aprender) mucho español en quince días.
2. ¿ Dónde —— (estar) ustedes?
3. Yo no —— (tener) tiempo.
4. El día —— (ser) muy agradable.
5. Luisa —— (estar) en el centro.

6. Miguel y yo no —— (terminar) la lección de mañana.
7. ¿ —— (dar) usted una vuelta con la señorita García?
8. Los padres —— (comprar) ropa para los niños.
9. Pedro y yo no —— (estar) en San Luis.
10. El señor Quiroga —— (tomar) el autobús.
11. Mi mamá no me —— (ayudar) mucho.
12. —— (haber) muchos días frescos.
13. Yo no —— (comer) en aquel restaurante.
14. ¿ —— (estudiar) ustedes la primera lección?

3. PROGRESSIVE PHRASES.

As you say the following sentences, fill the blank with the proper person-number form of **estar,** *and put the verb in parentheses in the progressive form. Then give the English.*

EXAMPLE:

La clase —— (imitar) a la profesora.

MODEL:

La clase **está imitando** a la profesora.
The class is imitating the teacher.

1. Las mujeres —— (comprar) sombreros.
2. ¿ Qué —— (aprender) ustedes en la clase de español?
3. Los niños —— (descansar) ahora.
4. Ella me —— (ayudar) a terminar.
5. ¿ En qué restaurante —— (comer) los amigos?
6. José y yo —— (estudiar) la segunda lección.
7. ¿ Dónde —— (trabajar) usted?
8. Yo —— (terminar) la primera página.
9. ¿ Qué —— (estudiar) usted?
10. Yo ya —— (hablar) español.
11. Los niños no —— (comer) bien.
12. —— (hacer) buen tiempo hoy.
13. Las señoritas —— (dar) una vuelta.
14. La señora —— (hablar) con mis padres.
15. ¿ En qué tienda —— (trabajar) Juan?

F. STUDY

1. *Review* SECTION A, *covering up the Spanish.*   **2.** *Prepare the* CONVERSATIONS *of* SECTION G.

G. CONVERSATIONS

1. *Reproduce the* BASIC DIALOGUE *in Spanish.*

2. *Using the* BASIC DIALOGUES *as your model, develop conversations of your own, such as:*

(*a*) Why you're studying Spanish.
(*b*) How you're studying Spanish.
(*c*) Have you learned today's lesson?
(*d*) How you're going to spend your holiday.

Verbs: Second Person; Type II Verbs; Verbs with Alternation of Root-Vowels; Verbs with **g**-Roots in the Present Tense.

A. BASIC DIALOGUES

1. The psychology of escape.

ENGLISH MEANING	AIDS TO LISTENING	SPANISH SPELLING

Record Side 2.

HENRY:

each time	káda béθ	cada vez
to begin, start	empeθár	empezar
(I) begin, start	empiéθo	empiezo
to feel	sentír	sentir
(I) feel	siénto	siento
desires to sleep	deséos de-dormír	deseos de dormir
Every time I start to study I feel like sleeping.	káda béθ k'empiéθo a-estudiár siénto deséos de-dormír.	Cada vez que empiezo a estudiar, siento deseos de dormir.
Am I sleepy now!	¡ ké suéño téngo aóra !	¡ Qué sueño tengo ahora !

PAUL:

you (do) not sleep	tú no-duérmes	tú no duermes
the night	la-nóche	la noche
Don't you sleep at night?	¿ tú no-duérmes por-la-nóche ?	¿ Tú no duermes por la noche ?

HENRY:

eight hours	ócho óras	ocho horas
Certainly I do! I sleep eight hours.	sí, kómo nó. duérmo ócho óras.	¡ Sí, cómo no ! Duermo ocho horas.

PAUL:

(it) is (a) question	es-kuestión	es cuestión
of psychology	de-sikolojía	de psicología
George says it's a matter of psychology.	jórje díθe k'es-kuestión de-sikolojía.	Jorge dice que es cuestión de psicología.

HENRY:

to understand	entendér	entender
I don't understand that.	no-entiéndo éso.	No entiendo eso.
Sleepiness is sleepiness, and psychology is psychology.	suéño es-suéño — i-sikolojía es-sikolojía.	Sueño es sueño, y psicología es psicología.

[33]

ENGLISH MEANING	AIDS TO LISTENING	SPANISH SPELLING

PAUL:

when one (does) not want — kuando-úno no-kiére — cuando uno no quiere

(he) tries to escape — tráta de-eskapár-se — trata de escaparse

George says that when a person doesn't want to do a thing he tries to escape. — díθe jórje ke-kuando-úno no-kiére aθér una-kósa — tráta d'eskapár-se. — Dice Jorge que cuando uno no quiere hacer una cosa, trata de escaparse.

HENRY:

(I) say — dígo — digo

a fool — un-tónto — un tonto

And *I* say that George is a fool. — i-yó dígo ke-jórje es-un-tónto. — Y yo digo que Jorge es un tonto.

PAUL:

on the contrary — al-kontrário — al contrario

(he) has rightness — tiéne rraθón — tiene razón

On the contrary, *I* think he's right. — al-kontrário, yó kréo ke-tiéne rraθón. — Al contrario, yo creo que tiene razón.

(I) do my work — ágo mi-trabájo — hago mi trabajo

easily — fáθil ménte — fácilmente

I don't generally do my work easily. — en-jenerál no-ágo mi-trabájo fáθil ménte. — En general no hago mi trabajo fácilmente.

HENRY:

What do you know about psychology, Paul? — ¿ ké sábes tú de-sikolojía, páblo. — ¿ Qué sabes tú de psicología, Pablo ?

PAUL:

I know — sé — sé

the people — la-jénte — la gente

I only know it's a thing that [the] people don't understand very well. — sólo sé k'es-una-kósa ke-la-jénte no-entiénde mui-bién. — Sólo sé que es una cosa que la gente no entiende muy bien.

HENRY:

to prefer — preferír — preferir

(I) prefer — prefiéro — prefiero

Well, I prefer not to talk about things I don't understand. — buéno, yó prefiéro no-ablár de-kósas ke-no-entiéndo. — Bueno, yo prefiero no hablar de cosas que no entiendo.

PAUL:

to go out — salír — salir

Then let's go out. — ¡ entónθes bámos a-salír. — Entonces vamos a salir.

We both prefer that. — los-dós preferímos éso. — Los dos preferimos eso.

HENRY:

And (what about) our work for tomorrow? — ¿ i-el-trabájo de-mañána ? — ¿ Y el trabajo de mañana ?

ENGLISH MEANING	AIDS TO LISTENING	SPANISH SPELLING

PAUL:

We('ll) do it afterwards.　　lo-aθémoş después.　　Lo hacemos después.

HENRY:

Good. I don't want to escape, but I *do* want to take a walk.　　múi ƀién: no-kiéro eskapár-me, pero-sí kiéro ɗár una-ƀuélta.　　Muy bien. No quiero escaparme, pero sí quiero dar una vuelta.

And do you know something?　　¿ i-sáƀes una-kósa ?　　Y ¿ sabes una cosa ?

I'm not sleepy any longer.　　yá no-téngo suéño.　　Ya no tengo sueño.

2. "When I want to eat I want to eat!"

PEDRO:

　is far　　está léjos　　está lejos

　the restaurant　　el-rrestauránte　　el restaurante

　Is the restaurant far?　　¿ está léjos el-rrestauránte ?　　¿ Está lejos el restaurante ?

ESTEBAN:

　Not very.　　nó múcho:　　No mucho.

PEDRO:

　to go on foot　　ír a-pié　　ir a pie

　If it isn't very far, why don't we walk (it)?　　si-no-está mui-léjos, ¿ por-ké no--ƀámos a-pié ?　　Si no está muy lejos, ¿ por qué no vamos a pie ?

ESTEBAN:

　much hunger　　múcha ámbre　　mucha hambre

　I'm very hungry, Pete.　　téngo múcha ámbre, pédro.　　Tengo mucha hambre, Pedro.

　I don't want to walk.　　no-kiéro ír a-pié.　　No quiero ir a pie.

　Let's go by bus this time.　　¡ ƀámos en-autoƀús ésta ƀéθ.　　Vamos en autobús esta vez.

PEDRO:

　at what hour　　a-ké óra　　a qué hora

　the meeting, appointment　　la-θíta　　la cita

　with Jim　　kon-jáime　　con Jaime

　What time's our meeting with Jim?　　¿ a-ké óra eş-la-θíta kon-jáime ?　　¿ A qué hora es la cita con Jaime ?

ESTEBAN:

　seven　　siéte　　siete

　Seven o'clock.　　a-las-siéte.　　A las siete.

PEDRO:

　six and (a) quarter　　séis i-kuárto　　seis y cuarto

　It's quarter past six now.　　son-las-séis i-kuárto aóra.　　Son las seis y cuarto ahora.

　to delay　　tarɗár　　tardar

　(it) delays　　tárɗa　　tarda

　to arrive　　ƚegár　　llegar

　How long does the bus take to get there?　　¿ kuánto tiémpo tárɗa el-autoƀús en-ƚegár aƚá ?　　¿ Cuánto tiempo tarda el autobús en llegar allá ?

[35]

ENGLISH MEANING	AIDS TO LISTENING	SPANISH SPELLING

ESTEBAN:

| minutes | minútos | minutos |
| Fifteen minutes. | kínθe minútos. | Quince minutos. |

PEDRO:

to think, intend, plan	pensár	pensar
(do you) think	piénsas	piensas
from six and (a) half	desde-las-séis i-média	desde las seis y media
What do you plan to do from six thirty till seven?	¿ ké piénsas aθér desde-las-séis i-média asta-las-siéte?	¿ Qué piensas hacer desde las seis y media hasta las siete?

ESTEBAN:

to be able	podér	poder
(we) can	podémos	podemos
We can begin to eat, man!	¡ ombre, podémos empeθár a--komér.	¡ Hombre, podemos empezar a comer !

PEDRO:

to ask, order	pedír	pedir
(do you) ask	pídes	pides
(Will) you order for Jim, too?	¿ tú pídes para-jáime también?	¿ Tú pides para Jaime también?

ESTEBAN:

| Yes, I think it's all right to order for Jim. | sí, kréo k'está biém pedír para--jáime: | Sí, creo que está bien pedir para Jaime. |

PEDRO:

| What complications! | ¡ ké komplikaθiónes! | ¡ Qué complicaciones ! |

ESTEBAN:

the fault	la-kúlpa	la culpa
It's not my fault.	yó no-téngo la-kúlpa.	Yo no tengo la culpa.
to wait	esperár	esperar
When I'm very hungry, I can't wait.	kuando-téngo múcha ámbre no--puédo esperár.	Cuando tengo mucha hambre, no puedo esperar.

3. "Haven't you got any clothes of your own?"

JORGE:

to come	benír	venir
(do you) come	biénes	vienes
Where are you coming from?	¿ de-dónde biénes tú?	¿ De dónde vienes tú?

ROBERTO:

(I) come	béngo	vengo
from no place	de-ningúna párte	de ninguna parte
I'm not coming from anywhere.	no-béngo de-ningúna párte.	No vengo de ninguna parte.
Where can I be coming from?	¿ de-dónde puédo benír.	¿ De dónde puedo venir?

ENGLISH MEANING	AIDS TO LISTENING	SPANISH SPELLING

JORGE:

Then what are you doing with that hat? — ¿ ké áθes kon-ése sombréro en-tónθes. — ¿ Qué haces con ese sombrero, entonces ?

ROBERTO:

It's Guillermo's. — eş-de-giĺérmo. — Es de Guillermo.

JORGE:

that necktie — ésa korƀáta — esa corbata

And (what about) that tie? — ¿ i-ésa korƀáta ? — ¿ Y esa corbata ?

ROBERTO:

pretty — boníta — bonita

It's very pretty. — eş-múi ƀoníta. — Es muy bonita.

JORGE:

to know — konoθér — conocer

known — konoθída — conocida

Very pretty, and very (well) known. — múi ƀoníta i-múi konoθída. — Muy bonita, y muy conocida.

ROBERTO:

a party — una-fiésta — una fiesta

this night — ésta nóche — esta noche

You know, George, I'm going to a party tonight . . . — sáƀes, jórje, ƀói a-una-fiésta ésta nóche . . . — Sabes, Jorge, voy a una fiesta esta noche . . .

JORGE:

Really ? — á, ¿ sí ? — ¿ Ah, sí ?

ROBERTO:

blue socks — kalθetínes aθúles — calcetines azules

And I need some blue socks. — i-neθesíto unos-kalθetínes aθúles. — Y necesito unos calcetines azules.

JORGE:

My socks too? No! — ¿ mis-kalθetínes también ? ¡ éso nó ! — ¿ Mis calcetines también ? ¡ Eso no !

Haven't you got (any) clothes? — ¿ tú no-tiénes rrópa ? — ¿ Tú no tienes ropa ?

ROBERTO:

that of you (all) — la-de-ustédes — la de ustedes

elegant, stylish — elegánte — elegante

Yours are more stylish. — la-de-ustédes eş-más-elegánte. — La de ustedes es más elegante.

JORGE:

Saturday — sáƀado — sábado

Today's Saturday and all of us are going out. — ói es-sáƀado i-ƀámos a-salír tódos. — Hoy es sábado y vamos a salir todos.

ENGLISH MEANING	AIDS TO LISTENING	SPANISH SPELLING
(you) can	puéđes	puedes
to use, wear	usár	usar
Dad	papá	papá
You can wear one of Dad's ties.	puéđes usár una-korƀáta đe--papá.	Puedes usar una corbata de papá.

ROBERTO:

those of Dad	laş-đe-papá	las de papá
Dad's aren't very stylish.	laş-đe-papá no-son-mui-elegán-tes.	Las de papá no son muy ele-gantes.

JORGE:

All right. You can wear my tie, but not the socks!	está ƀién: puéđes usár mi--korƀáta, ¡ pero-los-kalθetíneş nó!	Está bien. Puedes usar mi corbata, pero ¡ los calcetines no!

ROBERTO:

Fine thing!	¡ ké ƀarƀaridáđ!	¡ Qué barbaridad!
to serve	serƀír	servir
(they) serve	sírƀen	sirven
What are [the] brothers for, then?	¿ para-ké sírƀen los-ermános entónθes.	¿ Para qué sirven los hermanos entonces?

NOTES ON PRONUNCIATION AND SPELLING

CONSONANTS

1. THE SPANISH g-SOUND.

Like the b-sound and the d-sound, this consonant has two varieties, which appear in the transcription as g and g. There is no great difference between these two varieties, which simply alternate in accordance with the sounds surrounding them. The difference in quality is not recognized in Spanish writing, which spells EITHER variety as gu before i or e, and g elsewhere.

(*1*) At the very beginning of a word-group, or after n, the g-sound is as in English *Gate*, *anGer*, formed with the back part of the mouth fully closed. We transcribe this variety as g. Examples:

TRANSCRIPTION

gráθias, inglés, téngo, béngo, đe-ningúna párte, bién gráθias, inglatérra

WRITTEN SPANISH

gracias, inglés, tengo, vengo, de ninguna parte, bien gracias, Inglaterra

(*2*) In any other surroundings, the g-sound is formed with the back part of the mouth not quite closed, so that the breath continues to pass through. We transcribe this variety as g. Examples:

TRANSCRIPTION

eş-đe-giĺérmo, migél; múcho gústo, tiéndaş grándes, álgo, segúndo, unos-amígos, dígo, ágo, l̇egár, elegánte

WRITTEN SPANISH

es de Guillermo, Miguel; mucho gusto, tiendas grandes, algo, segundo, unos amigos, digo, hago, llegar, elegante

[38]

2. THE SPANISH k-SOUND.

This closely resembles the sounds of English *CoKe*. It is spelled **qu** before **i** or **e**, and **c** elsewhere. (Remember that **c** spells the θ-sound before **i** or **e**.) Examples:

TRANSCRIPTION

de-akí, kínθe, kiéro, ké, akélos, késo; kalór, la-káma, kansádos, θínko, fréskos, konoθída, la-kúlpa, kuátro, kuestión, kréo, el-klíma, la-kláse, la-lekθión

WRITTEN SPANISH

de aquí, quince, quiero, qué, aquellos, queso; calor, la cama, cansados, cinco, frescos, conocida, la culpa, cuatro, cuestión, creo, el clima, la clase, la lección

VOWELS

3. THE SPANISH VOWEL i.

This vowel-sound has two varieties:

(*1*) As a full vowel, either stressed or unstressed, it approximates the sound of English *machIne*. It is written **i** in all cases except one: the Spanish word for *and* is spelled **y**. Examples:

TRANSCRIPTION

θínko, la-θíta, dormír, en-méjiko, mi-pádre, kiróga, i-yó

WRITTEN SPANISH

cinco, la cita, dormir, en México, mi padre, Quiroga, y yo

(*2*) As a half-vowel, unstressed and occurring just before or just after a full vowel — that is, in a DIPHTHONG —, it approximates the sound in English *vIew, voId*. This variety is written **i** normally, but **y** at the end of a word. Examples:

TRANSCRIPTION

también, niébe, a-pié, gráθias, estúdia, estudiár, la-lekθión, bakaθiónes; séis, ai-múchos, jáime, soi-españóla, bói a-kása, estói muibién

WRITTEN SPANISH

también, nieve, a pie, gracias, estudia, estudiar, la lección, vacaciones; seis, hay muchos, Jaime, soy española, voy a casa, estoy muy bien

4. THE SPANISH VOWEL u.

Like the vowel **i**, this sound has two varieties. Both are written as **u**.

(*1*) As a full vowel, either stressed or unstressed, it approximates the sound of English *prUne*. Examples:

TRANSCRIPTION

me-ayúda, aθúles, la-kúlpa, minútos, la-película, ustéd, un-ermáno, usár

WRITTEN SPANISH

me ayuda, azules, la culpa, minutos, la película, usted, un hermano, usar

(*2*) As a half-vowel, unstressed and occurring just before or just after a full vowel in a DIPHTHONG, it approximates the sound in English *qUake, loUd*. This variety is also written **u**. Examples:

TRANSCRIPTION

luébe, después, suéño, kuátro, kuárto, kuánto; en-autobús, el-rrestauránte

WRITTEN SPANISH

llueve, después, sueño, cuatro, cuarto, cuánto; en autobús, el restaurante

B. STUDY

Review SECTION A, *covering up the English.*

C. LISTENING IN

1. *Review* SECTION A, *repeating the Spanish and giving the English.*

2. *With book closed, listen in as Raúl and Ricardo talk about going to the party tonight.*

Record Side 2.

RAÚL: ¿ Tú vas a la fiesta esta noche ?

RICARDO: Quiero ir a la fiesta pero no puedo.

RAÚL: ¿ Por qué no puedes ir a la fiesta ?

RICARDO: Estoy esperando a unos amigos que van a llegar de Londres.

RAÚL: ¿ A qué hora llegan esos amigos de Londres ?

RICARDO: Llegan a las siete o a las siete y media.

RAÚL: Los amigos de Londres también pueden ir a la fiesta.

RICARDO: ¿ Con quién vas tú a la fiesta ?

RAÚL: Voy con Carmen Díaz. Es muy bonita.

RICARDO: ¿ A qué hora empieza la fiesta ?

RAÚL: No sé a qué hora empieza.

RICARDO: ¿ Qué piensas hacer ahora ?

RAÚL: Quiero ir al centro a comprar unos calcetines y una corbata. Necesito calcetines azules. Mi hermano Pedro usa mis corbatas. Cada vez que tengo que salir, necesito comprar otra corbata.

RICARDO: Eso es muy malo. ¿ No tiene ropa Pedro ?

RAÚL: Dice que no tiene ropa. También dice que prefiere mi ropa porque es más elegante. Pedro es un tonto.

RICARDO: ¿ Qué clase de corbata quieres comprar ?

RAÚL: Una corbata azul.

RICARDO: Yo también quiero ir al centro.

RAÚL: ¿ Prefieres ir a pie o en autobús ?

RICARDO: Vamos en autobús.

RAÚL: Pero hombre, la tienda no está lejos y tenemos mucho tiempo.

RICARDO: Bueno, entonces, podemos ir a la tienda a pie.

RAÚL: Y también los autobuses tardan mucho. No llegan cuando uno está esperando. ¿ No sabes eso ?

RICARDO: Sí, tienes razón. Cada vez que espero el autobús, tarda mucho en llegar.

D. GRAMMATICAL ANALYSIS

VERBS

1. THE SECOND PERSON.

Until the present unit you have used only **usted** (plural **ustedes**) as the equivalent of English *you.* This is a courtesy title which is followed by a THIRD-PERSON verb-form (**usted tiene, ustedes están,** etc.). In this unit, however, you have been using the pronoun **tú,** also meaning *"you."* This is the FAMILIAR form for addressing one person, which a speaker of Spanish uses when he talks to a member of his family, to a close friend, or to a child.

(*1*) **Familiar Singular.** The pronoun **tú** is a SECOND-PERSON SINGULAR pronoun, and any verb of which it is the subject has the SECOND-PERSON SINGULAR ending. In the present tense of all verbs this ending is **-s,** as you have seen in such verb-forms as **sabes, tienes, vienes,** etc.

(*2*) **Familiar Plural.** Spanish also has SECOND-PERSON PLURAL forms, which are used for familiar address in Spain but not at all commonly in Spanish America. Speakers of American Spanish use the third-person plural **ustedes** for addressing *any two or more* persons, regardless of familiarity. You recall the sentence **"Las de ustedes son más elegantes,"** in which the **ustedes** refers to the two brothers of the speaker.

2. TYPE II VERBS WITH VOWEL -i-.

In TYPE II verbs having the vowel **-i-** before the **-r-** of the general form (**decir, pedir, salir,**

The arts and crafts and hand labour move on side by side with industrialization, a curious fact as readily seen in Spain, in Mexico, in Venezuela, and elsewhere in the Spanish-speaking world. These two pictures from Bolivia illustrate primitive yet effective methods in agriculture and crafts. Above: Two Indian women weave fabrics on a hand loom. Below: Workers on the Altiplano (high plateau) break ground for the spring planting.

Above: Boiled chicle — base for chewing gum — is poured into a mould in the Guatemala forests from which it comes. Below: Costa Rican workers harvest bananas. (Notice: The fruit grows upwards, never down.) On the opposite page: A rubber tapper, in the jungle near Beni, Bolivia, prepares to coagulate the milk into a bale over the fire.

Above: Sheep from the Argentine pampas, the stockgrower's paradise. Purebreds on a farm near Cochabamba in Bolivia.

venir, etc.), this type-vowel becomes -e- (as in other TYPE II verbs) when it is the last vowel of a present-tense form. Thus we get: sal**ir**, sal**imos** *but* sal**e**, sal**es**, sal**en**.

3. VERBS WITH ALTERNATION OF ROOT-VOWEL.

You have already used such present-tense forms as "prefiero, siento, empieza, puedes, llueve, duermo," etc., in all of which the root contains a combination of two vowels (a DIPHTHONG), different from the single vowel appearing in the root of other forms of these verbs such as "preferimos, sentir, podemos, dormir," etc. You may also have noted that all the forms with diphthongs are among those present-tense forms which, like "aprendo, ayuda, hablan," etc., are stressed on the root.

We describe the behavior of these verbs by stating that some (though not all) Spanish verbs of both TYPES I and II show the following alternations of the root-vowel according as the root is unstressed or stressed:

UNSTRESSED	STRESSED
-e-	-ie-
-o-	-ue-

Here is a list of the verbs with this feature that you have met so far. (The hyphen after the type-vowel in the parenthesized form stands for all person-number forms stressed on the root and therefore having the diphthong: for example, **empieza-** stands for **empieza, empiezas, empiezan,** and **empiezo.**)

TYPE I
empezar (empieza-)
pensar (piensa-)

TYPE II
dormir (duerme-)
entender (entiende-)

llover	(llueve-)
poder	(puede-)
preferir	(prefiere-)
querer	(quiere-)
sentir	(siente-)
tener	(tiene-)
venir	(viene-)

Since the feature of root-vowel alternation cannot be predicted from the general form alone — compare, for example, esperar (espera-), comer (come-) — we will use the above formula to list those verbs which have it.

A small number of TYPE II verbs, all of which have the type-vowel -i- in the general form, show the following root-vowel alternation instead of the commoner one with diphthongs:

UNSTRESSED	STRESSED
-e-	-i-

Thus far you have seen the following three: decir (dice-); pedir (pide-); servir (sirve-).

4. g-ROOTS IN THE PRESENT TENSE.

Some very common Spanish verbs show a variation in their root, consisting of a -g- following or replacing its final consonant. In the present tense, this g-root occurs in the FIRST-SINGULAR form of the following verbs you have met:

hacer: hago
salir: salgo
decir (dice-): digo
tener (tiene-): tengo
venir (viene-): vengo

The g-root of **decir** has the alternate stressed vowel -i-, but in the g-roots of **tener** and **venir,** even though stressed, there is no diphthong as there is in the regular root when stressed.

E. GRAMMATICAL DRILLS

1. PRESENT-TENSE FORMS OF VERBS WITH ROOT-VOWEL ALTERNATION.

As you say the following sentences aloud, supply the proper person-number form of the present tense of the verb in parentheses. Then give the English.

EXAMPLE:

¿ A qué hora (empezar) la película ?

MODEL:

    ¿ A qué hora **empieza** la película?
    What time does the film begin?

1. ¿ Por qué no (querer) ustedes ir en autobús?
2. ¿ No (entender) usted a la profesora?
3. Este señor dice que no (poder) esperar.
4. Yo no (dormir) durante el día.
5. Estos muchachos (tener) sueño cuando (empezar) a estudiar.
6. Manuel no (poder) ir a comer con ustedes.
7. ¿ Cuántas horas (dormir) tú por la noche?
8. Mi hijo Jorge no (querer) estudiar.
9. Tú y yo (poder) empezar a comer.
10. ¿ (pedir) yo para Jaime también?
11. Yo no (entender) esta lección.
12. ¿ Para qué (servir) las hermanas?
13. ¿ Qué (pensar) usted de este clima?
14. Gloria y yo (poder) empezar a trabajar a las ocho.
15. Yo (preferir) no hablar de eso.
16. María (sentir) deseos de dormir.
17. ¿ Qué (pensar) tú hacer durante las vacaciones?
18. José dice que (preferir) descansar ahora.
19. Usted y yo (servir) como profesores de inglés.
20. Rosita y yo (pensar) terminar ese trabajo después.
21. Jaime (pedir) queso cada vez que come.
22. ¿ Para qué (servir) estas cosas?
23. Los muchachos no aprenden porque no (entender).
24. Yo no (sentir) deseos de trabajar hoy.
25. Mi mamá y yo (entender) el español.
26. Tú y yo (pedir) para los otros.
27. Mis padres (poder) estar aquí a las cuatro.
28. Mis hijos y yo (querer) aprender el español.
29. Pedro dice que (sentir) deseos de comer.
30. Yo (dormir) en la clase de aquel profesor.
31. Mis amigos y yo (preferir) las tiendas del centro.

2. PRESENT-TENSE FORMS OF tener, venir, salir, hacer, decir.

    Go through the five sentences that follow, and make **yo** *the subject of each. Second, make* **tú** *the subject. Third, make it* **Gloria**; *fourth,* **Gloria y yo**; *and fifth,* **Gloria y Juan**. *Each time through, supply the proper person-number of the verb in parentheses, and say the English.*

EXAMPLE:

    . . . (tener) tres hijos.

MODEL:

    Yo tengo tres hijos.
    I have three children.

1. . . . no (tener) la culpa.
2. . . . no (venir) de ninguna parte.
3. . . . no (salir) por la noche.
4. . . . (hacer) el trabajo fácilmente.
5. . . . (decir) que no hay tiempo para eso.

F. STUDY

    1. *Review* SECTION A *again, with the Spanish covered.*

    2. *Prepare the* CONVERSATIONS *of* SECTION G.

G. CONVERSATIONS

    1. *Reproduce the* BASIC DIALOGUES *in Spanish.*
    2. *Using the* BASIC DIALOGUES *as your model, develop conversations of your own, such as:*
    (*a*) Arguing with your brother or sister, who wants to borrow your clothes.

    (*b*) Planning to meet a friend at a restaurant; how you're going to get there, what time, etc.

Review.

Unit One.   Unit Two.   Unit Three.   Unit Four.

UNIT

5

A. REVIEW OF UNIT 1

I. SPEAKING SPANISH.

1. *Review thoroughly* SECTION A *of* UNIT 1, *making sure you can say the English with the English text covered and the Spanish with the Spanish text covered.*

2. *Give answers to the following questions:* (*Any answer that makes sense is all right, provided it's in the form of a full sentence. It shouldn't be just* **Sí,** **No,** *or some other monosyllable. You don't need to confine yourself to the vocabulary of* UNIT 1; *use any words you know by now.*)

1. ¿ Como está usted ?
2. ¿ A dónde va usted ?
3. ¿ Es ésta la sala número cinco ?
4. ¿ Quién es el profesor ?
5. ¿ Cómo es el profesor ?
6. ¿ De dónde es usted, señorita ?
7. ¿ Cómo se llama usted ?
8. ¿ Tiene usted hermanos, señorita ?
9. ¿ Dónde están los padres de Silvia ?
10. ¿ Es mexicano el padre de Luisa ?
11. ¿ Tiene usted hijos ?
12. ¿ Es simpática la hermana de Ricardo ?
13. ¿ Habla usted español, señor Ross ?
14. ¿ Es usted español ?
15. ¿ Habla usted inglés, señor Centeno ?
16. ¿ Es usted un profesor de inglés ?
17. ¿ Cómo se llama la hija del profesor González ?
18. ¿ Hablan inglés los amigos de usted ?
19. ¿ Cómo se llama la hermana de la señora Evans ?
20. ¿ Son simpáticos los hijos del profesor ?
21. ¿ Cómo se llama el hermano de usted ?
22. ¿ Hablan español los padres de Ricardo ?
23. ¿ Cómo están ustedes ?
24. ¿ Están aquí los padres de usted ?
25. ¿ Cómo estás ?
26. ¿ A dónde van ustedes ?
27. ¿ Está aquí Miguel ?
28. ¿ De dónde son ustedes ?
29. ¿ Cómo se llaman los hijos del señor Quiroga ?
30. ¿ A dónde vas ahora ?
31. ¿ Tienen ustedes hijos ?
32. ¿ Dónde está el autobús ?
33. ¿ Tiene hijos el señor López ?
34. ¿ Dónde está la casa del señor Ross ?
35. ¿ Es usted de Londres ?
36. ¿ Dónde están los hermanos de usted ?
37. ¿ Son ustedes de aquí ?
38. ¿ De dónde es Luisa ?
39. ¿ Quién es usted ?
40. ¿ A dónde va el profesor ?

3. *Ask the questions that would get the following answers:* (*Here is a clue to framing the question: if the answer begins with* **Sí** *or* **No,** *the question is of the "Yes or No" type, containing no question word; otherwise it does contain a question word such as* **dónde, quién, cómo.**)

1. El autobús está en la esquina.
2. Muy bien, gracias, ¿ y usted ?
3. No, ésta es la sala número tres.
4. Sí, mis hijos están aquí ahora.
5. No, el profesor no está aquí.
6. Soy de San Luis, señora.
7. No, no tengo hermanas.
8. Somos de México.
9. Mi padre se llama Ricardo.
10. Sí, hablo español.
11. Mis padres están en Inglaterra.
12. Voy a la esquina a tomar el autobús.
13. Sí, hablan muy bien el inglés.
14. Es muy simpático.

[43]

15. Yo me llamo Ricardo Ross.
16. Yo soy de Londres.
17. Mis padres son mexicanos.
18. Los hermanos de Ricardo son muy simpáticos.
19. Somos de San Luis Potosí en México.
20. Sí, señor, soy mexicana.
21. Es muy simpática la señora López.
22. Sí, somos cinco hijos.
23. Miguel y Luisa están en el centro.
24. Está en la casa.
25. El señor y la señora González tienen cuatro hijos.
26. La hija del señor López se llama Silvia.
27. Las mujeres son mexicanas.
28. Miguel Centeno es de San Luis.
29. No, yo sólo hablo español.
30. Sí, tengo dos hermanos y una hermana.

4. *After hearing again the* LISTENING-IN *Section of* UNIT 1, *give answers to the following questions based directly on it:*

1. ¿ Quién es el señor González ?
2. ¿ Es un profesor de inglés ?
3. ¿ Habla inglés el profesor ?
4. ¿ Habla bien el inglés ?
5. ¿ Es simpática la señora González ?
6. ¿ Tienen hijos el señor y la señora González ?
7. ¿ Cuántos hijos tienen ?
8. ¿ Cuántos hombres y cuántas mujeres ?
9. ¿ Cómo se llama la hija ?
10. ¿ Dónde están los hijos del profesor ?
11. ¿ Están en España ?
12. ¿ Los hijos hablan español ?
13. ¿ De dónde es el señor ?
14. ¿ Tiene hermanos el señor ?
15. ¿ Cuántos hermanos tiene ?
16. ¿ Es mexicana la señorita ?
17. ¿ Hablan inglés los mexicanos ?

II. WRITING SPANISH.

The following sentences are variations on the content of the BASIC DIALOGUES *of* UNIT 1. *Write them out in Spanish. Parentheses around an English word mean that it isn't expressed in the Spanish version; brackets around a word not normally present in the English mean that it* **is** *expressed in the Spanish.*

1. Good morning, Mrs. González.
2. Have you (any) brothers (and sisters) ?
3. We have (a) house in London.
4. How are you, Mr. López ? — I'm very well, thank you.
5. My parents are in England.
6. Is Luisa nice ? — Yes indeed !
7. Where are we now ?
8. Richard Ross is from London.
9. I'm not from here.
10. Where is [the] Mr. López from ?
11. Where is [the] Mr. González going ?
12. The bus is at (**en**) the corner.
13. There comes [the] Miss Sylvia.
14. Good-bye, Mrs. Quiroga.
15. My name is Sylvia Evans.
16. Who is the professor ?
17. Where's [the] Miss Evans ?
18. The professor isn't very nice.
19. I'm not [the] Miss Ross.
20. How do you do, sir ?
21. This isn't [the] room number five.
22. Where's the bus ? — There it comes.
23. Who is going to the corner ?
24. We have seven children: three boys and four girls.
25. The brothers (and sisters) are very nice.
26. I have one sister and one brother.
27. Where are Miguel and Richard ?
28. Do you speak Spanish ? — Yes indeed.
29. What's your name ?
30. Where are you from ?
31. Are you Mexican ? — Yes, ma'am, I'm Mexican.
32. My father is in St. Louis.
33. London is in England.
34. Do you have a brother or a sister ?

B. REVIEW OF UNIT 2

I. SPEAKING SPANISH.

1. *Review thoroughly* SECTION A *of* UNIT 2, *just as you did for* UNIT 1.

2. *Give complete answers to the following questions:*

1. ¿ Es usted de este país ?
2. ¿ Es de México el señor González ?
3. ¿ Qué país es más grande, España o Inglaterra ?
4. ¿ Es grande la casa de ustedes ?
5. ¿ Cómo es el clima de Inglaterra ?
6. ¿ Hay nieve en el sur ?
7. ¿ Qué tiempo hace en el invierno ?
8. ¿ Qué tienda es aquella que está en la esquina ?
9. ¿ Tiene hambre usted ?
10. ¿ Es agradable el invierno ?
11. ¿ Qué tiempo hace en la primavera ?
12. ¿ Cómo es la casa de usted ?
13. ¿ Qué tiempo hace en el otoño ?
14. ¿ Llueve mucho aquí ?
15. ¿ Qué tiempo hace en el verano ?
16. ¿ Tiene usted sed ?
17. ¿ Qué va usted a tomar ?
18. ¿ Es buena la tienda ?
19. ¿ Está en el centro la casa de ustedes ?
20. ¿ Quiere usted tomar algo ?
21. ¿ Cómo son los días de la primavera ?
22. ¿ Cómo son los días del invierno ?
23. ¿ Cómo son los días del otoño ?
24. ¿ Cómo son los días del verano ?
25. ¿ Qué va usted a comprar en la tienda ?
26. ¿ Tiene usted un sombrero de verano ?
27. ¿ Qué número de teléfono tiene Luisa ?
28. ¿ Tiene usted teléfono ?

3. *Ask questions that will get the following answers:*

1. Mi país es muy grande.
2. Hace calor hoy.
3. En el sur el clima es muy agradable.
4. La primavera es fresca.
5. El clima de aquí no es bueno.

6. Llueve mucho en aquel país.
7. Voy a tomar una limonada.
8. Quiero comprar un sombrero.
9. Esa tienda no es muy buena.
10. Voy a casa a descansar.
11. Sí, tengo teléfono.
12. Sí, lo llamo por teléfono mañana.
13. Esta casa es de Pedro.
14. Estos señores son hermanos.
15. No, señorita. Soy española.
16. El día es muy agradable.
17. No hay teléfono aquí.
18. Es muy bonita la casa.
19. Son hermosas las señoritas.
20. Es agradable la señora del profesor.
21. La casa que está en la esquina es de aquellos señores.
22. Los españoles hablan español.
23. Los días del verano son agradables.
24. Sí, usted es muy simpático.
25. El hermano es más simpático que la hermana.
26. No, tengo más sed que hambre.
27. No, no tengo sueño.

4. *After hearing again the* LISTENING-IN *Section of* UNIT 2, *give answers to the following questions based directly on it.*

1. ¿ Qué tiempo hace en el invierno ?
2. ¿ Hay nieve ?
3. ¿ Hace viento ?
4. ¿ Es agradable el invierno ?
5. ¿ Llueve mucho en el otoño ?
6. ¿ Cuándo hace calor ?
7. ¿ Cómo es el invierno en el país de Miguel ?
8. ¿ Tiene hambre Harry ?
9. ¿ Qué quiere tomar Harry ?
10. ¿ Hay limonada en esa tienda ?
11. ¿ A dónde van entonces ?
12. ¿ Qué quiere comprar Miguel ?
13. ¿ No tiene sombrero Miguel ?
14. ¿ Cómo es el sombrero de Miguel ?
15. ¿ Quiere tomar el autobús Miguel ?
16. ¿ Cómo es el autobús ?

17. ¿ Dónde está la tienda ?
18. ¿ De quién es la tienda ?
19. ¿ Tienen que hablar español ?
20. ¿ Qué tiene Miguel ?
21. ¿ A dónde quiere ir Miguel ?
22. ¿ Tiene Miguel el número de teléfono de Harry ?
23. ¿ Qué número es ?

II. WRITING SPANISH.

The following sentences are variations on the content of the BASIC DIALOGUES *of* UNIT 2. *Write them out in Spanish.*

1. These gentlemen are brothers.
2. What are you saying, Miss ?
3. Are the professor's children here ?
4. We have to learn that for tomorrow.
5. What are you going to have, Dick ?
6. I'm more hungry than thirsty.
7. (Girl speaking:) I'm not Mexican, I'm Spanish.
8. The Mexicans also speak Spanish.
9. What's the weather like in that country ?
10. Is it like the climate [of] here ? — More or less.
11. They say that it doesn't rain much in the south.
12. It's cold in the winter.
13. It's warm in the summer.
14. The spring is cool and beautiful.
15. It's very windy here.
16. In general the autumn is dry.
17. There aren't (any) big shops in the town.
18. Peter and Dick are sleepy.
19. My parents are Spanish.
20. Those two ladies are Spanish too.
21. There isn't (any) snow in the summer.
22. These lessons are very easy.
23. That young lady isn't very intelligent.
24. That house is beautiful, and this (one) too.
25. The climate [of] here is very agreeable.
26. How is the autumn in this country ?
27. That cheese is dry.
28. We have three professors of Spanish. — Are they Spanish ?
29. There isn't (any) telephone here.
30. I want to buy something in that shop (over there).
31. It's very windy in the spring.
32. Who speaks English here ?
33. José's brothers are very nice.
34. The weather is beautiful now.
35. This is my father's hat.

C. REVIEW OF UNIT 3

I. SPEAKING SPANISH.

1. *Review thoroughly* SECTION A *of* UNIT 3, *just as you have done for* UNITS 1 *and* 2.

2. *Give answers to the following questions:*

1. ¿ Qué estás haciendo ?
2. ¿ Qué lección estás estudiando ?
3. ¿ Qué va usted a hacer mañana ?
4. ¿ Descansa usted durante el día ?
5. ¿ Qué lección es ésta ?
6. ¿ Es una lección de inglés ?
7. ¿ Qué has aprendido durante estos días ?
8. ¿ Cuántas páginas tiene esta lección ?
9. ¿ Está usted cansado de estudiar ?
10. ¿ Estudian mucho ustedes ?
11. ¿ Cómo está la mamá de Pedro hoy ?
12. ¿ Quieres dar una vuelta ?
13. ¿ Qué película están dando en el Regis ?
14. ¿ Por qué estudia usted el español ?
15. ¿ Cómo son los amigos de usted ?
16. ¿ Quiere usted trabajar en México ?
17. ¿ Cuánto tiempo necesita usted para aprender una lección de español ?
18. ¿ Es difícil esta lección ?
19. ¿ Son difíciles las lecciones en general ?
20. ¿ Es éste el tercer año que usted estudia el español ?
21. ¿ Cuánto ha aprendido usted ?
22. ¿ Es inteligente Jorge ?
23. ¿ Cuántos muchachos hay en esta clase ?

24. ¿ Hay muchachas en esta clase ?
25. ¿ Quién está hablando ?
26. ¿ Es fácil hablar español ?
27. ¿ Qué necesita usted ?
28. ¿ Qué va usted a hacer después de la clase ?
29. ¿ Tiene usted otra clase después de ésta ?
30. ¿ Cuántas clases tiene usted hoy ?
31. ¿ Es fácil imitar a la profesora ?
32. ¿ Cuántos días de vacaciones vamos a tener ?
33. ¿ Va usted a ver esa película ?
34. ¿ Son amigos de usted esos señores ?
35. ¿ Cree usted que son agradables las vacaciones ?

3. *Ask questions that will get the following answers:*

1. Llueve más en la primavera que en el otoño.
2. En general el tiempo es agradable.
3. No, yo tengo sed.
4. Quiero tomar una limonada.
5. Quiero ver la película que están dando en el Regis.
6. Sí, usted tiene que hablar español.
7. Imitamos a la profesora.
8. Voy a casa a descansar.
9. Las primaveras son frescas.
10. En general el otoño es seco.
11. Yo me llamo Miguel González.
12. Ésta es la tercera lección.
13. Están dando la película *Tú y Yo* en el centro.
14. Estoy estudiando el español porque me gusta.
15. Necesito tres días para aprender una lección.
16. Ese señor es el padre de Luisa.
17. Voy a descansar mucho durante las vacaciones.
18. Estoy descansando.
19. La casa es grande.
20. La lección es difícil.
21. La cuarta lección es fácil.
22. No quiero ver esa película.
23. No como en la cama.

4. *After hearing again the* LISTENING-IN *Section of* UNIT 3, *give answers to the following questions based directly on it:*

1. ¿ Qué está haciendo Manuel ?
2. ¿ Por qué no estudia Manuel la lección de inglés ?
3. ¿ Cree Jorge que Manuel es un muchacho inteligente ?
4. ¿ De qué está cansado Manuel ?
5. ¿ Es fácil la lección ?
6. ¿ Cuántas páginas ha terminado Jorge ?
7. ¿ Cuánto tiempo necesita Jorge para aprender una lección ?
8. ¿ Cómo es la segunda lección ?
9. ¿ Cómo es la tercera lección ?
10. ¿ Cómo es la cuarta lección ?
11. ¿ Dónde estudia Manuel ?
12. ¿ Cuándo se levanta Manuel de la cama ?
13. ¿ Cuánto inglés han aprendido ?
14. ¿ En cuánto tiempo ?
15. ¿ Cómo es la profesora ?
16. ¿ Por qué no está bien Manuel ?
17. ¿ Qué necesita Manuel ?
18. ¿ Cuántos días de vacaciones necesita Manuel ?
19. ¿ Qué tiempo hace ?
20. ¿ Cómo es el día ?
21. ¿ Está cansado Manuel ?

II. WRITING SPANISH.

The following sentences are variations on the content of the BASIC DIALOGUES *of* UNIT 3. *Write them out in Spanish.*

1. I've learned the third lesson.
2. Have you finished the first two pages ?
3. I say, that's good !
4. Why does she help me ?
5. They say [that] that picture is very good.
6. I'm tired of these things.
7. I haven't studied today's lesson.
8. Let's take a walk now.
9. What picture are they showing in town ?
10. She says [that] it's to make me study.
11. I'm studying Spanish because I want to learn it.
12. How much time do we have ? — It's hard to say [it].
13. How much time do you think [that] we need ?

14. This is my third year of Spanish.
15. Dick is an intelligent boy.
16. What does the teacher say?
17. It's easy to do this.
18. The children are learning [the] Spanish.
19. We all imitate the teacher.
20. You've already learned a lot.
21. Aren't you (people) tired?
22. Yes, and the teacher is tired too.
23. I think [that the] English is hard.
24. What are you going to do today?
25. What are you (people) going to do during the summer?
26. I get up to take a walk.
27. During the holidays I'm going to see some friends.
28. Where are the friends? — They're in Madrid.
29. We all speak English.
30. It's good weather today.
31. The picture is called *The Bandit of the Rio Grande*.
32. That bed isn't very good.
33. The first two years are easy.
34. The third year and the fourth year are hard.
35. Thanks to my sister, I've already learned that.

D. REVIEW OF UNIT 4

I. SPEAKING SPANISH

1. *Review* SECTION A *of* UNIT 4 *just as you did for* UNITS 1-3.

2. *Give answers to the following questions:*

1. ¿ A qué hora empieza usted a estudiar?
2. ¿ Cuántas horas duerme usted?
3. ¿ Qué hace usted por la noche?
4. ¿ Qué hace usted cuando está cansado?
5. ¿ Duerme usted en la clase?
6. ¿ Cuándo trata uno de escaparse?
7. ¿ Qué dice Jorge?
8. ¿ Tiene usted sueño después de comer?
9. ¿ Qué tiene usted que hacer ahora?
10. ¿ Tiene usted amigos tontos?
11. ¿ Quién tiene razón?
12. ¿ Qué entiende usted de psicología?
13. ¿ Es fácil entender a la profesora cuando habla?
14. ¿ Sale usted por la noche?
15. ¿ Qué prefiere usted hacer ahora?
16. ¿ Has terminado el trabajo de hoy?
17. ¿ Qué piensas hacer mañana?
18. ¿ Está lejos la casa de usted?
19. ¿ Va usted a la clase a pie o en autobús?
20. ¿ Es ésta la primera vez que usted habla español?
21. ¿ Es agradable tener cita con una señorita bonita?
22. ¿ A qué hora es la cita con Jaime?
23. Tenemos cita a las siete, y son las siete menos cuarto. ¿ Cuántos minutos tenemos?
24. ¿ Cuánto tiempo tarda usted en llegar a la clase?
25. ¿ A qué hora llega el autobús?
26. ¿ Qué vas a pedir en el restaurante?
27. ¿ Quién tiene la culpa?
28. ¿ Es fácil esperar cuando uno tiene hambre?
29. ¿ Cuántos minutos tienes que esperar?
30. ¿ De dónde vienes?
31. ¿ Tú usas sombrero?
32. ¿ Usa usted las corbatas de sus amigos?
33. ¿ Va usted a una fiesta esta noche?
34. ¿ Con quién va usted a la fiesta?
35. ¿ Cuántas corbatas tiene usted?
36. ¿ Usa usted calcetines?

3. *Ask questions that will get the following answers:*

1. Comemos a las seis.
2. Comemos en el restaurante.
3. Aprendemos mucho en la clase de español.
4. Pedro me ayuda con la lección.
5. Estudiamos en mi casa.
6. Imitamos a la profesora.
7. La película termina mal.
8. El hermano de Jorge trabaja en el centro.

9. En la clase de español aprendemos el español.
10. Estoy estudiando la segunda lección.
11. La señora está hablando con mis padres.
12. Pedro no ha terminado el trabajo.
13. Está haciendo el trabajo de hoy.
14. Mañana es sábado.
15. La casa de la señorita está muy lejos.
16. No es buena la cama.
17. El día es muy agradable.
18. Yo no he comido en aquel restaurante.
19. Duermo ocho horas.
20. No, no entiendo muy bien.
21. Pienso estudiar después de comer.
22. Yo quiero ir a pie.
23. Tenemos cita con Jaime.
24. La cita es a las ocho.
25. El autobús tarda quince minutos en llegar.
26. Vengo de la clase.
27. El sombrero es de Guillermo.
28. No puedo ir porque tengo que trabajar.
29. Los amigos llegan a las nueve.
30. La fiesta empieza a las nueve.
31. Pensamos salir a las cuatro.
32. El autobús no ha llegado.
33. La fiesta no ha terminado.
34. No quiero ir a pie porque estoy cansado.

1. *After hearing again the* LISTENING-IN *Section of* UNIT 4, *give answers to the following questions based directly on it:*

1. ¿ Quiere ir a la fiesta Ricardo ?
2. ¿ Puede ir a la fiesta Ricardo ?
3. ¿ Por qué no puede ir a la fiesta ?
4. ¿ De dónde van a llegar los amigos de Ricardo ?
5. ¿ A qué hora van a llegar los amigos ?
6. ¿ Con quién va Raúl a la fiesta ?
7. ¿ Cómo es la señorita Carmen ?
8. ¿ A qué hora empieza la fiesta ?
9. ¿ Qué va a comprar Raúl en el centro ?
10. ¿ Qué clase de calcetines necesita ?
11. ¿ Por qué necesita calcetines ?
12. ¿ Qué necesita hacer cada vez que sale ?
13. ¿ No tiene ropa el hermano de Raúl ?
14. ¿ Por qué prefiere Pedro la ropa de Raúl ?
15. ¿ Cómo van al centro los dos amigos ?
16. ¿ Está lejos la tienda ?
17. ¿ Qué es lo que no hacen los autobuses ?
18. ¿ Tarda mucho en llegar el autobús ?

II. WRITING SPANISH.

The following sentences are variations on the content of the BASIC DIALOGUES *of* UNIT 4. *Write them out in Spanish.*

1. Every time I study I feel like eating.
2. Am I hungry now!
3. I don't understand that.
4. Do you think [that] George is a fool?
5. On the contrary, he's a very intelligent boy.
6. I do my work with (some) friends.
7. What do you know about Dick Ross?
8. I only know that he's a friend of Jim's.
9. What do you plan to do today?
10. I eat from six thirty to seven.
11. Let's go out.
12. How long does the bus take?
13. It's quarter past five.
14. They have (an) appointment with the professor.
15. Let's go (and) see a romantic film this time.
16. It isn't very far.
17. What time does the bus leave?
18. I'm tired, but I want to take a walk.
19. Is tomorrow's work hard? — No, not very.
20. I think [that] George is right.
21. When I'm cold I'm not thirsty.
22. Is your (girl) friend beautiful? — Yes, very.
23. I feel like ordering for Jim.
24. Can you wait until three o'clock?
25. I prefer to go on foot.
26. Do you know where I can buy (some) ties and socks?
27. Whose is that blue hat? It's not very pretty.
28. It's hard to rest in the Spanish class.
29. [The] Mexican children speak Spanish.
30. Whose are those neckties? — They're not Jim's.
31. It's not my fault.

[49]

32. What day is today? — It's Saturday, man!
33. We're going to a party tonight.
34. Dad's clothes aren't very elegant.
35. What are those things for?

36. I don't know where the restaurant is.
37. Are there (any) good shops in the town?
38. I try to speak Spanish but I can't.
39. I think [that] it's (a) question of psychology.

SPANISH–ENGLISH VOCABULARY

FOR UNITS 1–4

A

a *preposition* to, *etc.*
adiós good-bye
agradable pleasant, agreeable
ahora now
al = **a** + **el**
algo something
allá there
amigo friend
año year
aprender to learn
aquel, -lla, -llo (aquél, *etc.***)** *demonstrative* that
aquí here
el **autobús** bus
ayudar to help
azul blue

B

barbaridad: qué barbaridad *exclamation*
bien well
bonito pretty
bueno (buen) good

C

cada each, every
los **calcetines** socks
el **calor** heat
cama bed
cansar to tire
casa house
centro centre
cinco five
cita meeting, appointment
la **clase** class
el **clima** climate
comer to eat
como like

cómo how
la **complicación** complication
comprar to buy
con *preposition* with, *etc.*
conocer to know
contrario contrary
corbata necktie
cosa thing
creer to believe, think
cuando (cuándo) when
cuánto how much, how many
cuarto quarter; fourth
cuatro four
la **cuestión** question
culpa fault

D

dar to give
de *preposition* of, from, *etc.*
decir (dice-) to say
del = **de** + **el**
descansar to rest
desde *preposition* from, *etc.*
deseo desire
después de after
el **día** day
difícil difficult, hard
digo (see decir)
dónde where
dormir (duerme-) to sleep
dos two
durante *preposition* during

E

el *article* the
elegante elegant, stylish
ella she
empezar (empieza-) to begin, start
en *preposition* in, *etc.*

entender (entiende-) to understand
entonces then
es (see ser)
escapar(se) to escape
ese, esa, eso (ése, *etc.***)** *demonstrative* that
España Spain
español, -ola Spanish
esperar to wait
esquina corner
estar to be
este, esta, esto (éste, *etc.***)** *demonstrative* this
estudiar to study

F

fácil easy
fácilmente easily
fiesta party
fresco cool
frío cold

G

general general
la **gente** people
gracias thanks
grande large, big
gustar to please
gusto pleasure

H

ha- (see haber)
haber to have
hablar to speak, talk
hacer to make; to do
hago (see hacer)
el **hambre** (*fem.*) hunger
hasta *preposition* until, *etc.*
hay there is, there are

[50]

he, hemos (*see* haber)
hermano, -na brother, sister
hermoso beautiful
hijo, -ja son, daughter
hombre man
hora hour
hoy today

I

imitar to imitate
Inglaterra England
inglés, -esa English
inteligente intelligent
invierno winter
ir to go

L

la, las *article* the
latino Latin
la lección lesson
lejos far
levantar to raise
limonada lemonade
lo *3rd-person pronoun*
Londres London
los *article* the

LL

llamar to call
llegar to arrive
llover (llueve-) to rain

M

malo bad
mamá mother
mañana tomorrow
más more
me *pronoun* me, *etc.*
medio half
menos less
mexicano Mexican
mi *possessive* my, *etc.*
minuto minute
muchacho boy
mucho much, many
mujer woman
muy very

N

necesitar to need
la nieve snow
ninguno no, none
niño child

no no, not
la noche night
número number

O

o or
ocho eight
otoño autumn
otro other

P

padre father
página page
el país country
papá Dad
para *preposition* for, *etc.*
la parte part, place
pedir (pide-) to ask, order
película picture, film
pensar (piensa-) to think, intend, plan
pero but
el pie foot
poder (puede-) to be able, can
por *preposition* by, *etc.*
porque because
preferir (prefiere-) to prefer
primavera spring
primero (primer) first
profesor, -ora teacher, professor
psicología psychology

Q

que *conjunction* that; *preposition*
  than, *etc.*
qué what
querer (quiere-) to want
queso cheese
quién who
quince fifteen

R

la razón rightness
el restaurante restaurant
romántico romantic
ropa clothing, clothes

S

sábado Saturday
saber to know

sala room
salir to go out
el sándwich sandwich
se *reflexive 3rd person pronoun*
sé (*see* saber)
seco dry
la sed thirst
segundo second
seis six
sentir (siente-) to feel
señor Mr., sir; gentleman
señora Mrs., madam; lady;
  wife
señorita Miss; young lady
ser to be
servir (sirve-) to serve
sí yes
siete seven
simpático nice
sólo only
sombrero hat
somos, son, soy (*see* ser)
su *3rd person possessive*
sueño sleepiness
el sur south

T

también also, too
tanto so much, so many
tardar to delay
teléfono telephone
tener (tiene-) to have
tengo (*see* tener)
tercero (tercer) third
terminar to finish
tiempo time; weather
tienda shop, store
todo all, whole
tomar to take
tonto fool
trabajar to work
trabajo work
tratar to try
tres three
tú *pronoun* you

U

uno (un) one; *article* a, *etc.*
usar to use, wear
usted you

V

va- (*see* ir)
las vacaciones holiday(s)
vecino neighbour
vengo (*see* venir)
venir (viene-) to come

ver to see
verano summer
la vez time
viento wind
voy (*see* ir)
vuelta walk

Y

y and
ya already
yo *pronoun* I

Visiting. Birthdays. Greetings. Introductions. Telling Time.   **UNIT**

Verbs: Present-Tense Forms; Present of **dar, ir, estar**; Present of **ser**, **oír, saber**; Familiar and Formal Commands.   **6**

BASIC DIALOGUES

1. "Let's go to Jim's house and meet his pretty cousin."

ENGLISH MEANING	AIDS TO LISTENING	SPANISH SPELLING

Record Side 2, after first spiral.

FERNANDO:

Let's go to Jim's.	¡ bámos a-kása de-jáime.	Vamos a casa de Jaime.
on (a) visit	de-bisíta	de visita
his cousin	su-príma	su prima
His cousin from Madrid is visiting (there).	está de-bisíta su-príma de-madríd.	Está de visita su prima de Madrid.

MARCELO:

never	núnka	nunca
I've never been to Jim's house.	yó núnka 'estádo en-kása de-jáime.	Yo nunca he estado en casa de Jaime.
Do you think it's all right?	¿ tú krées k'está bién?	¿ Tú crees que está bien?

FERNANDO:

(do) not be	no-séas	no seas
companions	kompañéros	compañeros
Don't be silly! We're classmates.	¡ no-séas tónto! somos-kompañéroṣ de-kláse.	¡ No seas tonto! Somos compañeros de clase.

MARCELO:

to return, go back	bolbér (buélbe-)	volver (vuelve-)
ten	diéθ	diez
I've got to go home at ten.	téngo ke-bolbér a-kása a-laṣ-diéθ.	Tengo que volver a casa a las diez.

FERNANDO:

nine	nuébe	nueve
twenty	béinte	veinte
It's twenty (minutes) to nine now.	son-laṣ-nuébe menoṣ-béinte aóra.	Son las nueve menos veinte ahora.
together	júntos	juntos
We('ll) go back together at quarter to ten.	bolbémos júntos a-laṣ-diéθ menos-kuárto.	Volvemos juntos a las diez menos cuarto.

ENGLISH MEANING	AIDS TO LISTENING	SPANISH SPELLING

MARCELO:

Let's go, then. — ¡bámos entónθes. — Vamos, entonces.

   tell — dí — di

Tell me, what's Jim's cousin like? — ¡dí-me, ¿ kómo eş-la-príma de--jáime? — Dime, ¿ cómo es la prima de Jaime?

FERNANDO:

   a photograph, a picture — una-fotografía — una fotografía

   a delight — un-enkánto — un encanto

In a picture Jim has she's really good-looking. — en-una-fotografía ke-tiéne jáime, es-un-enkánto. — En una fotografía que tiene Jaime, es un encanto.

MARCELO:

How old is she? — ¿ kuántos áños tiéne? — ¿ Cuántos años tiene?

FERNANDO:

I think she's eighteen or nineteen. — kréo ke-tiéne dieθ-i-ócho o-dieθ--i-nuébe áños. — Creo que tiene dieciocho o diecinueve años.

MARCELO:

What's her name? — ¿ kómo se-ĺáma? — ¿ Cómo se llama?

FERNANDO:

Her name's Gloria. — se-ĺáma glória. — Se llama Gloria.

MARCELO:

   have — tén — ten

   care — kuidádo — cuidado

   there — aí — ahí

   a car — un-kóche — un coche

Be careful! There comes a car. — ¡tén kuidádo! aí biéne un--kóche. — ¡Ten cuidado! Ahí viene un coche.

What are you thinking about? — ¿ en-ké estás pensándo? — ¿ En qué estás pensando?

FERNANDO:

   to prepare — preparár — preparar

About a (piece of) work I'm preparing for Professor Rodríguez. — en-un-trabájo k'estói preparándo para-el-profesór rrodrí-geθ. — En un trabajo que estoy preparando para el profesor Rodríguez.

MARCELO:

I (can) believe that! — ¡yá lo-kréo! — ¡Ya lo creo!

   to live — bibír — vivir

   on the right — a-la-derécha — a la derecha

   true — berdád — verdad

Jim lives on the right, doesn't he? — jáime bíbe a-la-derécha, ¿ berdád? — Jaime vive a la derecha, ¿ verdad?

FERNANDO:

   on the left — a-la-iθkiérda — a la izquierda

ENGLISH MEANING	AIDS TO LISTENING	SPANISH SPELLING
No, he lives here on the left.	nó, bíƀe akí a-la-iθkiérda.	No, vive aquí a la izquierda.
I see	béo	veo
I see his house now.	yá ƀéo su-kása.	Ya veo su casa.

MARCELO:

if (he) is not	si-no-está	si no está
What('ll) we do if he's not (in)?	¿ ké aθémos si-no-está?	¿ Qué hacemos si no está?

FERNANDO:

(you) are not	no-éres	no eres
You're not very smart.	no-éreṣ mu'intelijénte.	No eres muy inteligente.
to enter, go in	entrár	entrar
To find out if he's not (in) we've got to go in the house, haven't we?	para-saƀér si-no-está, tenémos k'entrár en-la-kása, ¿ berdad?	Para saber si no está, tenemos que entrar en la casa, ¿ verdad?

MARCELO:

to inspire	inspirár	inspirar
You're inspired!	¡ estás inspirádo!	¡ Estás inspirado!

FERNANDO:

And rightly (so).	i-kon-rraθón:	Y con razón.

MARCELO:

to hear	oír	oír
hear, listen	óye	oye
go in	éntra	entra
Listen, you go in first!	¡ óye, éntra.tú priméro!	Oye, ¡ entra tú primero!

FERNANDO:

(do) not speak	no-áƀles	no hables
so loud	tan-álto	tan alto
Don't talk so loud!	¡ no-áƀles tan-álto!	¡ No hables tan alto!
There comes Mrs. (Castro).	aí ƀiéne la-señóra.	Ahí viene la señora.

FERNANDO:

Good evening, Mrs. (Castro).	buénaṣ nóches señóra.	Buenas noches, señora.

SEÑORA:

Good evening, Fernando.	buénaṣ nóches fernándo.	Buenas noches, Fernando.
How are you?	¿ kómo está ustéd.	¿ Cómo está usted?

FERNANDO:

Very well, thanks, how are you?	múi ƀién grácias: ¿ i-ustéd?	Muy bien, gracias, ¿ y usted?

SEÑORA:

Well, thank you.	bién gráθias:	Bien, gracias.

FERNANDO:

to present to you	presentár-le	presentarle
I want to introduce my friend Marcelo Sánchez.	kiéro presentár-le a-mi-amígo marθélo sáncheθ.	Quiero presentarle a mi amigo Marcelo Sánchez.

[55]

ENGLISH MEANING	AIDS TO LISTENING	SPANISH SPELLING
Señora:		
How do you do, Marcelo?	múcho gústo marθélo.	Mucho gusto, Marcelo.
Marcelo:		
How do you do, Mrs. (Castro)?	múcho gústo señóra.	Mucho gusto, señora.
Fernando:		
Is Jim (in), Mrs. (Castro)?	¿ está jáime, señóra ?	¿ Está Jaime, señora ?
Señora:		
a moment	un-moménto	un momento
Wait (just) a moment.	¡ espéren ustédes un-moménto.	Esperen ustedes un momento.
come here	bén aká	ven acá
Frankie, come here.	pakíto, ¡ bén aká.	Paquito, ven acá.
go	bé	ve
Go (and) see if Jim's at home.	¡ bé a-bér si-jáime está en-kása.	Ve a ver si Jaime está en casa.
Paquito:		
on (a) drive	de-paséo	de paseo
He's out driving with Gloria.	está de-paséo kon-glória.	Está de paseo con Gloria.
within, in	déntro	dentro
They('ll) be back in twenty minutes or so.	buélben déntro de-béinte minútos, más o-ménos.	Vuelven dentro de veinte minutos, más o menos.
Señora:		
don't go away	no-se-báyan	no se vayan
Don't go, gentlemen. Wait a few minutes.	¡ no-se-báyan, señóres. ¡ espéren unos-minútos.	No se vayan, señores. Esperen unos minutos.
Fernando:		
we regret it	lo-sentímos	lo sentimos
We're very sorry, Mrs. (Castro).	lo-sentímos múcho, señóra.	Lo sentimos mucho, señora.
late	tárde	tarde
It's late already.	yá es-tárde.	Ya es tarde.
Señora:		
Then come back tomorrow to meet Gloria.	¡ buélban mañána entónθes, a--konoθér a-la-señoríta glória.	Vuelvan mañana, entonces, a conocer a la señorita Gloria.
Fernando:		
With great pleasure, Mrs. (Castro).	kon-múcho gústo señóra.	Con much gusto, señora.
Good-bye.	adiós.	Adiós.
Marcelo:		
Good-bye, Mrs. (Castro).	adiós señóra.	Adiós, señora.

2. "Why talk about old age?"

Alfonso:		
the birthday	el-kumpleáños	el cumpleaños
my grandfather	mi-abuélo	mi abuelo

ENGLISH MEANING	AIDS TO LISTENING	SPANISH SPELLING
Today's my grandfather's birth-day.	ói es-el-kumpleáñoş de-mi--aƀuélo.	Hoy es el cumpleaños de mi abuelo.
ninety	nobénta	noventa
He's ninety years (old).	tiéne nobénta áños.	Tiene noventa años.

IGNACIO:

don't tell me	no-me-díga	no me diga
old	biéjo	viejo
No! That's what you call old.	¡ no-me-díga ! éso se-láma ser--ƀiéjo.	¡ No me diga ! Eso se llama ser viejo.

ALFONSO:

young	jóƀen	joven
My grandmother's younger.	mi-aƀuéla eş-más jóƀen.	Mi abuela es más joven.
eighty	ochénta	ochenta
She's eighty-five.	éĺa tiéne ochénta i-θínko.	Ella tiene ochenta y cinco.

IGNACIO:

I haven't got any grandparents.	yó yá no-téngo aƀuélos.	Yo ya no tengo abuelos.

ALFONSO:

Are your parents old ?	¿ som-biéjoş los-pádreş de-ustéd ?	¿ Son viejos los padres de usted ?

IGNACIO:

my mother	mi-mádre	mi madre
fifty	θinkuénta	cincuenta
sixty	sesénta	sesenta
Not so very. My mother's fifty-eight, and my father's sixty-two.	nó tánto: mi-mádre tiéne θinkuénta i-ócho —i-mi-pádre tiéne sesénta i-dós.	No tanto. Mi madre tiene cin-cuenta y ocho, y mi padre tiene sesenta y dos.

ALFONSO:

seventy	seténta	setenta
I don't want to live after seventy.	yó no-kiéro biƀír despuéş de--los-seténta.	Yo no quiero vivir después de los setenta.

IGNACIO:

let's talk	aƀlémos	hablemos
so serious	tan-sérias	tan serias
Let's not talk about such serious things.	¡ no-aƀlémoş de-kósas tan-sérias.	No hablemos de cosas tan serias.
in health	de-salúd	de salud
You're in good health ?	¿ ustéd está ƀién de-salúd ?	¿ Usted está bien de salud ?

ALFONSO:

(I) give thanks	dói gráθias	doy gracias
to God	a-diós	a Dios
Very good, thank the Lord !	¡ múi ƀién : dói gráθias a-diós. . .	¡ Muy bien ! Doy gracias a Dios.

ENGLISH MEANING	AIDS TO LISTENING	SPANISH SPELLING
IGNACIO:		
appetite	apetíto	apetito
You have (a) good appetite?	¿ tiéne ƀuén apetíto?	¿ Tiene buen apetito?
ALFONSO:		
Very good!	¡ múi ƀuéno:	¡ Muy bueno!
IGNACIO:		
let's go out	salgámos	salgamos
to celebrate	θeleƀrár	celebrar
Then let's go out (and) celebrate your grandfather's birthday.	¡ entónθes salgámos a-θeleƀrár el-kumpleáñoş de-su-aƀuélo.	Entonces salgamos a celebrar el cumpleaños de su abuelo.

3. "How do they tell time in Spanish?"

TOM:		
thirty	tréinta	treinta
"Thirty minutes are half (an) hour."	tréinta minútos son-média óra.	« Treinta minutos son media hora.»
"Sixty minutes are one hour."	sesénta minútos son-úna óra.	« Sesenta minutos son una hora. »
HENRY:		
forty	kuarénta	cuarenta
"Forty-five minutes are three quarters of (an) hour."	kuarénta i-θínko minútos son--trés kuártoş de-óra.	« Cuarenta y cinco minutos son tres cuartos de hora. »
TOM:		
by (good) fortune	por-fortúna	por fortuna
alone	sólos	solos
Fortunately we're alone.	por-fortúna estámos sólos.	Por fortuna estamos solos.
HENRY:		
big persons	persónaş grándes	personas grandes
Two grown-ups learning to tell time!	¡ dós persónaş grándes aprendiéndo a-deθír la-óra!	¡ Dos personas grandes aprendiendo a decir la hora !
TOM:		
to forget	olƀidár	olvidar
In Spanish, let's not forget that.	en-español, n'olƀidémos éso.	En español, no olvidemos eso.
HENRY:		
to follow, to come next	segír (síge-)	seguir (sigue-)
To work, Thomas! What comes next?	¡ a-traƀajár, tomás. ¿ ké síge?	¡ A trabajar, Tomás! ¿ Qué sigue ?
TOM:		
"Five past two; five to two."	laş-dós i-θinko — las-dós menos--θínko.	« Las dos y cinco; las dos menos cinco. »

ENGLISH MEANING	AIDS TO LISTENING	SPANISH SPELLING

HENRY:
"Quarter past four; quarter to four."
las-kuátro i-kuárto — las--kuátro menos-kuárto.
« Las cuatro y cuarto; las cuatro menos cuarto. »

TOM:
the right
Tongue-twisters, too? No fair!
el-derécho
¿ trabalénguas también? ¡ no--ái derécho !
el derecho
¿ Trabalenguas también? ¡ No hay derecho !

HENRY:
to listen
Listen to this: "*It is* one (o'clock)" but "*They are* two (o'clock)."
eskuchár
eskúche ésto. éş la-úna, pero--són laş-dós.
escuchar
Escuche esto: « *Es* la una » pero « *son* las dos. »

TOM:
English is easier.
el-inglés eş-mas-fáθil.
El inglés es más fácil.

HENRY:
hear, listen
Hey, what time is it?
óiga
¡ óiga, ¿ ké óra és ?
oiga
Oiga, ¿ qué hora es ?

TOM:
Seriously?
¿ en-sério ?
¿ En serio ?

HENRY:
Seriously.
en-sério.
En serio.

TOM:
In Spanish or in English?
¿ en-español o-en-inglés.
¿ En español o en inglés ?

HENRY:
In English.
en-inglés.
En inglés.

TOM:
the watch
I haven't got (a) watch !
el-rrelój
¡ no-téngo rrelój !
el reloj
¡ No tengo reloj !

NOTES ON PRONUNCIATION AND SPELLING

CONSONANTS

1. THE SPANISH j-SOUND.

This consonant is formed by tightening the back part of the mouth while still allowing the breath to pass through. Its commonest spelling is **j**, and we so transcribe it always. In some words however it is written **g** before **i** or **e**; in **México, mexicano,** and a very small number of other words it is written **x**. Examples:

TRANSCRIPTION

mujéres, trabajár, jáime, los-íjos, biéjo, jóben; pájınas, sikolojía, la-jénte, en-jenerál; méjiko, mejikáno

WRITTEN SPANISH

mujeres, trabajar, Jaime, los hijos, viejo, joven; páginas, psicología, la gente, en general; México, mexicano

NOTE: Many speakers, especially in Spanish America, pronounce the j-sound so lightly that it approximates the sound spelled h in English. This pronunciation may be safely imitated.

SPELLINGS OF THE SOUNDS: θ, k, j, g

VOWEL	i	e	a	o	u
θ-SOUND	ci	ce	za	zo	zu
k-SOUND	qui	que	ca	co	cu
j-SOUND	ji, gi	je, ge	ja	jo	ju
g-SOUND	gui	gue	ga	go	gu

2. THE LETTER h.

This letter, which appears in written Spanish at the beginning of many words, and in the middle of some words, represents NO SPOKEN SOUND AT ALL. Examples of words spelled with h:

TRANSCRIPTION

ermános, íjos, ermósa, ómbres, ámbre, aḅlár, ké óra, ái, ói, aóra

WRITTEN SPANISH

hermanos, hijos, hermosa, hombres, hambre, hablar, qué hora, hay, hoy, ahora

3. THE SPANISH r-SOUND.

This consonant is formed with a single flap of the tongue-tip against the roof of the mouth. It is always spelled r, and we so transcribe it. Examples:

TRANSCRIPTION

número, el-ḅeráno, prefiéro, el-imbiérno, deθírlo, kuárto, kuátro, profesór, sombréro, dormír, traḅajár, serḅír

WRITTEN SPANISH

número, el verano, prefiero, el invierno, decirlo, cuarto, cuatro, profesor, sombrero, dormir, trabajar, servir

4. THE SPANISH rr-SOUND.

This consonant, which is meaningfully distinct from the r-sound mentioned above, is formed by vibrating the tongue-tip against the roof of the mouth in a TRILL. It is spelled rr between vowels, and r elsewhere — that is, in surroundings where the r-sound never occurs, as for instance at the beginning of a word. We transcribe it always as rr. Examples:

TRANSCRIPTION

rrikárḍo, rraθón, el-rrestauránte, rromántikas, rrópa, rrelój; tiérra, arróθ, θerrádas, inglatérra

WRITTEN SPANISH

Ricardo, razón, el restaurante, románticas, ropa, reloj; tierra, arroz, cerradas, Inglaterra

B. STUDY

Review SECTION A, *covering up the English.*

C. LISTENING IN

1. *Review* SECTION A, *repeating the Spanish and giving the English.*

2. *Listen in as* (a) *Carlos introduces his friend Manuel to Señora López, and* (b) *a boy asks his father some questions about age.*

Record Side 2, after first spiral.

(a)

CARLOS: Señora López, quiero presentarle a mi compañero Manuel Fernández.

SEÑORA: Mucho gusto, señor Fernández.

MANUEL: Mucho gusto en conocer a usted, señora.

CARLOS: Manuel es el primo de Guillermo Fernández. Usted conoce a Guillermo, ¿ verdad ?

SEÑORA: Sí, lo conozco muy bien. Ha estado muchas veces en esta casa. Es un amigo de mi hijo Roberto.

CARLOS: Manuel ha venido a pasar unos días aquí. Tiene vacaciones ahora.

SEÑORA: ¿ Entonces usted no vive aquí, señor Fernández ?

MANUEL: No, señora. Vivo en Madrid.

SEÑORA: ¿ Es ésta la primera vez que viene usted a visitar a su primo Guillermo ?

MANUEL: No, señora. Es la tercera vez.

CARLOS: ¿ Qué hora es, Manuel ?

MANUEL: No tengo reloj.

SEÑORA: Son las cuatro menos veinte.

CARLOS: Es tarde, señora. Tenemos una cita con dos amigas a las cuatro.

MANUEL: ¿ Dónde está el coche, Carlos ? Creo que está aquí a la izquierda.

CARLOS: ¿ Qué hacemos ahora ? ¿ Volvemos a casa de Guillermo ? ¿ O damos un paseo en el coche ?

MANUEL: Yo prefiero ir a casa porque tengo que salir esta noche.

CARLOS: Está bien entonces. Vamos a casa de Guillermo.

(b) (Not recorded)

HIJO: Papá, ¿ es vieja una persona que tiene treinta o cuarenta años ?

PAPÁ: No, hijo. Esas personas son jóvenes. Hasta los cincuenta o sesenta años uno no es viejo.

HIJO: ¿ Cuántos años tienen mis abuelos ?

PAPÁ: El abuelo tiene setenta y cinco años, y la abuela tiene setenta.

HIJO: Entonces los abuelos son viejos.

PAPÁ: No son jóvenes.

HIJO: ¿ Hay mucha gente que vive hasta los ochenta o noventa años ?

PAPÁ: No mucha.

HIJO: Entonces es cosa seria tener cumpleaños.

D. GRAMMATICAL ANALYSIS

I. VERBS: PRESENT-TENSE FORMS

(*1*) Present of **dar, ir, estar.** By now you should be familiar with the present-tense forms of the following common verbs:

```
dar:  da-    (IST SING. doy)
ir:   va-    (IST SING. voy)
estar: está- (IST SING. estoy)
```

In these verbs the stress is on the type-vowel throughout the tense. When this happens, the first-singular form ends in **-oy** rather than just **-o.** Compare also **ser:** IST SING. **soy.**

(*2*) Present of **ser.** In this unit you have met the second-person singular form of **ser,** namely **eres.** We can now give a formula for the present tense of this verb, stating the two forms that do not fit the pattern:

```
ser:  so-  (2ND SING. eres, 3RD SING. es)
```

(*3*) Present of **oír.** In the root-stressed forms of the present tense of **oír,** the root has the shape **oy-** instead of just **o-,** thus:

```
oír:  oye-
```

This verb also has a g-root, as seen in the first-singular form **oigo.**

(*4*) Present of **saber, ver.** The present of **saber** and **ver** is normal except in the first-singular forms:

```
saber: sabe- (IST SING. sé)
ver:   ve-   (IST SING. veo)
```

II. VERBS: COMMANDS

In English, commands are expressed by using the general form of the verb — "*Come in,*" "*Be careful,*" "*Wait here,*" etc. The Spanish verb has particular forms for expressing commands, many of which have appeared in the BASIC DIALOGUES of this unit.

1. THE IMPERATIVE.

Familiar Address. When a "command" to do something is given to a person addressed familiarly as **tú,** Spanish uses the IMPERATIVE form of the verb. This imperative form appears in the following sentences:

Oye, ¡ entra tú primero !
¡ Habla más alto !
¡ Vuelve más tarde !
¡ Empieza ahora !

In regular verbs, the imperative form consists simply of stressed root plus type-vowel; it has no person-number ending, and therefore it happens to be identical to the third-singular form of the present tense. Note especially that the root-vowel, in verbs that have alternation (**volver, empezar,** etc.), is the same as it is in the root-stressed forms of the present tense.

A few common verbs have irregular imperative forms of one single syllable. You have seen the following four:

decir: di   Dime, ¿ cómo es la prima de Jaime ?
ir: ve   Ve a ver si Jaime está en casa.
tener: ten   ¡ Ten cuidado !
venir: ven   Paquito, **ven** acá.

2. OTHER COMMAND-FORMS.

(*1*) **Formal Address.** When a "command" to do or not to do something is given to a person (or persons) formally addressed as **usted(es),** Spanish uses special COMMAND-FORMS of the present tense. Some of these forms occur in the following sentences:

Espere usted un momento.
¡ No me **diga** !
Vuelvan mañana, entonces.
Oiga, ¿ qué hora es ?

The distinguishing feature of these forms is the EXCHANGE OF TYPE-VOWEL between the two types — a criss-crossing whereby TYPE I verbs show -e- and TYPE II verbs show -a-.

Also if a verb has a g-root (**decir, oír,** etc.), this g-root appears instead of the normal root in the command-forms. At the bottom of this page is given a summary of several verbs, setting the command-forms beside the straight present. The verbs **ser** and **ir** have command-form roots which are different from those of the present tense:

ser: sea-   **ir: vaya-**

(*2*) **Familiar Address:** "don't"- commands. The Spanish imperative, which we analyzed in preceding paragraphs, is never used with a negative word such as **no.** Thus, when a command NOT to do something is given, even to a person addressed familiarly as **tú,** the special command-forms of the present tense are used instead of the imperative:

¡ **No hables** tan alto !
No seas tonto.

THE PRESENT TENSE AND THE SPECIAL COMMAND–FORMS

	GENERAL FORM	STRAIGHT PRESENT	COMMAND-FORM
TYPE I	esperar	espera-	espere-
	hablar	habla-	hable-
	dar	da-	de-
	pensar	piensa-	piense-
TYPE II	comer	come-	coma-
	volver	vuelve-	vuelva-
	dormir	duerme-	duerma-
	pedir	pide-	pida-
TYPE II WITH g-ROOT	tener	tiene-, **tengo**	**tenga-**
	venir	viene-, **vengo**	**venga-**
	decir	dice-, **digo**	**diga-**
	hacer	hace-, **hago**	**haga-**
	salir	sale-, **salgo**	**salga-**
	oír	oye-, **oigo**	**oiga-**

In these negative commands the second-person singular ending **-s** appears, just as it does in the straight present tense.

Comparative Usage

When proposing or suggesting that something be done (or not done) by a group including himself, an English speaker uses *let's* before the verb. Spanish uses either of two expressions:

(*1*) English *let's* + VERB = Spanish VERB IN THE FIRST-PLURAL COMMAND-FORM:

Let's not talk about such serious things.
No **hablemos** de cosas tan serias.

In Spanish, let's not forget that!
En español, ¡ no **olvidemos** eso !

Let's go out and celebrate the birthday.
Salgamos a celebrar el cumpleaños.

Let's go to Jim's.
Vamos a casa de Jaime.

Even in this first-plural form where the root is not stressed, a **g**-root appears if the verb has one (**salgamos, digamos, tengamos,** etc.).

The last example, with **vamos,** shows that in the one case of the verb **ir,** the straight present-tense form is used (and not the command-form with **vaya-**).

(*2*) English *let's* + VERB = Spanish **vamos a** + GENERAL FORM OF VERB. The Spanish expression **vamos a** means literally *"let's go (and)."*

Let's take a walk.
Vamos a dar una vuelta.

Then let's go out.
Entonces **vamos a salir.**

E. GRAMMATICAL DRILLS

1. PRESENT OF **ir, dar, ver, ser, estar, saber, oír.**

Go through the seven sentences which follow. First, (a) make **yo** *the subject of each sentence. (b) Make the subject* **tú;** *(c) make it* **Carlos;** *(d) make it* **Carlos y yo;** *and (e) make it* **Carlos y María.** *Each time through, supply the proper person-number form of the verb in parentheses, and say the English.*

EXAMPLE:

. . . (ir) al centro.

MODEL:

(*a*) **Yo voy** al centro.
I'm going into town.

1. . . . (ir) a comprar ropa.
2. . . . (dar) una vuelta después de comer.
3. . . . no (ver) la casa.
4. . . . no (ser) de Madrid.
5. . . . (estar) preparando la lección.
6. . . . no (saber) dónde vive Jaime.
7. . . . no (oír) a la profesora.

2. "do"- COMMANDS.

A. *Use each of the verbal phrases that follow in a command in which you tell your brother, sister or close friend "what to do." Give the English.*

MODEL:

ayudar a esa señora

ANSWER:

¡ **Ayuda** a esa señora !
Help that lady!

1. hablar más alto
2. tomar una limonada
3. aprender la lección
4. comprar unas corbatas
5. descansar por quince minutos
6. tener cuidado
7. oír esto
8. comer en este restaurante
9. estudiar con Pedro
10. terminar el trabajo hoy
11. trabajar hasta las seis

12. usar la corbata de Pedro
13. entrar con esa gente
14. olvidar el trabajo
15. empezar la lección de mañana
16. ir a ver si está Jaime
17. llegar a tiempo
18. llamar a Juanita
19. decir la verdad
20. dar una vuelta con Miguel
21. imitar al profesor
22. pensar en otra cosa
23. tratar de entrar allá
24. volver a casa ahora
25. esperar unos minutos
26. venir acá

B. *Take the phrases of A, and make them into requests in which you tell a person you address formally "what to do." If you include the word* **usted,** *be sure you put it after the verb. You needn't say the English again.*

EXAMPLE:

ayudar a esa señora

MODEL:

¡ **Ayude** (usted) a esa señora !

C. *Take the phrases of A again, and make them into suggestions in which you include yourself, thus telling what "let's do." Express each one in two ways (see model).*

EXAMPLE:

ayudar a esa señora

MODEL:

¡ **Ayudemos** a esa señora !
OR
¡ **Vamos a ayudar** a esa señora !

3. "don't"- COMMANDS.

A. *Make each of the verbal phrases that follow into a command in which you tell your brother, sister or close friend "what not to do." Give the English.*

EXAMPLE:

hablar inglés

MODEL:

¡ **No hables** inglés !
Don't speak English!

1. aprender todo eso
2. llegar tarde
3. decir eso
4. comprar esos calcetines
5. ser tonto
6. tomar tanta limonada
7. descansar ahora
8. hacer eso
9. comer tanto
10. estudiar demasiado
11. terminar la página
12. trabajar tanto
13. dormir en esa cama
14. empezar a hablar
15. esperar el autobús
16. ir a ver esa película
17. pedir demasiado
18. pensar en aquello
19. venir hoy
20. usar el teléfono
21. entrar en esa casa
22. olvidar el número
23. volver tarde
24. salir de la casa

B. *Make each of the same phrases into a request in which you tell a person you address formally "what not to do." If you include the word* **usted,** *be sure you put it after the verb. You needn't say the English again.*

EXAMPLE:

hablar inglés

MODEL:

¡ **No hable** (usted) inglés !

The bullfight, the rodeo are characteristically Spanish. Above: A matador plays a bull for the kill in the ring in Mexico City. The great Mexican, Spanish, and South American bullfighters make, with the seasons, a circuit of the bull rings of the Spanish-speaking world. Below: Chilean huasos (cowboys) enter the ring at a colourful rodeo in Valdivia.

Soccer and swimming are favourite sports wherever Spanish is spoken. Above: Peru meets Argentina in a soccer match at the Lima Stadium. Below: "Horseshoe" Beach near Lima. Right background: A roller skating rink.

The Spanish-speaking world is indeed that of the theatre, of music, and of the dance. Spain, Mexico, and the Argentine produce many films of their own. Below: An open-air, Sunday-morning band concert in Bolívar Square, Caracas, Venezuela. It's interesting to note that you can hear good music by good bands at weekly concerts almost anywhere in the Spanish-speaking world.

Above: A "criolla", in the native dress of the pampas, sings a plaintive tango for the audience of a music hall in Buenos Aires. Below: Gypsies in the famous caves of Granada — most romantic city of Spain — dance for a distinguished visitor.

4. TWO-DIGIT NUMBERS.

Say the following numbers in Spanish:

16	82	23
21	97	52
38	44	86
45	71	17
53	36	94
64	69	77
79	95	68

5. TIME OF DAY.

    A. SPEAKER A: ¿ Es la una ?
        "   B: No, son las dos.
        "   C: ¿ Son las dos ?
        "   D: No, son las tres.

Continue this "conversation" until it ends with somebody saying **"No, es la una."**

B. *Answer each of the questions that follow with all of the different times of day listed herewith:* (*1*) 6:10; (*2*) 3:15; (*3*) 9:02; (*4*) 1:05; (*5*) 10:30; (*6*) 5:45; (*7*) 2:08; (*8*) 4:15; (*9*) 10:10.

EXAMPLE:

    ¿ A qué hora llegan ? — (*1*) 6:10, *etc.*

MODEL:

    Llegan a las **seis y diez,** etc.

1. ¿ A qué hora sale el autobús ?
2. ¿ A qué hora empieza la película ?
3. ¿ A qué hora come usted ?
4. ¿ A qué hora es la cita ?
5. ¿ A qué hora quieres volver ?
6. ¿ A qué hora piensas llegar ?
7. ¿ A qué hora empieza usted a trabajar ?

F. STUDY

1. *Review* SECTION A, *with the Spanish covered.* **2.** *Prepare the* CONVERSATIONS.

G. CONVERSATIONS

1. *Reproduce the* BASIC DIALOGUES *in Spanish.*

2. *Using the* BASIC DIALOGUES *as your model, develop conversations such as:*

(*a*) Going to a friend's house to see someone that's visiting there; talking about the friend, where he lives, what the visitor is like, etc.

(*b*) Discussing people's age: your age, your parents', your grandparents', your cousins', your brothers' and sisters'.

(*c*) Quizzing somebody on telling time in Spanish: various times of day; how many minutes in a half hour, etc., etc.

Getting Married.   Giving Gifts.   Writing a Letter.   Daily Routine.
Personal Pronouns.   The Verb-Object Pronoun Series: First, Second,
and Third Persons.   Position of Verb-Object Pronouns.

UNIT

7

A. BASIC DIALOGUES

1. Going to buy a wedding present, or "All the boys are getting married."

ENGLISH MEANING	AIDS TO LISTENING	SPANISH SPELLING

Not Recorded: see 2 (page 69).

PHIL:

this afternoon	ésta tárde	esta tarde
What are you going to do this afternoon?	¿ ké bá ustéd 'aθér ésta tárde?	¿ Qué va usted a hacer esta tarde?

PAUL:

a gift, a present	un-rregálo	un regalo
I'm going to town to buy a present.	bói al-θéntro a-komprár un--rregálo.	Voy al centro a comprar un regalo.
to accompany, to go with	akompañár	acompañar
Don't you want to go with me?	¿ no-kiére akompañár-me?	¿ No quiere acompañarme?

PHIL:

Glad to.	kon-múcho gústo.	Con mucho gusto.
Who's the present for?	¿ para-kién es-el-rregálo?	¿ Para quién es el regalo?

PAUL:

For Carlos Mann.	para-kárloş mán.	Para Carlos Mann.

PHIL:

to happen	pasár	pasar
What's happening to Carlos?	¿ ké le-pása a-kárlos?	¿ Qué le pasa a Carlos?
(I) have seen	e-bísto	he visto
I haven't seen him lately.	no-lo-e-bísto en-éstoş días.	No lo he visto en estos días.

PAUL:

Don't you know [it]?	¿ no-lo-sábe ustéd?	¿ No lo sabe usted?
to get married	kasár-se	casarse
August	agósto	agosto
He's getting married the first of August.	se-kása el-priméro de-agósto.	Se casa el primero de agosto.

PHIL:

To whom, man?	¡ ombre, ¿ kon-kién?	Hombre, ¿ con quién?

PAUL:

You don't know her.	ustéd no-la-konóθe.	Usted no la conoce.

[66]

ENGLISH MEANING	AIDS TO LISTENING	SPANISH SPELLING
She's not from here.	no-és de-akí.	No es de aquí.
fourteen	katórθe	catorce
We're going to give Carlos a party on the fourteenth.	el-día katórθe le-bámos a-dár una-fiésta a-kárlos.	El día catorce le vamos a dar una fiesta a Carlos.

PHIL:

to invite	imbitár	invitar
yet	todabía	todavía
You haven't invited me yet.	ustédes no-me-an-imbitádo todabía.	Ustedes no me han invitado todavía.

PAUL:

well	pués	pues
Well, we're inviting you now.	pues-lo-estámos imbitándo aóra.	Pues, lo estamos invitando ahora.

PHIL:

little	póko	poco
the world	el-múndo	el mundo
Thanks. Little by little everybody's getting married.	gráθias. póko a-póko se-bá kasándo tódo el-múndo.	Gracias. Poco a poco se va casando todo el mundo.

PAUL:

few	pókos	pocos
the unmarried	los-soltéros	los solteros
Yes, there are very few of us bachelors (left) now.	sí, somos-múi pókos los--soltéros aóra.	Sí, somos muy pocos los solteros ahora.
almost, nearly	kási	casi
Nearly everybody has married.	kási tódos se-an-kasádo.	Casi todos se han casado.

PHIL:

to defend	defendér (defiénde-)	defender (defiende-)
rather, quite	bastánte	bastante
Women, women! I defend myself from them pretty well.	¡ ái, las-mujéres! yó me-defiéndo bastánte bién de-éḷas.	¡ Ay, las mujeres! Yo me defiendo bastante bien de ellas.

PAUL:

You certainly do!	¡ éso sí!	¡ Eso sí!

PHIL:

the same	lo-mísmo	lo mismo
I can't say the same of you.	no-puédo deθír lo-mísmo de--ustéd.	No puedo decir lo mismo de usted.
between	éntre	entre
girl	chíka	chica
tall and blond	álta i-rrúbia	alta y rubia
Tell me, what is there between you and that tall blond girl?	¡ díga-me, ¿ ké ái entre-ustéd i-ésa chíka álta i-rrúbia?	Dígame, ¿ qué hay entre usted y esa chica alta y rubia?

[67]

ENGLISH MEANING	AIDS TO LISTENING	SPANISH SPELLING

PAUL:

nothing	náda	nada
Nothing serious.	náda de-sério.	Nada de serio.
But what blond are you talking about?	¿ pero-de-ké rrúbia está ablándo.	Pero ¿ de qué rubia está hablando?

PHIL:

| The Costales girl. | de-la-chíka kostáles. | De la chica Costales. |

PAUL:

| to seem | pareθér | parecer |
| She seems to me very nice. | me-paréθe mui-simpátika. | Me parece muy simpática. |

PHIL:

to notice	fijár-se	fijarse
I've noticed that.	m'e-fijádo en-éso.	Me he fijado en eso.
I've seen you together often.	los-e-bísto júntoṣ múchaṣ béθes.	Los he visto juntos muchas veces.

PAUL:

by (the) way	a-propósito	a propósito
By the way, I've got to telephone her.	a-propósito, téngo ke-l̇amár-la por-teléfono.	A propósito, tengo que llamarla por teléfono.
(Will) you wait for me a minute?	¿ m'espéra un-moménto?	¿ Me espera un momento?

PHIL:

to hurry	apurár-se	apurarse
soon	prónto	pronto
Hurry up. We've got to start pretty soon.	¡ apúre-se. tenémos ke-salír mui-prónto.	Apúrese. Tenemos que salir muy pronto.

PAUL:

| to shut, to close | θerrár (θiérra-) | cerrar (cierra-) |
| What time do the shops close? | ¿ a-ké óra se-θiérran las-tiéndas? | ¿ A qué hora se cierran las tiendas? |

PHIL:

to open	abrír	abrir
open, opened	abiértas	abiertas
They're open till five thirty.	están abiértas asta-las-θínko i-média.	Están abiertas hasta las cinco y media.

PAUL:

to bathe oneself	bañár-se	bañarse
to shave oneself	afeitár-se	afeitarse
I've got to bathe and shave first.	téngo ke-bañár-me i-afeitár-me priméro.	Tengo que bañarme y afeitarme primero.
Don't you have anything to do?	¿ ustéd no-tiéne náda ke-aθér?	¿ Usted no tiene nada que hacer?

[68]

ENGLISH MEANING	AIDS TO LISTENING	SPANISH SPELLING

PHIL:

to write	eskribír	escribir
a letter	una-kárta	una carta
I can write a letter.	puédo eskribír una-kárta.	Puedo escribir una carta.
to meet each other	enkontrár-se (enkuéntra-)	encontrarse (encuentra-)
We('ll) meet here in half (an) hour.	nos-enkontrámos akí déntro de--média óra.	Nos encontramos aquí dentro de media hora.
All right ?	¿ está bién ?	¿ Está bien ?

PAUL:

| until later | asta-luégo | hasta luego |
| Right. See you later. | está bién. asta-luégo. | Está bien. Hasta luego. |

PHIL:

| I say, Paul ! Don't you know what day it is ? | ¡ óiga, páblo ! ¿ no-sábe ustéd ké día es-ói ? | ¡ Oiga, Pablo ! ¿ No sabe usted qué día es hoy ? |

PAUL:

| Tuesday | mártes | martes |
| It's Tuesday, why ? | es-mártes. ¿ por-ké ? | Es martes. ¿ Por qué ? |

PHIL:

| July | júlio | julio |
| It's the Fourth of July, (a) holi-day. | es-el-kuátro de-júlio, día de--fiésta. | Es el cuatro de julio, día de fiesta. |

PAUL:

| Oh oh ! And all the shops are closed. | ¡ ái ! i-tódaṣ las-tiéndas están θerrádas. | ¡ Ay ! Y todas las tiendas están cerradas. |

Record Side 3.

2. "What is life? Mostly work."

JAVIER:

| the morning | la-mañána | la mañana |
| What time do you get up in the morning ? | ¿ a-ké óra te-lebántas por-la--mañána ? | ¿ A qué hora te levantas por la mañana ? |

LEONARDO:

| I don't get up at the same time every day. | no-me-lebánto a-la-míṣma óra tódoṣ loṣ-díaṣ. | No me levanto a la misma hora todos los días. |

JAVIER:

| Why (not) ? Don't you work ? | ¿ kómo es-éso. ¿ no-trabájas ? | ¿ Cómo es eso ? ¿ No trabajas ? |

LEONARDO:

| Not these days. | en-éstoṣ díaṣ nó. | En estos días no. |

JAVIER:

| Then what *do* you do ? | ¿ ké áθes entónθes. | ¿ Qué haces, entonces ? |

LEONARDO:

| I'm studying. | estói estudiándo. | Estoy estudiando. |

[69]

ENGLISH MEANING	AIDS TO LISTENING	SPANISH SPELLING

JAVIER:
What time do your classes begin? | ¿ a-ké óra empiéθan tus-kláses. | ¿ A qué hora empiezan tus clases ?

LEONARDO:
eleven | ónθe | once
Some days at nine, others at eleven. | únoṣ días a-laṣ nuébe — ótros a-las-ónθe. | Unos días a las nueve, otros a las once.

JAVIER:
life | bída | vida
What (a) life! | ¡ ké bída ! | ¡ Qué vida !
I have to get up at half past six every morning. | yó téngo ke-lebantár-me a-las--séis i-média tódaṣ laṣ--mañánas. | Yo tengo que levantarme a las seis y media todas las mañanas.

LEONARDO:
early | tempráno | temprano
That's very early. | eṣ-múi tempráno. | Es muy temprano.
to lie down | akostár-se (akuésta-) | acostarse (acuesta-)
What time do you go to bed? | ¿ a-ké óra te-akuéstas. | ¿ A qué hora te acuestas ?

JAVIER:
before | ántes | antes
twelve | dóθe | doce
Sometimes before twelve, and sometimes after twelve. | a-béθes ánteṣ de-laṣ-dóθe — i-a--béθeṣ despuéṣ de-laṣ-dóθe. | A veces antes de las doce, y a veces después de las doce.

LEONARDO:
to pass, to spend | pasár | pasar
You spend the whole day working, don't you? | pásas tódo el-día trabajándo, ¿ berdád? | Pasas todo el día trabajando, ¿ verdad?

JAVIER:
certain, sure | θiérto | cierto
That's right. | es-θiérto: | Es cierto.

LEONARDO:
Why does a (person) work so much? | ¿ para-ké trabája úno tánto? | ¿ Para qué trabaja uno tanto ?

JAVIER:
useful | útil | útil
To live, to do something useful. | para-bibír, par'aθér álgo útil. | Para vivir, para hacer algo útil.

LEONARDO:
to occupy, to take up | okupár | ocupar
too much | demasiádo | demasiado
Yes, but work takes too much time. | sí, pero-el-trabájo okúpa de-masiádo tiémpo. | Sí, pero el trabajo ocupa demasiado tiempo.

[70]

ENGLISH MEANING	AIDS TO LISTENING	SPANISH SPELLING
precisely, exactly	preθísa ménte	precisamente
to complain	kejár-se	quejarse
That'(s) exactly (what) I'm complaining about.	preθísa ménte de-éso me-kéjo.	Precisamente de eso me quejo.

JAVIER:

What does a (person) need more time for?	¿ para-ké neθesíta úno más tiémpo?	¿ Para qué necesita uno más tiempo?

LEONARDO:

to enjoy oneself	dibertír-se (dibiérte-)	divertirse (divierte-)
To have a good time.	para-dibertír-se.	Para divertirse.

JAVIER:

And to complain, the way you're doing now.	i-para-kejár-se, komo-estás aθiéndo tú aóra.	Y para quejarse, como estás haciendo tú ahora.

LEONARDO:

You're right	tiénes rraθón	Tienes razón
the cinema	el-θíne	el cine
Do you want to go to the cinema?	¿ kiéres ír al-θíne?	¿ Quieres ir al cine?

JAVIER:

I don't think so.	kréo ke-nó.	Creo que no.
to remember	akordár-se (akuérda-)	acordarse (acuerda-)
Remember I get up early.	akuérda-te ke-yó me-lebánto tempráno.	Acuérdate que yo me levanto temprano.

NOTES ON PRONUNCIATION AND SPELLING

CONSONANTS

1. THE SPANISH n-SOUND.

This consonant has two varieties, both spelled n in written Spanish. There is no great difference between them: they simply alternate in accordance with the sounds surrounding them. Since you will normally produce each variety automatically, we transcribe both merely as n.

(*1*) In most surroundings the n-sound closely resembles the English sound in *NiNe*, though it is formed with the tongue-tip pressed against the teeth rather than above the teeth as in English. Examples:

TRANSCRIPTION

niébe, número, kansádo, están, entónθes, aprendiéndo

WRITTEN SPANISH

nieve, número, cansado, están, entonces, aprendiendo

(*2*) When it occurs just before a k-sound, g-sound, or j-sound, either within a word or at a word-boundary, the n-sound is like the sound spelled *n* in English *thiNk*, or *ng* in English *siNG*. Examples:

TRANSCRIPTION

enkánto, un-kóche, tén kuidádo; inglés, ningúna, bién gráθias; en-jenerál, kon-jáime

WRITTEN SPANISH

encanto, un coche, ten cuidado; inglés, ninguna, bien gracias; en general, con Jaime

NOTE: Many speakers, especially in Spanish America, use this variety of the n-sound whenever it occurs at the end of a word. If you hear this pronunciation you may safely imitate it.

2. REPLACEMENT OF THE n-SOUND BY THE m-SOUND.

The Spanish n-sound NEVER occurs before the sounds p or b. As a result, when a word normally ending in n is followed by a word beginning with p or b, the final n is replaced by m. Our transcription shows this, though in written Spanish the spelling with **n** is kept. Examples:

TRANSCRIPTION

biém péðro, um-buém beθíno, som-bakaθiónes, som-biéjos

WRITTEN SPANISH

bien Pedro, un buen vecino, son vacaciones, son viejos

Within a word, the sequence mb is spelled **mb** in some words and **nv** in other words. Examples:

TRANSCRIPTION

ómbre, ámbre, también; el-imbiérno, imbi-tándo

WRITTEN SPANISH

hombre, hambre, también; el invierno, invi-tando

WORD-GROUPS

1. MAJOR AND MINOR WORD-GROUPS.

A MAJOR word-group of Spanish is a sequence of words within which a speaker would not usually make a pause. In the transcription, the major word-groups are those within which no punctuation (other than hyphens) appears.

The major groups in turn consist of sequences of single words and MINOR word-groups — that is, certain phrases between the words of which it would be abnormal for a speaker to pause. Only one of the words of a minor group has a stressed vowel. In the transcription, the words making up MINOR groups are joined together by hyphens. In speaking the dialogues, try especially never to hesitate where a hyphen occurs.

2. ELISION.

When, within a word-group, a word ENDING in a vowel-sound is followed by a word BEGINNING with a vowel-sound (for example **va usted, poco a poco, qué hay**), the two vowel-sounds are normally "slurred" together so that the transition from one to the other is smooth and unbroken. When the two vowels are the same, AND NEITHER IS STRESSED, only a single vowel-sound is heard in normal speech (**hacerme estudiar, Jaime está,** etc.). Written Spanish does not recognize this "elision." In our transcription, however, within a MINOR word-group where any pause would be abnormal, we use an apostrophe to replace the first of the two identical vowels, in order to remind you that making the elision is especially important in those places. Examples:

TRANSCRIPTION

k'está, par'aθér-me, l'amérika, 'aprendíðo, 'estáðo, n'olbidémos, 'aθér, m'e-fijáðo

WRITTEN SPANISH

que está, para hacerme, la América, ha aprendido, he estado, no olvidemos, a hacer, me he fijado

B. STUDY

Review SECTION A, *with the English covered.*

C. LISTENING IN

1. *Review* SECTION A, *repeating the Spanish and giving the English.*

2. *Listen in as Luis complains to Miguel about routine.*

Record Side 3.

LUIS: Estoy cansado de hacer las mismas cosas todos los días.

MIGUEL: Hay ciertas cosas que uno tiene que hacer. ¿Por qué se queja usted?

LUIS: Yo me quejo de todo. ¿No se ha fijado en eso?

MIGUEL: Sí, me he fijado.

LUIS: No hay bastante tiempo en el día para hacer todas las cosas.

MIGUEL: ¿No le gusta estar ocupado todo el día?

LUIS: No, no me gusta estar ocupado todo el día. Quiero tener tiempo para divertirme.

MIGUEL: ¿Cómo se divierte usted?

LUIS: Pues, a veces me gusta no hacer nada.

MIGUEL: Dígame, ¿qué cosas tiene usted que hacer durante el día?

LUIS: Tengo que levantarme temprano cada día.

MIGUEL: ¿A qué hora se levanta cada día?

LUIS: Me levanto a las siete.

MIGUEL: No es muy temprano.

LUIS: Después me baño y me afeito. ¿**Por** qué tienen que afeitarse todos los días los hombres? Ocupa demasiado tiempo.

MIGUEL: ¿Cómo puede usted quejarse de eso?

LUIS: Porque no tengo tiempo en la mañana y no me gusta apurarme.

MIGUEL: Puede usted levantarse más temprano. ¿Qué hace después de afeitarse?

LUIS: Después de afeitarme como algo y **voy a** trabajar.

MIGUEL: ¿A qué hora sale del trabajo?

LUIS: Salgo del trabajo a las cinco.

MIGUEL: ¿A qué hora come usted **por la noche**?

LUIS: En general como a las seis.

MIGUEL: ¿Come usted solo?

LUIS: A veces me acompañan unos **amigos**, y a veces me invitan otros amigos.

MIGUEL: Ésa es la vida de un soltero. ¿**Por** qué no se casa usted?

LUIS: Voy a casarme uno de estos días.

MIGUEL: ¿Qué hace usted después de **comer**?

LUIS: Voy al cine o escribo cartas.

MIGUEL: ¿A qué hora se acuesta?

LUIS: Me acuesto antes de las doce.

MIGUEL: Ésas son las mismas cosas que hace todo el mundo. No sé por qué se queja usted.

D. GRAMMATICAL ANALYSIS
PERSONAL PRONOUNS

English has three sets of personal pronouns: one used as subjects (*I*, *he*, etc.), a second as objects (*me*, *him*, etc.), and a third in the reflexive function (*myself*, *himself*, etc.).

Spanish has just two sets of personal pronouns, and there is no single Spanish counterpart to any given English pronoun, or vice versa.

1. THE VERB-OBJECT PRONOUN SERIES.

In Spanish the idea of "pronoun object of a verb" is expressed by unit forms which we will call the VERB-OBJECT PRONOUNS. The forms of this series all consist of a single syllable, THEY ARE NEVER STRESSED, and they never occur apart from a verb. Thus, having no independent existence, a verb object pronoun must be thought of as a PREFIX or SUFFIX (as the case may be) of the verb.

Since the verb-object pronouns distinguish the three grammatical persons which we have seen in verb SUBJECTS, we may make our analysis primarily on this basis.

(*1*) **First Person.** When the pronoun-reference is to the speaker(s), Spanish distinguishes singular and plural by using the form **me** for singu-

[73]

lar and **nos** for plural, as seen in the following examples (not all of which occur in the BASIC DIALOGUES):

> Yo me llamo Ricardo Ross.
> ¡ No me diga!
> Dime ¿ cómo es la prima de Jaime?
> Dígame ¿ qué hay entre usted y esa rubia?
> Ustedes no **nos** han invitado todavía.
> Tenemos que bañar**nos** y afeitar**nos** primero.
> Mi mamá me ayuda.
> No me gustan las películas románticas.
> Yo me defiendo de las mujeres.
> ¿ No quiere acompañar**nos**?
> **Nos** encontramos aquí dentro de media hora.

In first-person pronouns, then, no distinction is made between reflexive object, indirect object, or direct object.

(2) **Second Person.** When the pronoun reference is to a single person addressed informally with second-person forms, the Spanish form is **te**:

> ¿ No **te** han invitado todavía?
> ¿ No **te** gusta la película?
> ¿ A qué hora **te** levantas por la mañana?

Likewise in the second-person, there is no distinction between reflexive, indirect, and direct object.

(3) **Third Person.** When the pronoun reference is to any third person or thing, including persons addressed formally as **usted(es)**, formal distinction is made between: *A*, REFLEXIVE OBJECT, *B*, INDIRECT OBJECT, and *C*, DIRECT OBJECT.

A. REFLEXIVE OBJECT. For reflexive reference there is only the one form **se**:

> Uno necesita más tiempo para divertir**se**.
> ¿ Cómo **se** llaman ustedes?
> ¿ A qué hora **se** cierran las tiendas?

The context always makes clear the meaning of the reflexive **se**, since a reflexive object is always identical with the subject of the verb.

B. INDIRECT OBJECT. The indirect object form is **le**, to which is added the plural sign **-s** for distinction of number:

> Quiero presentar**le** a mi amigo Marcelo Sánchez.
> Se casan Carlos y Elena; quiero dar**les** un regalo.
> ¿ Qué **le** pasa a Carlos?
> El día catorce **le** vamos a dar una fiesta a Carlos.

The form **le(s)** has no single meaning of its own, but rather has a meaning reflected on it by the context in which it is used. In the first example above, the speech situation is such that **le** can only refer to the person being addressed (formally).

The last two examples show that even where a NOUN indirect object is present (**a Carlos**), an indirect object pronoun referring to that noun is also used.

C. DIRECT OBJECT. The direct object forms are the only ones which agree in GENDER with the noun they refer to: **lo** for masculines, **la** for feminines. (Some speakers make a further distinction between reference to things and to persons in the masculine, using **lo** in referring to things and **le** in referring to persons.) As with the indirect object forms, **-s** is added when the reference is plural. The following examples show how the direct-object pronoun takes its meaning from the context of the speech situation:

> No **lo** he visto en estos días.
> *referring to Carlos Mann*
> Usted no **la** conoce.
> *referring to Carlos' fiancée*
> Vamos a ver**la**.
> *referring to* **la película**
> A propósito, tengo que llamar**la** por teléfono.
> *referring to the Costales girl*
> **Lo** llamo por teléfono mañana.
> *referring to* **usted**
> Pues **lo** estamos invitando ahora.
> *referring to* **usted**
> ¿ No **lo** sabe usted?
> *referring to the fact that Carlos is getting married*
> **Lo** sentimos mucho, señora.
> *referring to the fact that they can't stay until Gloria gets home*

The last two examples show that when the reference is to a fact or a situation, rather than to a specific person or thing, the form used is **lo**, which in this case is actually GENDERLESS, not masculine.

2. POSITION OF VERB-OBJECT PRONOUNS.

Regarding the position of a verb-object pronoun relative to the verb it accompanies, the following statements apply equally to all the forms in the series:

(*1*) The pronoun is SUFFIXED when the verb is in the GENERAL FORM:

Es difícil decirlo.
. . . Y para quejarse.
Creo que es para hacerme estudiar.

(*2*) The pronoun is also SUFFIXED when the verb is in the IMPERATIVE, or in the COMMAND-FORM when expressing a "do"-command:

Dime ¿ cómo es la prima de Jaime?
Dígame ¿ qué hay entre usted y esa rubia?
Acuérdate que yo me levanto temprano.
Apúrese.

(*3*) The pronoun is PREFIXED when the verb is in a TENSE-FORM, including the COMMAND-FORM when expressing a "don't"-command:

¿ Por qué **lo** ayuda?
Precisamente de eso **me** quejo.
¡ No **me** diga!
No **se** vayan, señores.

Finally, in the case of a verb phrase made up of a tense-form of one verb plus the general form or the progressive form of another verb, the pronoun may be EITHER suffixed to the second or prefixed to the first:

¿ No quiere acompañar**me**?
OR
¿ No **me** quiere acompañar?

Tengo que llamar**la**.
OR
La tengo que llamar.

Quiero presentar**le** . . .
OR
Le quiero presentar . . .

Estamos invitánd**olo** . . .
OR
Lo estamos invitando . . .

Va casánd**ose** . . .
OR
Se va casando . . .

A prefixed pronoun is written separately from the verb, while a suffixed pronoun is not.

Comparative Usage of Reflexive Verbs

Since Spanish uses the reflexive pattern more extensively than English, you have already met with several verbal expressions which are reflexive in Spanish but not so in the corresponding English. You recall the following instances:

What time do you go to bed?
¿ A qué hora **te** acuestas?

Remember that I get up early.
Acuérdate que yo **me** levanto temprano.

We'll meet here in half an hour.
Nos encontramos aquí dentro de media hora.

. . . And to complain.
. . . Y para quej**arse**.

What time do the shops close?
¿ A qué hora **se** cierran las tiendas?

Hurry up.
Apúr**ese**.

I've noticed that.
Me he fijado en eso.

Whom's he marrying?
¿ Con quién **se** casa?

Don't go (away), gentlemen.
No **se** vayan, señores.

Since the direct object of the Spanish verb is the reflexive pronoun itself, a word which in English is direct object of the verb is introduced in Spanish by a PREPOSITION (**con**, **en**, etc.).

The last example illustrates the verb **ir** used with a reflexive "object," which serves to express the particular idea of "*go away*" or "*leave.*"

E. GRAMMATICAL DRILLS

1. PRONOUN POSITION.

As you say the following sentences, insert a verb-object pronoun in the proper place, the first time through making yourself the object of the action, the second time your brother or friend, and the third time the two of you together. Give the English.

EXAMPLE:

¿ No conoce Luisa ?

MODEL:

¿ No **me** conoce Luisa ?
Doesn't Louise know me ?

1. No han invitado todavía.
2. Están esperando unos amigos.
3. Miguel no quiere acompañar.
4. Los señores Quiroga no conocen.
5. ¿ No quiere esperar Roberto ?
6. A veces acompañan unos amigos.

2. PRONOUN VERB-OBJECTS REPLACING NOUNS.

A. *Take each of the noun phrases that follow and frame a question beginning with ¿ Conoce usted . . . , then answer the question in the affirmative, replacing the noun by the corresponding verb-object pronoun.*

EXAMPLE:

a mis padres

MODEL:

Q. — ¿ **Conoce usted** a mis padres ?
A. — Sí, **los conozco.**

1. aquellos países
2. la casa
3. esas tiendas
4. el coche
5. a María
6. el centro
7. a estos señores
8. al profesor Chávez

B. *Follow the same procedure as in A, beginning the question with ¿ Has visto . . . , then answer in the negative.*

EXAMPLE:

el autobús

MODEL:

Q. — ¿ **Has visto** el autobús ?
A. — No **lo he visto.**

1. a mi hermana
2. mi sombrero
3. este reloj
4. a esos hombres
5. la casa de Pedro
6. los calcetines
7. las fotografías
8. al señor Rodríguez
9. aquellas tiendas
10. el coche de mis padres
11. a la señorita Fernández
12. a mis hijos
13. a la señora
14. a Juan y a Julio
15. la nieve
16. esas cosas

C. *Follow the same procedure again, beginning the question with ¿ Van ustedes a comprar . . . , then answer in the affirmative, giving both possible positions of the verb-object pronoun.*

EXAMPLE:

la casa

MODEL:

Q. — ¿ **Van ustedes a comprar** la casa ?
A. — Sí, **vamos a comprarla.**
    OR
    Sí, **la vamos a comprar.**

1. ese queso
2. las corbatas
3. esta ropa
4. el restaurante
5. los calcetines
6. la tienda
7. las camas
8. los sombreros
9. esas cosas
10. el coche

D. *For the items that follow, first read the question as it is, then answer with a "do"-command, and then with a "don't"-command, using the informal in both.*

EXAMPLE:

¿ Compro el regalo ?

MODEL:

Q. — ¿ Compro el regalo ?
Shall I buy the present?
A1. — Sí, cómpralo.
A2. — No, **no lo compres.**

1. ¿ Llamo a los niños ?
2. ¿ Como el queso ?
3. ¿ Compro esta corbata ?
4. ¿ Tomo la limonada ?
5. ¿ Uso la corbata de José ?

Now, beginning the question with ¿ **Compro** *. . . , do the same thing with items 1–10 of* **C** *above, making the commands formal.*

Q. — ¿ Compro el regalo ?
A1. — Sí, cómprelo (usted).
A2. — No, **no lo compre (usted).**

3. REFLEXIVE VERBS.

A. *Take each of the phrases that follow and frame a question with the first part, making* **usted** *the subject. Then answer the question, using the phrase in the second part (or some other phrase of the same type).*

EXAMPLE:

cómo llamarse — Juan López, *etc.*

MODEL:

Q. — ¿ Cómo **se llama usted?**
A. — (Yo) **me llamo** Juan López.

1. a qué hora levantarse — a las siete, *etc.*
2. cuándo bañarse — por la mañana, *etc.*
3. de qué estarse quejando — del calor, *etc.*
4. cuándo ir a casarse — en agosto, *etc.*
5. qué día pensar irse — el dos de julio, *etc.*

B. *Go through the same phrases the same way again, successively making the subject of the question* **ella, tú, yo, ustedes, ellas.**

4. MORE REFLEXIVE VERBS.

A. *Take each of the following verbal phrases and make a statement with* **yo** *as the subject, and then give the English equivalent.*

EXAMPLE:

llamarse Carlos

MODEL:

Yo me llamo Carlos.
My name's Charles.

1. no acordarse del número
2. levantarse muy temprano
3. no haberse afeitado hoy
4. pensar casarse pronto
5. fijarse en las señoritas
6. quejarse de todo
7. tener que apurarse
8. defenderse de las mujeres
9. estarse divirtiendo mucho
10. no haberse bañado todavía
11. acostarse a las diez

B. *Go through the same phrases again, successively making the subject* **tú, usted,** *and* **mis hermanos y yo.**

F. STUDY

1. *Review* SECTION A, *with the Spanish covered.* **2.** *Prepare the* CONVERSATIONS.

G. CONVERSATIONS

1. *Reproduce the* BASIC DIALOGUES *in Spanish.*
2. *Using the* BASIC DIALOGUES *as your model, develop conversations such as:*
(*a*) Telling about your school day, or your work day, or your daily routine.

(*b*) Talking about a friend of yours that's getting married, and about the girl he's marrying. Or is your friend a girl?

(*c*) Going into town to buy a present for your friend.

[77]

Personal Pronouns, continued. Two Verb Objects together. Emphasis
on a Personal Pronoun. Pronouns in Verbless Expressions.

A. BASIC DIALOGUES
1. "I hate winter."

ENGLISH MEANING	AIDS TO LISTENING	SPANISH SPELLING

Record Side 3, after first spiral.

CÉSAR:

to me	a-mí	a mí
to you	a-tí	a ti
I don't like winter.	a-mí no-me-gústa el-imbiérno.	A mí no me gusta el invierno.
Do you?	¿ i-a-tí?	¿ Y a ti?

ROBERTO:

a season	una-estaθión	una estación
For me it's a season of the year (just) like the others.	para-mí es-una-estaθión del-áño komo-las-ótras.	Para mí es una estación del año como las otras.
Why don't you like winter?	¿ por-ké no-te-gústa el-im-biérno?	¿ Por qué no te gusta el invierno?

CÉSAR:

the ice	el-iélo	el hielo
Because of the cold, and the ice and snow.	por-el-frío, i-tambiém por-el-iélo i-la-niébe.	Por el frío, y también por el hielo y la nieve.
to take a step	dár um-páso	dar un paso
the street	la-káĺe	la calle
without breaking	sin-rrompér	sin romper
the head	la-kaƀéθa	la cabeza
You can't take a step in the street without breaking your neck.	úno no-puéde dár um-páso en--la-káĺe sin-rrompér-se la--kaƀéθa.	Uno no puede dar un paso en la calle sin romperse la cabeza.

ROBERTO:

in accord, in agreement	de-akuérdo	de acuerdo
with you	kon-tígo	contigo
I don't agree with you.	no-estói de-akuérdo kon-tígo.	No estoy de acuerdo contigo.
strong	fuérte	fuerte
[The] cold makes you strong.	el-frío te-áθe fuérte.	El frío te hace fuerte.
It's good for your health.	eş-mui-ƀuéno para-la-salúd.	Es muy bueno para la salud.

CÉSAR:

I don't feel very strong in the winter.	yó no-me-siénto mui-fuérte en--el-imbiérno.	Yo no me siento muy fuerte en el invierno.

ENGLISH MEANING	AIDS TO LISTENING	SPANISH SPELLING

ROBERTO:

with me	kon-mígo	conmigo
With me it's just the opposite.	kon-mígo pása tódo lo-kontrário.	Conmigo pasa todo lo contrario.
I like [the] cold better than [the] heat.	me-gústa más el-frío k'el-kalór.	Me gusta más el frío que el calor.

CÉSAR:

| I never complain of [the] heat. | yó núnka me-kéjo del-kalór. | Yo nunca me quejo del calor. |

ROBERTO:

| All the seasons have something good. | tódas las-estaθiónes tiénen álgo buéno. | Todas las estaciones tienen algo bueno. |

CÉSAR:

ideal	ideál	ideal
the tropics	el-trópiko	el trópico
For me the ideal climate's that of the tropics.	para-mí el-klíma ideál es-el-del-trópiko.	Para mí el clima ideal es el del trópico.

ROBERTO:

| some | algúnos | algunos |
| Remember what some (people) say. | akuérda-te de-lo-ke-díθen algúnos. | Acuérdate de lo que dicen algunos. |

CÉSAR:

| What do they say? | ¿ ké díθen ? | ¿ Qué dicen ? |

ROBERTO:

| a superior culture | una-kultúra superiór | una cultura superior |
| That [the] cold countries have a superior culture. | ke-los-países fríos tiénen una-kultúra superiór. | Que los países fríos tienen una cultura superior. |

CÉSAR:

nonsense	tonterías	tonterías
happy	felíθ	feliz
Nonsense. The people in the tropics live more happ(il)y, and with less work.	¡ tonterías ! la-jénte del-trópiko bíbe mas-felíθ, i-kon-ménos trabájo.	Tonterías. La gente del trópico vive más feliz, y con menos trabajo.

ROBERTO:

to stay, to remain	kedár-se	quedarse
the north	el-nórte	el norte
Why do you stay in the north, then ?	¿ por-ké te-kédas en-el-nórte entónθes.	¿ Por qué te quedas en el norte, entonces ?

CÉSAR:

| next | próksimo | próximo |
| Next winter I'm going to the South. | el-imbiérno próksimo me-bói al-súr. | El invierno próximo me voy al sur. |

2. "That's the last time I'll lend Jim my fountain pen."

ENGLISH MEANING	AIDS TO LISTENING	SPANISH SPELLING

JOE:

last	última	última
to lend	prestár	prestar
my fountain pen	mi-plúma fuénte	mi pluma fuente
(That)'s the last time I('ll) lend my fountain pen to Jim.	eṣ-la-última β́θ ke-le-présto mi--plúma fuénte a-jáime.	Es la última vez que le presto mi pluma fuente a Jaime.

LOU:

| to find | enkontrár (enkuéntra-) | encontrar (encuentra-) |
| Why? (Can)'t you find it? | ¿ por-ké? ¿ no-la-enkuéntras? | ¿ Por qué? ¿ No la encuentras? |

JOE:

to carry, to take	ḷebár	llevar
with himself	kon-sígo	consigo
No. Every time I lend it to him, he takes it (away) with him.	nó. káda β́θ ke-se-la-présto, se-la-ḷéba kon-sígo.	No. Cada vez que se la presto, se la lleva consigo.

LOU:

Why does he ask for your pen?	¿ por-ké te-píde la-plúma?	¿ Por qué te pide la pluma?
he	él	él
Hasn't he got (one)?	¿ él no-tiéne?	¿ Él no tiene?

JOE:

to ask	preguntár	preguntar
idea	idéa	idea
Don't ask me. I have no idea.	¡ no-me-lo-pregúntes. no-téngo idéa.	No me lo preguntes. No tengo idea.
on purpose	a-propósito	a propósito
It seems as though he does it on purpose.	paréθe ke-lo-áθe a-propósito.	Parece que lo hace a propósito.

LOU:

in itself	en-sí	en sí
importance	importánθia	importancia
to explain	esplikár	explicar
The thing in itself is of no importance, but I (can)'t explain it.	la-kósa en-sí no-tiéne importánθia, pero-no-me-lo--esplíko. . . .	La cosa en sí no tiene importancia, pero no me lo explico.

JOE:

nor I	ni-yó	ni yo
neither	tampóko	tampoco
Neither (can) I. Jim's a good fellow.	ni-yó tampóko. jáime es-una--β́uéna persóna:	Ni yo tampoco. Jaime es una buena persona.

ENGLISH MEANING	AIDS TO LISTENING	SPANISH SPELLING
LOU:		
to show	enseñár	enseñar
Where are the pictures you want to show me?	¿ dónde están las-fotografías ke--me-kiéres enseñár.	¿ Dónde están las fotografías que me quieres enseñar?
JOE:		
to look for	buskár	buscar
over there	por-alí	por allí
Look for them over there.	¡ búska-las por-alí.	Búscalas por allí.
under	debájo	debajo
some books	unoş-líbros	unos libros
They're under some books.	están debájo de-unoş-líbros.	Están debajo de unos libros.
LOU:		
Hey Joe, what's this?	¡ óye josé, ¿ ké es-ésto?	Oye, José, ¿ qué es esto?
JOE:		
What?	¿ ké kósa?	¿ Qué cosa?
LOU:		
the name	el-nómbre	el nombre
A fountain pen with Jim's name on it.	una-plúma fuénte ke-léba el--nómbre de-jáime.	Una pluma fuente que lleva el nombre de Jaime.
JOE:		
Can't be!	¡ no-puéde sér!	¡ No puede ser!
LOU:		
thus, so	así	así
Well it is. Your name isn't James Aguilar.	pues-así és. tú no-te-lámas jáime agilár.	Pues así es. Tú no te llamas Jaime Aguilar.
JOE:		
poor	póbre	pobre
Poor Jim! Now I understand why he [has] asked to borrow my pen.	¡ póbre jáime. aóra entiéndo por-ké me-a-pedído prestáda la-plúma.	¡ Pobre Jaime! Ahora entiendo por qué me ha pedido prestada la pluma.
LOU:		
I think he won't ask you for it again.	kréo ke-yá no-buélbe a-pedír--te-la.	Creo que ya no vuelve a pedír-te-la.

3. "Tell me your name and I can't tell you where you're from."

ALEJANDRO:		
By the way, do you know the Rodríguez-MacKennas?	a-propósito, ¿ konóθe ustéd a--los-rrodrígeθ makéna?	A propósito, ¿ conoce usted a los Rodríguez-MacKenna?
HENRY:		
I haven't (had) the pleasure.	no-téngo el-gústo.	No tengo el gusto.

ENGLISH MEANING	AIDS TO LISTENING	SPANISH SPELLING
rare, strange	rráro	raro
But where does that queer name come from?	¿ pero-de-dónde biéne ése nómbre tan-rráro.	¿ Pero de dónde viene ese nombre tan raro ?
Scots, Scottish	eskoθés	escocés
Are they a Spaniard and a Scots-woman ?	¿ son-un-españól i-una-eskoθésa ?	¿ Son un español y una esco-cesa ?

ALEJANDRO:

the land	la-tiérra	la tierra
No. They're both from the land of O'Higgins.	nó. loṣ-dós son-de-la-tiérra de-ojígins.	No. Los dos son de la tierra de O'Higgins.

HENRY:

impossible	imposíble	imposible
Both from Ireland? Impossible.	¿ loṣ-doṣ de-irlánda ? imposíble.	¿ Los dos de Irlanda ? Imposible.

ALEJANDRO:

a famous personage	um-personáje famóso	un personaje famoso
the history	la-istória	la historia
Bernardo O'Higgins is a famous figure in the history of Chile.	bernárdo ojígins es-um-personáje famóso en-la-istória de-chíle.	Bernardo O'Higgins es un per-sonaje famoso en la historia de Chile.

HENRY:

even funny	ásta graθióso	hasta gracioso
(That) seems to me very odd; funny even.	me-paréθe mui-rráro i-ásta graθióso.	Me parece muy raro y hasta gracioso.
Chilean	chiléno	chileno
Bernardo O'Higgins a Chilean !	¡ bernárdo ojígins un-chiléno !	¡ Bernardo O'Higgins en chi-leno !

ALEJANDRO:

to read	leér	leer
to contain	kontenér (kontiéne-)	contener (contiene-)
foreign	estranjéro	extranjero
(Just) read [the] Chilean history. It contains a lot of "foreign" names.	¡ léa ustéd la-istória de-chíle. kontiéne múchoṣ nómbres estranjéros.	Lea usted la historia de Chile. Contiene muchos nombres « ex-tranjeros ».

HENRY:

Are foreign names found only in Chile ?	¿ sólo en-chíle s'enkuéntran nómbres estranjéros ?	¿ Sólo en Chile se encuentran nombres extranjeros ?

ALEJANDRO:

No, there are (some of) them everywhere.	¡ nó ómbre. los-ái en-tódas pártes.	No, hombre. Los hay en todas partes.
for example	por-ejémplo	por ejemplo
Italian	italiáno	italiano

ENGLISH MEANING	AIDS TO LISTENING	SPANISH SPELLING
For example, in [the] Argentina there are a lot of Italian names.	por-ejémplo, en-l'arjentína ai--múchoş nómbres italiános.	Por ejemplo, en la Argentina hay muchos nombres italianos.

HENRY:

for them	para-éĺos	para ellos
for us	para-nosótros	para nosotros
So for them it's the same as for us.	entónθes para-éĺos eş-lo-míşmo ke-para-nosótros.	Entonces para ellos es lo mismo que para nosotros.
A foreign name doesn't mean anything.	un-nómbre estranjéro no-kiére deθír náda.	Un nombre extranjero no quiere decir nada.

ALEJANDRO:

Yes, that's about it.	sí, más o-ménos.	Sí, más o menos.

HENRY:

Gosh!	¡ ké karái!	¡ Qué caray!
to take a trip	aθér um-biáje	hacer un viaje
Some day I'm going to take a trip through Spanish America.	algún día hói 'aθér um-biáje por l'américa cspañola.	Algún día voy a hacer un viaje por la América Española.

NOTES ON PRONUNCIATION AND SPELLING

CONSONANTS

THE LETTER X.

The letter **x** appears in the written form of many Spanish words borrowed from Latin. Between vowels **x** represents the consonant combination ks, as in English. Before another consonant, it represents merely the s-sound. Examples:

TRANSCRIPTION

próksimo; esplikár, estranjéro

WRITTEN SPANISH

próximo; explicar, extranjero

Some speakers pronounce ks even before another consonant in words spelled with **x**, saying for example eksplikár, ekstranjéro. If you hear this pronunciation, you may safely imitate it.

SYLLABLES

1. SYLLABLE BOUNDARIES.

A Spanish word has as many syllables as it has full vowel-sounds or diphthongs. Within a word, boundaries between syllables occur BEFORE single consonant-sounds or such pairs of consonant-sounds as may also occur at the beginning of a word. Examples (in written Spanish):

co/no/cer, a/que/lla, vie/nes, ca/be/za, i/de/al, tró/pi/co, su/pe/rior, pro/pó/si/to, ce/rra/das, gra/cias, va/ca/cio/nes, ha/bla/mos, fo/to/gra/fí/as, Ro/drí/guez, no/so/tros, lec/ción, in/glés, ex/tran/je/ro, in/vier/no, rom/per/se, nom/bre, is/to/ria, en/ton/ces, a/pren/dien/do, en/cuen/tran

Throughout a major word-group, the boundaries of spoken syllables occur according to the above principle, as though the entire group were a single word. For example, in the sentence

Po/de/mo/s em/pe/za/r a /co/me/r a /la/s o/cho

the final consonants of **podemos, empezar, comer** and **las** are all spoken as part of the first syllable of the following word.

2. THE MARKING OF STRESS IN WRITTEN SPANISH.

The stressed syllable of every Spanish word of more than one syllable is shown in its written form, through a system of the use versus the non-use of the accent-mark (´). This system may be stated as follows:

(*1*) **Words stressed on their LAST syllable.** These are written with the accent-mark over the stressed vowel when that vowel is final in the word, or is followed by **n** or **s**:

TRANSCRIPTION

akí, así, josé, aĺá, está, también, están, rraθón, estaθión, inglés, después, tomás, adiós, autobús

WRITTEN SPANISH

aquí, así, José, allá, está, también, están, razón, estación, inglés, después, Tomás, adiós, autobús

Otherwise, such words are NOT written with the accent-mark:

TRANSCRIPTION

ustéd, salúd, rrelój, jenerál, español, sentír, señór, felíθ, estói, karái

WRITTEN SPANISH

usted, salud, reloj, general, español, sentir, señor, feliz, estoy, caray

(*2*) **Words stressed on their NEXT–TO–LAST syllable.** These are NOT written with the accent-mark when they end in a vowel, followed or not by **n** or **s**:

TRANSCRIPTION

kási, tiéne, kabéθa, beráno, díθen, enkuéntran, rréjis, puédes, kósas, salgámos

WRITTEN SPANISH

casi, tiene, cabeza, verano, dicen, encuentran, Regis, puedes, cosas, salgamos

Otherwise, such words are written with the accent-mark over the stressed vowel:

TRANSCRIPTION

fáθil, difíθil, útil, gonθáleθ, lópeθ, sáncheθ

WRITTEN SPANISH

fácil, difícil, útil, González, López, Sánchez

(*3*) **Words stressed on their SECOND–FROM–LAST syllable.** These are all written with the accent-mark over the stressed vowel:

TRANSCRIPTION

número, simpátiko, película, teléfono, trópiko, última, díga-me, búska-las, pedír-te-la

WRITTEN SPANISH

número, simpático, película, teléfono, trópico, última, dígame, búscalas, pedírtela

(*4*) Any word which contains a syllable boundary occurring between a stressed **i** or **u** and another vowel, is written with an accent-mark over the stressed **i** or **u**:

TRANSCRIPTION

días, frío, fotografía, todabía, país, oír, rraúl

WRITTEN SPANISH

días, frío, fotografía, todavía, país, oír, Raúl

In this way the stressed **i** or **u** is distinguished in writing from the half-vowel of a diphthong, as for example in **gracias, Gloria, contrario, duermo, restaurante, después.**

(*5*) A number of one-syllable and two-syllable words are written with the accent-mark over their stressed vowel merely to distinguish their written appearance from that of an identically spelled word having a different meaning or a different grammatical function. This is true of all question-words (for example **qué, quién, cómo, dónde,** cuánto); of demonstrative words separated from their nouns (ésta, aquéllos, ése, etc.), of the pronouns tú, mí, sí; of más, *more;* of the verb-form sé, *I know* (cf. the pronoun se); of sólo, *only* (cf. solo, *alone*); of sí, *yes* (cf. si, *if*); and of a few others.

B. STUDY

Review SECTION A, *with the English covered.*

C. LISTENING IN

1. *Review* SECTION A, *repeating the Spanish and giving the English.*

2. *Listen in as* (*1*) *Manuel and an Englishman discuss climates, and* (*2*) *Luis offers to lend Antonio a pen.*

Record Side 3, after first spiral.

(*1*)

MANUEL: En mi país sólo tenemos dos estaciones del año, el invierno y el verano.

UN INGLÉS: ¿ Ah, sí ? ¿ Cómo son las dos estaciones?

MANUEL: En el invierno llueve mucho. El verano es seco.

EL INGLÉS: A nosotros nos parece raro porque aquí tenemos cuatro estaciones.

MANUEL: La primavera es muy bonita aquí.

EL INGLÉS: El otoño también es hermoso, pero a veces hace mucho calor.

MANUEL: La gente de cada país cree que tiene un clima ideal.

EL INGLÉS: Sí, a nosotros nos gustan la nieve y el hielo, y a ustedes no. Nosotros decimos que el frío es bueno para la salud.

MANUEL: La vida del trópico es agradable también. La gente del trópico vive muy feliz. No necesitan trabajar mucho.

EL INGLÉS: Estoy de acuerdo con usted. Es agra-dable la vida del trópico. El invierno próximo voy a hacer un viaje por esos países.

MANUEL: Y yo quiero pasar el invierno en un país frío. Quiero ver la nieve y el hielo.

(*2*) (*Not recorded*)

ANTONIO: Nunca puedo usar una pluma fuente sin romperla.

LUIS: ¿ Cómo es eso ?

ANTONIO: No me lo explico.

LUIS: ¿ Tiene usted pluma ahora ?

ANTONIO: No, no tengo.

LUIS: Si quiere mi pluma se la presto con mucho gusto.

ANTONIO: Gracias, pero yo nunca le pido la pluma a un amigo.

LUIS: Yo tengo dos. Le presto la que no es muy buena.

ANTONIO: ¿ La tiene aquí ? Enséñemela.

LUIS: No sé dónde está en este momento. Voy a preguntarle a Roberto si la tiene.

ANTONIO: Roberto no está en la casa ahora.

LUIS: Entonces vamos a ver si encontramos la pluma. ¿ Cree que está bien ?

ANTONIO: Creo que sí. Pero ¿ qué hacemos si se la ha llevado consigo ?

LUIS: Entonces tenemos que esperar, ¿ verdad ?

D. GRAMMATICAL ANALYSIS

PERSONAL PRONOUNS (CONT'D.)

1. The Verb-Object Series (*Continued*).

Two Verb-Object Pronouns Together. In the following sentences two verb-object pronouns are present with the same verb:

> No **me lo** preguntes.
> Pero no **me lo** explico.
> { Creo que ya no vuelve a pedír**tela**.
> { Creo que ya no **te la** vuelve a pedir.

In these expressions one of the pronouns represents the indirect object, the other the direct object. In every case, whether the pronouns are prefixed or suffixed, the indirect object form (which may be also reflexive) precedes the direct.

When both pronoun objects are THIRD-PERSON, the indirect object form is **se** WHETHER REFLEXIVE OR NOT, as shown in the following sentence:

> Cada vez que **se la** presto, **se la** lleva consigo.

2. The Supplementary Pronoun Series.

We now turn to the set of Spanish personal pronouns which are used in all patterns other than that of verb-object. These are independent forms, not prefixes or suffixes. Again we base our analysis on distinction of the three grammatical persons.

(*1*) **First Person.** When the pronoun-reference is to the speaker(s), Spanish distinguishes singular from plural. In the singular, the form **mí** is used after any preposition, and the form **yo** elsewhere:

> Para **mí** el clima ideal es el del trópico.
> A **mí** no me gusta el invierno.
> **Yo** quiero trabajar en la América Española.
> Están dando la película *Tú y Yo*.
> Ni **yo** tampoco.

In the plural, the forms used in all patterns — **nosotros, nosotras** — show agreement with the gender of the speakers:

> Entonces para ellos es lo mismo que para **nosotros**.
> María no puede ir con **nosotras**.

(*2*) **Second Person.** When reference is to a single person addressed informally with second-person forms, the Spanish forms are **ti** after prepositions, and **tú** elsewhere:

> Esto no es para **ti**, Ricardo.
> ¿ Y a **ti** ?
> **Tú** no te llamas Jaime Aguilar.
> Oye ¡ entra **tú** primero !

(*3*) **Third Person.** When the pronoun reference is to any third person — other than those addressed formally as **usted**(**es**) — and when it is NOT REFLEXIVE, the forms used in all patterns — **él, ella, ellos, ellas** — show agreement of both gender and number:

> ¿ **Él** no tiene ?
> **Ella** me ayuda.
> Entonces para **ellos** es lo mismo que para nosotros.
> Yo me defiendo bastante bien de **ellas**.

However, if the reference is REFLEXIVE, that is, to the subject of the verbal expression in which the pronoun occurs, there is only the one form **sí,** which distinguishes neither gender nor number:

> La cosa en **sí** no tiene importancia.

Finally, let us observe that the forms **mí, ti,** and **sí** appear with the suffix **-go** when they follow the preposition **con,** the whole phrase being written as a single word.

> **Conmigo** pasa todo lo contrario.
> No estoy de acuerdo **contigo.**
> Cada vez que se la presto, se la lleva **consigo.**

A. **Emphasis on a Personal Pronoun.** In order to give "contrastive emphasis" to a personal pronoun, an English speaker simply applies stress to a regularly used pronoun. In Spanish, however, it is not possible to apply stress to a verb-object pronoun. Therefore, in order to achieve desired emphasis, Spanish adds a stressed supplementary pronoun while retaining the unstressed verb-object form, as in the following examples:

> *I haven't seen* **her.**
> No **la** he visto **a ella.**

> **I** *don't like winter.*
> **A mí no me** gusta el invierno.

Since it is obviously impossible to give contrastive emphasis to a subject which is merely implied by the person-number ending of a verb (**digo,** *I say*), Spanish for this purpose adds a supplementary pronoun as subject. You have seen many such cases, such as the following:

> *And* **I** *say that George is a fool.*
> Y **yo** digo que Jorge es un tonto.

> *And to complain, the way* **you're** *doing now.*
> Y para quejarse, como estás haciendo **tú** ahora.

> *Hasn't* **he** *got one?*
> ¿ **Él** no tiene ?

B. **Personal Pronouns in Verbless Expressions.** In many situations where English uses *do* without any other verb, Spanish uses a completely verbless expression. If such a verbless expression involves a personal pronoun, the form used is naturally one of the supplementary set:

> *Do you?*
> ¿ **Y a ti?**

> *Neither do I.*
> Ni **yo** tampoco.

> *Who wants to go?* — *We don't.*
> ¿ Quién quiere ir ? — **Nosotros** no.

> *Do they know that?* — **He** *doesn't, but* **she** *does.*
> ¿ Saben eso ? — **Él** no, pero **ella** sí.

The last two examples show that the supplementary pronoun is followed by **no** in negative patterns, and by **sí,** *yes* in cases of contrast with a previous negative.

E. GRAMMATICAL DRILLS

1. TWO VERB-OBJECT PRONOUNS TOGETHER.

A. *Read the question as it is, also giving the English. Then answer by changing the indirect object and by replacing the italicized noun object with the appropriate pronoun.*

EXAMPLE:

> — ¿ Te presta *el reloj?*
> *Does he lend you the watch?*

MODEL:

> Sí, **me lo** presta.

1. ¿ No te quiere decir *el número?*
2. ¿ Te está explicando *la lección?*
3. ¿ Te ha presentado *a esas señoritas?*
4. ¿ No te han enseñado *la casa?*
5. ¿ Van a darte *los regalos?*

B. *Repeat the preceding series of questions and answers, making the indirect object in the question* **le,** *referring to "you."*

MODEL:

> — ¿ Le presta *el reloj?*
> *Does he lend you the watch?*

ANSWER:

> Sí, **me lo** presta.

C. *Repeat the questions and answers again, making the indirect object* **le,** *referring to "him" or "her."*

EXAMPLE:

> — ¿ Le presta *el reloj?*
> *Does he lend him (her) the watch?*

MODEL:

> — Sí, **se lo** presta.

D. *Repeat, making the indirect object* **les,** *referring to "you (people)."*

EXAMPLE:

> — ¿ Les presta *el reloj?*
> *Does he lend you the watch?*

MODEL:

> — Sí, **nos lo** presta.

E. *Repeat, making the indirect object* **les,** *referring to "them."*

EXAMPLE:

— ¿ Les presta *el reloj?*
Does he lend them the watch?

MODEL:

— Sí, **se lo** presta.

2. SUPPLEMENTARY PRONOUNS.

In speaking the sentences that follow, replace the italicized English pronoun by the required Spanish one. Give the English.

EXAMPLE:

No voy con *him.*

MODEL:

No voy con **él.**
I'm not going with him.

1. A *me* no me gusta la nieve.
2. A *you* no te gusta ese restaurante.
3. A *him* no le gusta el invierno.
4. A *her* le gusta levantarse temprano.
5. ¿ A *you* le gusta este país?
6. A *us* nos gusta mucho la casa.
7. A *them* no les gustan estas corbatas.
8. ¿ Me llevo esto con *me?*
9. No puedes llevártelo con *you.*
10. Juan se va a llevar esto con *him.*
11. María se va a llevar esto con *her.*
12. Llévese usted esto con *you.*
13. Los niños van a llevárselo con *them.*
14. ¿ Qué dicen de *me, you, you (people), him, her, them, us?*
15. Quieren hablar con *me, you, you (people), him, her, them, us.*
16. José quiere comprar eso para *me, you, you (people), him, her, them, us.*

3. SUPPLEMENTARY PRONOUNS IN VERBLESS EXPRESSIONS.

In connection with each of the sentences that follow, give the Spanish for each of the English expressions listed with it.

EXAMPLE:

— ¿ Quién tiene mi reloj? — I haven't.

MODEL:

— Yo no.

1. ¿ Quién tiene mi sombrero? — (*a*) I haven't. (*b*) He hasn't. (*c*) She hasn't. (*d*) We haven't. (*e*) They haven't. (*f*) Jim hasn't.
2. Yo quiero ver esa película. — (*a*) Do you too? (*b*) So do I. (*c*) So do they. (*d*) So do we. (*e*) So does he. (*f*) So does she. (*g*) I don't. (*h*) So does Luis.
3. Yo no soy de Inglaterra. — (*a*) Are you? (*b*) Aren't you either? (*c*) I'm not either. (*d*) She isn't either. (*e*) He isn't either. (*f*) Neither are we. (*g*) Neither are they.
4. Anita habla muy bien el inglés. — (*a*) I don't. (*b*) I do too. (*c*) So do we. (*d*) But you don't. (*e*) So do they. (*f*) Do you too?
5. Yo no he estado en esa casa. — (*a*) She hasn't either. (*b*) But they have. (*c*) Neither has he. (*d*) But I have. (*e*) They haven't either. (*f*) But she has. (*g*) Neither have we. (*h*) But he has. (*i*) But we have.

4. ASKING: pedir OR preguntar?

The verb **pedir** means "*request,*" and the verb **preguntar** means "*inquire.*" English, however, most frequently uses *ask* to express either of those two meanings. *As you read the following sentences aloud, choose the form in parentheses which Spanish would use.*

EXAMPLE:

Jaime siempre (me pide — me pregunta) prestada la ropa.

MODEL:

Jaime siempre me **pide** prestada la ropa.

1. (Pídeles — Pregúntales) el número de la casa.
2. Es la segunda vez que Juan (me pide — me pregunta) dónde vivo.
3. No sé de dónde es ese señor, pero se lo voy (a pedir — a preguntar).
4. Cada hora mi hijo (me pide — me pregunta) algo de comer.

[88]

5. Mis hermanos (me piden — me preguntan) prestadas las corbatas.

6. Siempre (me piden — me preguntan) cuándo me voy a casar.

7. (Pidámosle — Preguntémosle) al señor Pérez si es chileno.

8. ¿ Por qué te han (pedido — preguntado) cuántos años tienes ?

9. Miguel tiene coche, ¿ verdad ?   — Sí, vamos (a pedírselo — a preguntárselo).

10. No (me pidas — me preguntes) eso, porque no lo sé.

11. (Pida — Pregunte) usted la hora.

12. No (me pidas — me preguntes) la pluma porque no la tengo.

F. STUDY

1. *Review* SECTION A, *with the Spanish covered.*   **2.** *Prepare the* CONVERSATIONS.

G. CONVERSATIONS

1. *Reproduce the* BASIC DIALOGUES IN SPANISH.

2. *Using the* BASIC DIALOGUES *as your model, develop conversations such as:*

(*a*) Discussing which you like best, winter or summer, cold weather or hot weather, and why.

(*b*) Lending something to somebody and not getting it back — for example a hat, a tie, a pen, a watch.

(*c*) Talking about foreign names in English-speaking and Spanish-speaking countries.

Studying Indoors and Out. Changing Quarters. Choosing Clothes.

Possessive Words: Choice of Basic Forms. English *of* in Possessive
Phrases. Substitution of the Definite Article for the Possessive Adjective. Alternatives for **suyo.**

A. BASIC DIALOGUES

1. "Pre-holiday blues."

ENGLISH MEANING	AIDS TO LISTENING	SPANISH SPELLING

Record Side 3, after second spiral.

AL:

to approach, to come near
aθerkár-se
acercarse

Well, Fred, holiday's getting close.
buéno, feðeríko, s'están aθerkándo laş-ƀakaθióne̦s.
Bueno, Federico, se están acercando las vacaciones.

FRED:

Thank the Lord.
gráθias a-ðiós.
Gracias a Dios.

I'm not in the mood for studying any more.
yá no-téngo kaƀéθa para- -estuðiár.
Ya no tengo cabeza para estudiar.

AL:

Neither am I.
ni-yó tampóko.
Ni yo tampoco.

FRED:

to enclose, to confine
enθerrár (enθiérra-)
encerrar (encierra-)

When the weather begins to be nice, I can't shut myself in with a book.
kuando-empiéθa 'aθér ƀuén tiémpo, no-puéðo enθerrár- -me kon-un-líƀro.
Cuando empieza a hacer buen tiempo, no puedo encerrarme con un libro.

AL:

in the open air
al-áire líƀre
al aire libre

Have you tried studying out- doors?
¿ as-tratáðo ð'estuðiár al-áire líƀre ?
¿ Has tratado de estudiar al aire libre ?

FRED:

various, several
bárias
varias

always
siémpre
siempre

Yes, several times, but it always makes me sleepy.
sí, báriaş ƀéθes, pero-siémpre me-ðá suéño.
Sí, varias veces, pero siempre me da sueño.

AL:

Of course !
¡ kláro.
¡ Claro !

to expect
esperár
esperar

the sun
el-sól
el sol

ENGLISH MEANING	AIDS TO LISTENING	SPANISH SPELLING
What can you expect with the sun and the heat and a book?	¿ké puédes esperár, kon-el-sól, el-kalór i-un-líbro.	¿Qué puedes esperar, con el sol, el calor y un libro?

FRED:

Doesn't the same (thing) happen to you?	¿a-tí no-te-pása lo-mísmo?	¿A ti no te pasa lo mismo?

AL:

point	púnto	punto
Yes, to a certain extent.	sí, asta-θiérto púnto:	Sí, hasta cierto punto.
But I'd rather do my work in the house and go out afterwards.	pero-yó prefiéro aθér mi-trabájo en-la-kása i-salír después.	Pero yo prefiero hacer mi trabajo en la casa y salir después.

FRED:

admirable	admiráble	admirable
You're wonderful!	¡éres admiráble, ermáno.	Eres admirable, hermano.
ought to be	débe sér	debe ser
That's the way [the] people ought to be.	así débe sér la-jénte.	Así debe ser la gente.

AL:

It's not your fault.	tú no-tiéneş la-kúlpa.	Tú no tienes la culpa.
It's hard to study here.	eş-difíθil estudiár akí.	Es difícil estudiar aquí.
much light	múcha lúθ	mucha luz
the room	el-kuárto	el cuarto
besides	además	además
small, little	pekéño	pequeño
There isn't much light in this room, and besides it's pretty small.	no-éntra múcha lúθ en-éste kuárto, i-además eş-mui- -pekéño.	No entra mucha luz en este cuarto, y además es muy pequeño.

FRED:

clean	límpio	limpio
dark	oskúro	oscuro
the floor	el-píso	el piso
It's clean, but it's dark, and it's on the third floor.	eş-límpio, pero-es-oskúro i-está en-el-terθér píso.	Es limpio, pero es oscuro y está en el tercer piso.

AL:

I say, what day do classes end?	¡óye, ¿ké día termínan las- -kláses?	Oye ¿qué día terminan las clases?

FRED:

at (the) beginnings	a-prinθípios	a principios
the month	el-més	el mes
The first of next month.	a-prinθípioş del-més ke-biéne.	A principios del mes que viene.
I don't know what day.	no-sé ké día.	No sé qué día.

AL:

at once, immediately	en-segída	en seguida

ENGLISH MEANING	AIDS TO LISTENING	SPANISH SPELLING
Are you planning to leave here right away?	¿ piénsas salír de-akí en-segída ?	¿ Piensas salir de aquí en seguida ?

FRED:

sure, certain	segúro	seguro
I certainly am!	¡ segúro ke-sí !	¡ Seguro que sí !
I'm not staying a minute longer.	no-me-kédo ni-un-minúto más.	No me quedo ni un minuto más.

AL:

to move, leave	desokupár	desocupar
Moving out of this room isn't going to be easy, you know	no-bá a-sér fáθil desokupár éste kuárto, ¿ sábes ?	No va a ser fácil desocupar este cuarto, ¿ sabes ?

FRED:

to assemble, to collect	juntár	juntar
A lot of things pile up in a year, don't they?	se-júntan múchas kósas en-un--áño, ¿ berdád ?	Se juntan muchas cosas en un año, ¿ verdad ?

AL:

worse	peór	peor
And (with) two living in a room it's worse.	i-bibiéndo dós en-un-kuárto es--peór.	Y viviendo dos en un cuarto es peor.
sure	segúro	seguro
which (ones)	kuáles	cuáles
mine	mías	mías
yours	túyas	tuyas
And I'm not sure what things are mine and what are yours.	ni-estói segúro ké kósas son--mías ni-kuáles son-túyas.	Ni estoy seguro qué cosas son mías ni cuáles son tuyas.

FRED:

a pair of shoes	um-pár de-θapátos	un par de zapatos
white	blánkos	blancos
Whose is this pair of white shoes?	¿ de-kién es-éste pár de-θapátos blankos?	¿ De quién es este par de zapatos blancos ?

AL:

Aren't they yours?	¿ no-son-túyos ?	¿ No son tuyos ?

FRED:

I haven't got (any) white shoes.	yó no-téngo θapátos blánkos.	Yo no tengo zapatos blancos.

AL:

it is necessary to ask	ái ke-preguntár	hay que preguntar
Then we('ll) have to ask Henry.	entónθes ái ke-preguntár-le a--enrríke.	Entonces hay que preguntarle a Enrique.
They may be his.	puéden sér de-él.	Pueden ser de él.

FRED:

tennis racquets	rrakétas de-ténis	raquetas de tenis

ENGLISH MEANING	AIDS TO LISTENING	SPANISH SPELLING
behind	detrás	detrás
the door	la-puérta	la puerta
Have you noticed there are three tennis racquets behind the door?	¿ te-as-fijádo en-ke-ái trés rrakétaş de-téniş detráş de-la--puérta ?	¿ Te has fijado en que hay tres raquetas de tenis detrás de la puerta ?
ours	nuéstras	nuestras
They're not ours.	no-son-nuéstras.	No son nuestras.

AL:

One's mine.	úna eş-mía.	Una es mía.
(they) must be	dében sér	deben ser
your girl-friend	tu-nóbia	tu novia
The other two must be your girl's.	las-ótraş dóş dében sér de-tu--nóbia.	Las otras dos deben ser de tu novia.

FRED:

Man, that's right!	¡ ombre, sí.	¡ Hombre, sí !
hers	súyas	suyas
Now I remember they are hers.	yá me-akuérdo ke-son-súyas.	Ya me acuerdo que son suyas.

AL:

to divide	dibidír	dividir
How('ll) we manage to divide all these ties (of) ours?	¿ kómo aθémos para-dibidír tódas éstas korbátaş nués--tras?	¿ Cómo hacemos para dividir todas estas corbatas nuestras ?

FRED:

the best	lo-mejór	lo mejor
the eyes	los-ójos	los ojos
to choose, to pick	eskojér	escoger
I think the best (thing) is to close our eyes and pick.	kréo ke-lo-mejór es-θerrár los--ójos i-eskojér.	Creo que lo mejor es cerrar los ojos y escoger.
Don't you think so?	¿ no-te-paréθe.	¿ No te parece ?

AL:

Something like that.	álgo así:	Algo así.
in all ways	de-tódoş módoş	de todos modos
Anyway it's going to be hard getting out of here quickly.	de-tódoş módoş bá a-sér difíθil salír de-akí prónto.	De todos modos va a ser difícil salir de aquí pronto.

2. "I haven't got a thing to wear."

JANE:

a (piece of) advice	un-konséjo	un consejo
Mary, give me some advice, will you?	maría, ¡ dá-me un-konséjo, ¿ kiéres.	María, dame un consejo ¿ quieres ?
dress	bestído	vestido
to put	ponér	poner
(I) put	póngo	pongo

ENGLISH MEANING	AIDS TO LISTENING	SPANISH SPELLING
What dress (shall) I put on to-night?	¿ ké bestído me-póngo ésta nóche?	¿ Qué vestido me pongo esta noche?
MARY:		
Tell me first where you're planning to go.	dí-me priméro a-dónde piénsas ír.	Dime primero a dónde piensas ir.
JANE:		
I really don't know.	es-ke-no-sé.	Es que no sé.
MARY:		
You don't know?	¿ no-sábes?	¿ No sabes?
Who are you going out with, then?	¿ kon-kiém bás a-salír, entónθes.	¿ Con quién vas a salir, entonces?
JANE:		
I can't tell you [it], Mary.	no-te-lo-puédo deθír, maría.	No te lo puedo decir, María.
a secret	un-sekréto	un secreto
It's a secret.	es-un-sekréto.	Es un secreto.
to offend	ofendér	ofender
Don't be offended.	¡ no-te-oféndas.	No te ofendas.
MARY:		
(I) know	konóθko	conozco
Do I know him?	¿ lo-konóθko yó?	¿ Lo conozco yo?
You're not thinking of going out with my boy-friend, at least?	¿ no-piénsas salír kon-mi-nóbio, kuando-ménos.	¿ No piensas salir con mi novio, cuando menos?
JANE:		
Not with yours.	kon-el-túyo nó.	Con el tuyo no.
MARY:		
Oh my! What women are!	¡ dióş mío! ¡ kómo són laş--mujéres!	¡ Dios mío! ¡ Cómo son las mujeres!
JANE:		
You've got to help me, Mary.	tiénes ke-ayudár-me, maría.	Tienes que ayudarme, María.
good taste	buén gústo	buen gusto
to dress	bestír (bíste-)	vestir (viste-)
You have very good taste in clothes.	tú tiéneş mui-buén gústo para--bestír.	Tú tienes muy buen gusto para vestir.
MARY:		
Thanks, Jane.	gráθias juána.	Gracias, Juana.
It's not hard when you know where you're going and who you're going out with.	no-éş difíθil kuando-sábe úno a-dónde bá i-kon-kién sále.	No es difícil cuando sabe uno a dónde va y con quién sale.
JANE:		
to cost	kostár (kuésta-)	costar (cuesta-)

[94]

ENGLISH MEANING	AIDS TO LISTENING	SPANISH SPELLING
I always have a hard time choosing a dress.	a-mí siémpre me-kuésta trabájo eskojér um-bestído.	A mí siempre me cuesta trabajo escoger un vestido.
to remove, to take off	kitár	quitar
I put one on and take it off right away.	me-póngo úno i-me-lo-kíto en--segída.	Me pongo uno y me lo quito en seguida.

MARY:

impression	impresión	impresión
What (kind of an) impression do you want to make on the poor (man)?	¿ ké impresión le-kiéres aθér al-póbre.	¿ Qué impresión le quieres hacer al pobre ?

JANE:

possible	posíble	posible
The best impression I can.	la-mejór impresióm posíble.	La mejor impresión posible.
It's the first time he's invited me to go out.	eş-la-priméra béθ ke-me-imbíta a-salír.	Es la primera vez que me invita a salir.

MARY:

Why don't you put on your white dress?	¿ por ké no-te-pónes el-bestído blánko.	¿ Por qué no te pones el vestido blanco ?

JANE:

It isn't clean.	no-está límpio.	No está limpio.

MARY:

put	pón	pon
black	négro	negro
Well, put on your black (one) then.	buéno, ¡ pón-te el-négro en--tónθes.	Bueno, ponte el negro, entonces.

JANE:

my handbag	mi-kartéra	mi cartera
I can't wear my black dress because my black handbag's old now.	no-puédo usár el-bestído négro por-ke-mi-kartéra négra yá está biéja.	No puedo usar el vestido negro porque mi cartera negra ya está vieja.

MARY:

those details	ésoş detáĺes	esos detalles
[The] men don't notice those details.	los-ómbreş no-se-fíjan en-ésoş detáĺes:	Los hombres no se fijan en esos detalles.

JANE:

This man notices everything.	éste señór se-fíja en-tódo.	Este señor se fija en todo.
Besides he likes [the] smart women.	además le-gústan laş-mujéres elegántes.	Además le gustan las mujeres elegantes.

MARY:

to offer	ofreθér	ofrecer
(I) offer	ofréθko	ofrezco

ENGLISH MEANING	AIDS TO LISTENING	SPANISH SPELLING
Well, if you haven't (a) handbag I (can) offer you mine.	buéno, si-no-tiénes kartéra te--ofréθko la-mía.	Bueno, si no tienes cartera te ofrezco la mía.

JANE:

Oh thanks, Mary.	¡ ái gráθiaş maría.	Ay gracias, María.
to return, to give back	deƀolƀér (deƀuélƀe-)	devolver (devuelve-)
I('ll) give it back to you tomorrow.	te-la-deƀuélƀo mañána.	Te la devuelvo mañana.
to deserve	mereθér	merecer
(I) deserve	meréθko	merezco
the favour.	el-faƀor	el favor
I don't deserve the favour.	no-meréθko el-faƀór.	No merezco el favor.

NOTES ON PRONUNCIATION AND SPELLING

INTONATION

The intonations, or pitch-patterns, of spoken Spanish are not wholly uniform from region to region or even from speaker to speaker in the same region. Nevertheless we have, in our transcription, used a system of punctuation intended to represent consistently certain prevalent intonation patterns which you are most likely to hear.

In the speech of all Spanish speakers at least three pitch levels are discernible: normal, high, and low. These three pitches combine into three significant types of intonation patterns which extend over full utterances. In all three types, initial unstressed syllables in an utterance are usually pitched lower than the prevalent, significant level.

1. THE DECLARATIVE INTONATION.

This pattern, marked by a period at the end in written Spanish, is pitched mainly at the normal level. When, as in most cases, it ends slightly lower than normal, we transcribe with a period at the end:

TRANSCRIPTION

yá no-téngo kaƀéθa para-estudiár.
en-jenerál no-ágo mi-traƀájo fáθil ménte.

WRITTEN SPANISH

Ya no tengo cabeza para estudiar.
En general no hago mi trabajo fácilmente.

When occasionally, the pitch rises slightly on the last stressed syllable and then returns to normal, we transcribe with three dots at the end:

TRANSCRIPTION

yó téngo más ámbre ke-séđ, pero-ƀámos . . .
la-kósa en-sí no-tiéne importánθia, pero-no-me-lo-esplíko . . .

WRITTEN SPANISH

Yo tengo más hambre que sed, pero vamos.
La cosa en sí no tiene importancia, pero no me lo explico.

When, again, the pitch starts higher and descends to lower than normal, but ends normal, we transcribe with a colon at the end:

TRANSCRIPTION

jáime es una-ƀuéna persóna:
los-ombreş no-se-fíjan en-ésoş detáĺes:

WRITTEN SPANISH

Jaime es una buena persona.
Los hombres no se fijan en esos detalles.

2. THE INTERROGATIVE INTONATION.

In this pattern the prevalent pitch is higher than normal. Written Spanish encloses an utterance which has this intonation between a pair of question-marks. In the transcription we use the initial (inverted) question-mark to indicate the prevalent high pitch. When this high pitch is raised even higher at the end, we transcribe with the final question-mark also:

TRANSCRIPTION

¿ tú pídes para-jáime también?
¿ ké día termínan las-kláses?

WRITTEN SPANISH

¿ Tú pides para Jaime también?
¿ Qué día terminan las clases?

When, on the other hand, the high pitch is not maintained, but drops toward normal at the end, we transcribe with a final period:

TRANSCRIPTION

¿ piénsas salír de-akí en-segída.
¿ por-ké no-te-gústa el-imbiérno.

WRITTEN SPANISH

¿ Piensas salir de aquí en seguida?
¿ Por qué no te gusta el invierno?

3. THE EXCLAMATORY INTONATION.

In this pattern the pitch begins higher than normal and descends. When it descends to LOWER than normal on the final stressed syllable (which is then also lengthened slightly by some speakers), we enclose the utterance between exclamation-marks, as does written Spanish:

TRANSCRIPTION

¡ ké komplikaθiónes!
¡ kómo son laş-mujéres!

WRITTEN SPANISH

¡ Qué complicaciones!
¡ Cómo son las mujeres!

When, however, the pitch merely descends to normal at the end, we transcribe with only the initial (inverted) exclamation-mark. Written Spanish frequently does not use the exclamation-marks in this case:

TRANSCRIPTION

¡ bámos a-dár una-buélta.
¡ léa ustéd la-istória de-chíle.

WRITTEN SPANISH

Vamos a dar una vuelta.
Lea usted la historia de Chile.

An utterance may contain more than one major word-group, with pauses indicating the boundaries. Such pauses are usually marked in written Spanish by commas. When the pause is preceded by normal pitch, we transcribe with a comma:

TRANSCRIPTION

sí, báriaş béθes, pero-siémpre me-dá suéño.
no-kiéro eskapár-me, pero-sí kiéro dár una-buélta.

WRITTEN SPANISH

Sí, varias veces, pero siempre me da sueño.
No quiero escaparme, pero sí quiero dar una vuelta.

When, occasionally, the pause is preceded by a rise to high pitch, we transcribe with a dash:

TRANSCRIPTION

en-jenerál áθe frío en-el-imbiérno — i-en-el-beráno áθe kalór.
únoş días a-laş-nuébe — ótros a-las-ónθe.

WRITTEN SPANISH

En general hace frío en el invierno, y en el verano hace calor.
Unos días a las nueve, otros a las once.

B. STUDY

Review SECTION A, *covering up the English.*

C. LISTENING IN

1. *Review* SECTION A, *repeating the Spanish and giving the English.*

2. *Listen in as Leonor and Gloria talk about clothes, tennis rackets, and pocketbooks:*

Record Side 4.

LEONOR: ¿ Te gustan los zapatos blancos ?

GLORIA: Sí, los zapatos blancos son muy bonitos cuando hace sol y cuando están limpios. Ese par tuyo es muy bonito.

LEONOR: Pero no son bonitos cuando llueve, y aquí llueve mucho.

GLORIA: A mí me gustan los vestidos blancos también. No me gusta ponerme un vestido oscuro en el verano.

LEONOR: Un vestido negro siempre hace una buena impresión.

GLORIA: Sí, es verdad que un vestido negro es elegante.

LEONOR: Mi novio se fija en todos esos detalles. A veces le pido su consejo antes de comprar ropa. Otras veces me ayuda él a escoger un vestido, o un sombrero.

GLORIA: ¿ Es por eso que siempre usas sombrero, porque le gusta a él ?

LEONOR: Sí, a mi novio le gustan las mujeres elegantes.

GLORIA: ¡ Dios mío ! Yo no me pongo un som- brero para darle gusto a un hombre ! Me gusta estar al aire libre, sin sombrero. Quiero sentir el aire y el sol.

LEONOR: Todo es cuestión de gusto.

GLORIA: Oye, ¿ me quieres prestar tu raqueta de tenis esta tarde ? La mía se va a romper muy pronto.

LEONOR: Te la presto con mucho gusto, **pero no es muy buena.** La tuya es mejor.

GLORIA: Muchas gracias, Leonor. ¿ Dónde está tu raqueta ?

LEONOR: Búscala por allí, detrás de la puerta. Me imagino que está ahí.

GLORIA: No la veo por aquí.

LEONOR: Entonces debe estar en el segundo piso.

GLORIA: Ah sí, aquí está. Parece que tengo los ojos cerrados.

LEONOR: Ahora puedes hacerme un favor a mí, si quieres.

GLORIA: ¿ Qué favor te puedo hacer ?

LEONOR: Voy a salir esta noche y necesito una cartera blanca. ¿ Tú tienes una ?

GLORIA: Yo no tengo pero mi hermana tiene dos.

LEONOR: ¡ Ah no ! ¡ No quiero usar la suya !

GLORIA: Yo siempre uso la ropa de ella.

LEONOR: No, muchas gracias, Gloria. Puedo usar otra cartera.

D. GRAMMATICAL ANALYSIS
POSSESSIVE WORDS

In addition to the "possessive" form with *'s*, English has special words to denote something as possessed by, or someone as related to, a particular person or persons — for example *my, mine; your, yours; his*, etc.

Similarly Spanish, in addition to the pattern expressing possession with **de** before a noun or pronoun, has special words which denote possession or relationship. However, the grammar of Spanish possessive words is sufficiently different from those of English that a careful analysis of the forms and patterns is necessary.

1. CHOICE OF BASIC FORM OF POSSESSIVES.

In Spanish the GENDER of the possessor is never distinguished by the form of the possessive word used. There is, however, distinction of the three grammatical PERSONS.

(*1*) **First Person.** When the possessor is the speaker(s), Spanish like English further distinguishes NUMBER by using forms of the basic **mío** for the singular, and of the basic **nuestro** for the plural.

(*2*) **Second Person.** When the possessor is a (singular) person addressed informally with second-person verb and pronoun forms, the basic possessive form used is **tuyo.**

(*3*) **Third Person.** When the possessor is third-person — including those addressed as **usted(es)** — the basic form is **suyo**, without distinction of the NUMBER of the possessor(s). This "blanket" form has no single meaning of its own, but rather has a meaning reflected on it by the context in which it is used.

2. USE OF SPECIFIC FORMS OF POSSESSIVES.

The specific form taken by the basic **mío, nuestro, tuyo,** or **suyo** depends on two factors: (*1*) the gender-number of the "thing possessed" and (*2*) the type of pattern in which the form occurs. Let us observe the following groups of sentences containing possessive words:

Ni estoy seguro qué cosas son **mías** ni cuáles son **tuyas.**
¿ Esos zapatos no son **tuyos** ?
Las tres raquetas no son **nuestras.**
Una de las raquetas es **mía.**
Las otras deben ser de Anita. — Sí, ya me acuerdo que son **suyas.**
¿ Cómo hacemos para dividir todas estas corbatas **nuestras** ?
¡ Dios **mío** !

In this group the possessive words either come JUST AFTER the noun they accompany, or are connected with it by a form of the verb ser. They act like four-form adjectives (such as **mucho, bueno,** etc.) in that they show gender-number agreement with the noun denoting the thing possessed.

Here is a contrasting group:

Yo prefiero hacer **mi** trabajo en casa.
Mi abuela es más joven.
Mis padres están en España.
Las otras dos deben ser de **tu** novia.
¿ Dónde están **tus** libros ?
Vamos a casa de Jaime; está de visita **su** prima de Madrid.
Jaime vive a la derecha; ya veo **su** casa.
Entonces salgamos a celebrar el cumpleaños de **su** abuelo.
¿ Van ustedes a ver a **sus** amigos ?

Here the possessive words stand JUST BEFORE the noun they accompany (this being the common type of possessive phrase you have used since UNIT 1). In this position the possessive words **mío, tuyo, suyo** show agreement of NUMBER in the usual way, but they appear in shortened forms — one syllable, UNSTRESSED — without the gender-marking vowel. (The form **nuestro** does not shorten in this position.)

Comparative Usage

(*1*) **English *of* in Possessive Phrases.** In phrases where the thing possessed is preceded by an indefinite article, demonstrative word, numeral, or the like, English uses *of* between the noun and the following possessive word. In Spanish there is no comparable use of **de** before the possessive word:

John wants to take some friends of his.
Juan quiere llevar a **unos amigos suyos.**

Three cousins of mine are visiting.
Están de visita **tres primos míos.**

How'll we manage to divide all these ties of ours?
¿ Cómo hacemos para dividir todas **estas corbatas nuestras** ?

(*2*) **Spanish Definite Article with Possessive Words.** In possessive phrases where no noun is expressed, Spanish (unlike English) places the appropriate form of the definite article before a possessive word as a replacement for the unexpressed noun:

*You're not thinking of going out with my boy-friend?
— Not with yours.*
¿ No piensas salir con mi novio ? — Con **el tuyo** no.

If you haven't got a handbag I can offer you mine.
Si no tienes cartera te ofrezco **la mía.**

(3) Spanish Alternatives for "suyo." Any form of the third-person possessive word **suyo** may be, and frequently is, replaced by a possessive phrase consisting of **de** + SUPPLEMENTARY PRONOUN, thus paralleling the normal possessive pattern of **de** + NOUN. Observe the following alternative expressions:

Then we'll have to ask Henry. They may be his.
Entonces hay que preguntarle a Enrique. Pueden
ser $\begin{cases} \text{suyas.} \\ \text{de él.} \end{cases}$

Are your parents old?
¿ Son viejos $\begin{cases} \text{sus padres?} \\ \text{los padres de usted?} \end{cases}$

Yours are more stylish.
$\left. \begin{array}{l} \textbf{La suya} \\ \textbf{La de ustedes} \end{array} \right\}$ es más elegante.

In contrast, the first and second-person possessives **mío, nuestro** and **tuyo** are never replaced by **de mí, de nosotros, de ti.**

(4) Non-Use of Possessives in Spanish. In sentences containing mention of a person and a part of his body, an article of his clothing or a common portable possession — in other words, sentences in which a "possessor-possessed relationship" is self-evident — Spanish (unlike English) uses no possessive word, but merely the definite article:

The best thing is to close our eyes and pick.
Lo mejor es cerrar **los** ojos y escoger.

I can't wear my black dress.
No puedo usar **el** vestido negro.

In such sentences there does often appear, however, an indirect-object reference to the possessor as the "person affected by the action":

Why does he ask you for your pen?
¿ Por qué **te** pide **la** pluma?

You can't take a step in the street without breaking your head.
Uno no puede dar un paso en la calle sin romperse **la** cabeza.

Why don't you put on your white dress?
¿ Por qué no **te** pones **el** vestido blanco?

Well, put on your black one, then.
Bueno, ponte **el** negro, entonces.

(In English, similar references to the "person affected" are often inherent in such words as *on, off, away*, etc. after the verb, as in the last two examples.)

On the other hand, if the possessor is not mentioned at all in the same phrase with the thing possessed, a possessive word naturally does occur:

. . . because my black handbag is old now.
. . . porque **mi** cartera negra ya está vieja.

All right, you can wear my tie.
Está bien, puedes usar **mi** corbata.

E. GRAMMATICAL DRILLS

1. POSSESSIVE FORMS.

Make possessive phrases using each of the nouns in the following list with each of the possessive words **mío, nuestro, tuyo, suyo.**

A. *First make short phrases with noun alone and possessive, putting the possessive before the noun and using the proper short form where required.*

EXAMPLE:
casa

MODEL:

mi casa — **nuestra** casa — **tu** casa — **su** casa

1. hermano	8. amigas
2. hijos	9. cama
3. padres	10. clase
4. país	11. lección
5. ropa	12. niño
6. sombreros	13. gustos
7. tienda	14. hermanas

15. compañero
16. amigos
17. calcetines
18. pies
19. trabajo
20. papá
21. raqueta
22. abuelos
23. apetito
24. mamá
25. coche
26. secretos
27. fotografías
28. reloj
29. salud
30. cartas
31. cuarto
32. regalo
33. vida
34. novio
35. zapatos
36. libros
37. nombre
38. pluma fuente
39. tierra
40. viajes
41. cartera
42. consejos
43. impresiones
44. vestidos
45. ojos

B. *Using each of the nouns (1–45 of A) make phrases including also such words as* **este, ese, uno, dos, muchos,** *etc., which will come before the noun, while the possessive, unshortened, comes after it.*

EXAMPLE:

casa

MODEL:

esta casa **mía** — **una** casa **nuestra** — **esa** casa **tuya** — **esta** casa **suya**

C. *Using each of the nouns (1–45 of A) make compound phrases joined by* **y** *or* **o,** *mentioning any two different possessors, and putting the noun only in the first element.*

EXAMPLE:

casa

MODEL:

mi casa **y la tuya** — **nuestra** casa **y la suya** — **tu** casa **o la suya** — **su** casa **o la mía**

2. NON-USE OF POSSESSIVES.

In saying the following sentences, supply the Spanish for the italicized English possessive words, by using the definite article and also inserting an indirect verb-object pronoun where the sense requires it:

EXAMPLE:

¡ Pon *your* sombrero !

MODEL:

¡ Pon**te el** sombrero !

1. Luis no ha puesto *his* corbata. (**puesto =** irregular completive form of **poner.**)
2. Paquito, no rompas *my* reloj.
3. ¿ Por qué quitas *your* zapatos ?
4. ¿ Dónde has puesto *your* pluma ?
5. ¿ No puede usted encontrar *your* sombrero ?
6. Mis hermanos siempre piden prestada *my* ropa.
7. ¡ No ponga usted *your* sombrero !
8. Ven acá, Juanito; quiero poner *your* zapatos nuevos.
9. ¡ Han quitado *our* fotografías ! (**quitar** here = "take away")
10. ¡ Quita *your* sombrero, hombre !
11. ¿ Por qué no usa Ricardo *his* corbata nueva ?
12. Cierra *your* ojos.

F. STUDY

1. *Review* SECTION A, *with the Spanish covered.*

2. *Prepare the* CONVERSATIONS.

G. CONVERSATIONS

1. *Reproduce the* BASIC DIALOGUES *in Spanish.*

2. *Using the* BASIC DIALOGUES *as your model, develop conversations such as:*

(*a*) Talking as if holiday time were near.

(*b*) Talking with a friend about going out: what you're going to wear; what you'd like your friend to lend you, etc.

Review.

Unit Six. Unit Seven. Unit Eight. Unit Nine.

UNIT
10

A. REVIEW OF UNIT 6

I. SPEAKING SPANISH.

1. *Review thoroughly* SECTION **A** *of* UNIT 6, *making sure you can say the English with the English text covered and the Spanish with the Spanish text covered.*

2. *Give answers to the following questions: (Any answer that makes sense is all right provided it's in the form of a full sentence. It shouldn't be just* **Sí, No,** *or some other monosyllable. You don't need to confine yourself to the vocabulary of* UNIT 6; *use any words you know by now.)*

1. ¿ A qué casa vamos ?
2. ¿ Quién está de visita en casa de Jaime ?
3. ¿ Cómo se llama la prima de Jaime ?
4. ¿ De dónde es Gloria ?
5. ¿ Cómo es Gloria ?
6. ¿ Has estado en casa de Jaime, Marcelo ?
7. ¿ Está bien entrar en casa de Jaime ?
8. ¿ Por qué está bien entrar en casa de Jaime ?
9. ¿ A qué hora tienes que volver a casa ?
10. ¿ Qué hora es ahora ?
11. ¿ A qué hora vamos a volver juntos ?
12. ¿ Vive a la derecha Jaime ?
13. ¿ Ves la casa ?
14. ¿ Qué tenemos que hacer para saber si está Jaime ?
15. ¿ Cómo se llama la mamá de Jaime ?
16. ¿ Quién va a ver si está en casa Jaime ?
17. ¿ Quién es Paquito ?
18. ¿ Están en casa Jaime y Gloria ?
19. ¿ Dónde están ?
20. ¿ Cuándo van a volver ?
21. ¿ Podemos esperar unos minutos ?
22. ¿ Por qué no podemos esperar ?
23. ¿ Cuándo volvemos a casa de Jaime ?
24. ¿ Quién tiene cumpleaños hoy ?

25. ¿ Cuántos años tiene el abuelo ?
26. ¿ Es vieja la abuela también ?
27. ¿ Cuántos años tiene la abuela ?
28. ¿ Tiene usted abuelos ?
29. ¿ Cuántos años tienen los abuelos de usted ?
30. ¿ Dónde viven sus abuelos ?
31. ¿ Son viejos los padres de usted ?
32. ¿ Cuántos años tienen sus padres, más o menos ?
33. ¿ Cómo está usted de salud ?
34. ¿ Tiene usted buen apetito ?
35. ¿ Cuántos minutos hay en media hora ?
36. ¿ En una hora cuántos minutos hay ?
37. ¿ Sabe usted decir la hora en español ?
38. ¿ Qué hora es ahora ?
39. ¿ Es más fácil el inglés o el español ?
40. ¿ Tiene usted reloj ?

3. *Ask the questions that would get the following answers:*

1. Vamos a casa de Jaime.
2. Gloria no vive en casa de Jaime. Sólo está de visita.
3. Sí, he estado en casa de Jaime muchas veces.
4. Está bien entrar en casa de Jaime porque somos compañeros de clase.
5. Tenemos que volver a casa a las diez.
6. Ahora son las nueve menos veinte.
7. Vamos a volver juntos a las diez menos cuarto.
8. La prima de Jaime es un encanto.
9. La prima de Jaime se llama Gloria.
10. No, Jaime vive a la izquierda.
11. ¡ No estoy hablando alto !
12. Este señor es mi amigo Marcelo Sánchez.
13. Paquito va a ver si está en casa Jaime.
14. Jaime está de paseo ahora.

15. Está de paseo con su prima Gloria.
16. No podemos esperar porque es tarde.
17. Sí, señora, podemos volver mañana.
18. El cumpleaños de mi abuelo es mañana.
19. Mi abuelo tiene noventa años.
20. Mi abuela es más joven que mi abuelo.
21. Ella tiene ochenta y cinco años.
22. Yo ya no tengo abuelos.
23. No, mis padres no son muy viejos.
24. Mi madre tiene cuarenta y ocho años.
25. Mi padre tiene cincuenta y dos años.
26. A mí me gusta hablar de cosas serias.
27. Estoy muy bien de salud, gracias.
28. Sí, tengo el apetito muy bueno.
29. Voy a salir a celebrar mi cumpleaños.
30. Hay treinta minutos en media hora.
31. Una hora tiene sesenta minutos.
32. Hay quince minutos en un cuarto de hora.
33. No, no estamos solos; aquí está el amigo Pedro.
34. Estamos aprendiendo a decir la hora en español.
35. Son las dos menos diez.
36. El inglés no es difícil.
37. El reloj del profesor es malo.
38. Yo no tengo reloj.
39. Tengo nueve compañeros de clase.
40. Tenemos cita a las cuatro.

4. *After hearing again the* Listening-In *Section of* Unit 6, *give answers to the following questions based directly on it:*

1. ¿ Cómo se llama la señora ?
2. ¿ Quién es Manuel Fernández ?
3. ¿ Conoce a Guillermo la señora López ?
4. ¿ Ha estado Guillermo en casa de la señora ?
5. ¿ Cómo se llama el hijo de la señora ?
6. ¿ Por qué ha venido aquí Manuel ?
7. ¿ Dónde vive Manuel ?
8. ¿ Cuántas veces ha visitado Manuel a su primo ?
9. ¿ Por qué no sabe la hora Manuel ?
10. ¿ Quién sabe la hora ?
11. ¿ Qué hora es ?
12. ¿ Con quién tienen cita Carlos y Manuel ?

13. ¿ A qué hora es la cita ?
14. ¿ Dónde está el coche ?
15. ¿ Por qué prefiere ir a su casa Manuel ?
16. ¿ Es vieja una persona que tiene treinta o cuarenta años ?
17. ¿ Cuántos años tiene el abuelo del muchacho ?
18. ¿ Cuántos años tiene la abuela ?
19. ¿ Son viejos los abuelos ?
20. ¿ Hay mucha gente que vive hasta los ochenta o noventa años ?

II. Writing Spanish.

The following sentences are variations on the content of the Basic Dialogues *of* Unit 6. *Write them out in Spanish. Parentheses around an English word mean that it* isn't *expressed in the Spanish version; brackets around a word not normally present in the English mean that it* is *expressed in the Spanish.*

1. Let's go and see [the] Grandfather.
2. Go to the right; don't go to the left.
3. Be careful, and don't be foolish.
4. Let's go into that shop.
5. Come back here in forty-five minutes.
6. Don't go away, gentlemen.
7. Don't talk so loud !
8. Let's not talk about those serious things.
9. Let's go out and celebrate your birthday.
10. Don't put the pictures there.
11. I say, what time is it ?
12. Fortunately I don't have a watch.
13. You're going to eat with Gloria ? No fair !
14. We've already learned that. What's next ?
15. Don't come late; come at 4:15.
16. She's my cousin, let's not forget that.
17. Don't get up at 11 o'clock tomorrow; get up at 8:30.
18. Let's go to class together.
19. What are you thinking about ?
20. I'm thinking about the winter, the cold, and the snow.
21. Are you going to meet Jim's cousin tonight ?
22. What's Jim's cousin like ? —She's very pretty.
23. You've never been in Mexico ?

24. Does Gloria live here? — No, she's only visiting.
25. Where does she live then, in Madrid?
26. I want to introduce my friends from Puerto Rico.
27. I'm very sorry, ma'am, but it's late already.
28. He's seventy-five years old? Don't tell me!
29. There are sixty minutes in an hour, and twenty-four hours in a day.
30. Are your parents in good health?
31. My grandmother is young; she's only sixty-six years old.
32. Can you wait a quarter of (an) hour?
33. Is Mario home? — No, he's taking a walk.
34. It's one o'clock, isn't it? — No, it's 2:20.
35. The house is on the left, I think.

B. REVIEW OF UNIT 7

I. SPEAKING SPANISH

1. *Review thoroughly* SECTION A *of* UNIT 7, *just as you have done for* UNIT 6.

2. *Give answers to the following questions:*

1. ¿ A dónde va usted esta tarde?
2. ¿ Para qué va usted al centro?
3. ¿ Quiere usted acompañarme al centro?
4. ¿ Para quién va usted a comprar un regalo?
5. ¿ Qué va a hacer el amigo Carlos?
6. ¿ Qué día se va a casar?
7. ¿ Con quién se va a casar?
8. ¿ Conoce usted a la muchacha con quien se va a casar?
9. ¿ Es soltero usted?
10. ¿ Piensa casarse usted uno de estos días?
11. ¿ Son casados todos los hermanos de usted?
12. ¿ Cómo es la chica Costales?
13. ¿ Le gusta a Pablo la chica Costales?
14. ¿ A qué hora se cierran las tiendas en el centro?
15. ¿ Tiene teléfono usted?
16. ¿ Qué número de teléfono tiene usted?
17. ¿ Se baña usted por la mañana o por la noche?
18. ¿ Tiene usted algo que hacer ahora?
19. ¿ Es día de fiesta hoy?
20. ¿ A qué hora te levantas por la mañana?
21. ¿ Te levantas a la misma hora todos los días?
22. ¿ Estudian o trabajan tus hermanos?
23. ¿ Dónde trabajan tus hermanos?
24. ¿ Dónde estudian tus hermanos?
25. ¿ A qué hora empiezan tus clases?
26. ¿ Empiezan a la misma hora todos los días?
27. ¿ A qué hora te acuestas?
28. ¿ Te gusta levantarte temprano?
29. ¿ Crees que el trabajo ocupa demasiado tiempo?
30. ¿ Te quejas cuando tienes que trabajar?

3. *Ask questions that will get the following answers:*

1. No voy a hacer nada esta tarde.
2. No, no me gusta comprar regalos.
3. El regalo es para mi mamá.
4. Carlos se casa el primero de agosto.
5. Se casa con la señorita González.
6. No, no me han invitado a la fiesta.
7. La fiesta es el martes.
8. Es alta y rubia la amiga de Pablo.
9. No me he fijado en el tiempo.
10. No me he fijado en la hora.
11. Tengo que llamar a una chica.
12. No, no puedo esperar.
13. Las tiendas se cierran a las cinco y media.
14. Antes de salir tengo que escribir una carta.
15. Nos encontramos en el centro.
16. Nos encontramos a las siete.
17. Voy a salir dentro de media hora.
18. Hoy es martes.
19. Mañana es día de fiesta.
20. Sí, vamos a tener ocho días de vacaciones.
21. Son las vacaciones de primavera.
22. Mis clases no empiezan a la misma hora todos los días.
23. Unos días empiezan a las nueve, otros a las once.
24. Yo me levanto a las siete.

25. Sí, me levanto a la misma hora cada día.
26. Me acuesto tarde.
27. Sí, yo creo que el trabajo ocupa demasiado tiempo.
28. Yo necesito más tiempo para divertirme.
29. Gracias, no quiero ir al cine.
30. No quiero ir al cine porque tengo que acostarme temprano.

4. *After hearing again the* LISTENING-IN *Section of* UNIT 7, *give answers to the following questions based directly on it:*

1. ¿ De qué está cansado Luis ?
2. ¿ En qué se ha fijado Miguel ?
3. ¿ Hay bastante tiempo en un día para Luis ?
4. ¿ Para qué quiere tener más tiempo Luis ?
5. ¿ Cómo se divierte Luis ?
6. ¿ Se levanta tarde Luis ?
7. ¿ A qué hora se levanta ?
8. ¿ Qué hace después de levantarse ?
9. ¿ Le gusta afeitarse ?
10. ¿ Por qué no le gusta afeitarse ?
11. ¿ Qué hace después de afeitarse ?
12. ¿ A qué hora sale del trabajo ?
13. ¿ A qué hora come por la noche ?
14. ¿ Come solo ?
15. ¿ Quiénes lo acompañan a veces ?
16. ¿ Es casado Luis ?
17. ¿ Cuándo se va a casar ?
18. ¿ Qué hace después de comer ?
19. ¿ A qué hora se acuesta ?
20. ¿ Qué dice Miguel de todo esto ?

II. WRITING SPANISH.

The following sentences are variations on the content of the BASIC DIALOGUES *of* UNIT 7. *Write them out in Spanish.*

1. What's happening to our friend Carlos ?
2. For whom is the present that you're going to buy ?
3. Is the Costales girl tall and blond ?
4. They haven't invited me to the party yet.
5. Who's Paul going to marry ? — I don't know.
6. Little by little we're all getting married.
7. You get up at ten o'clock ? What (a) life !
8. Ask Juana where she's going.
9. Tell them where I live.
10. We go to bed early every day.
11. What's going to happen on September 12th ?
12. What's the matter with you ?
13. Nothing serious. I'm going to get married on August 1st.
14. But that's very serious !
15. Tomorrow is (a) holiday, don't you remember ?
16. Why do you have to shave first ?
17. By the way, have you telephoned them ?
18. Do you know them ? — I don't think so.
19. Hasn't Mary arrived yet ? — No, I'm waiting for her now.
20. I have to write a letter and I can't write it.
21. Hurry up, man ! I can't wait all [the] day.
22. Haven't you anything to do ?
23. Yes, but I don't want to do it.
24. Where's Peter ? Have you seen him ?
25. I never see him [in] these days.
26. I don't like to think about all the work that I have to do.
27. Why don't you do it then ?
28. Sometimes I do it. Haven't you noticed ?
29. What are those children complaining about ?
30. We need more time to amuse ourselves.

C. REVIEW OF UNIT 8

I. SPEAKING SPANISH

1. *Review thoroughly* SECTION A *of* UNIT 8, *just as you have done for* UNITS 6 *and* 7.

2. *Give answers to the following questions:*

1. ¿ A usted le gusta el invierno ?
2. ¿ Por qué (no) le gusta el invierno ?
3. ¿ Le gusta más el frío o el calor ?
4. ¿ Por qué le gusta más el frío (el calor) ?

5. ¿ Por qué es agradable la vida del trópico ?
6. ¿ Qué dicen de los países fríos ?
7. ¿ Está usted de acuerdo con eso ?
8. ¿ Por qué (no) está usted de acuerdo ?
9. ¿ Ha pasado usted algún invierno en el sur ?
10. ¿ Por qué no encuentra José su pluma fuente ?
11. ¿ Por qué cree José que se la ha llevado Jaime ?
12. ¿ Quién encuentra una pluma ?
13. ¿ Dónde la encuentra Luis ?
14. ¿ De quién es esta pluma ?
15. ¿ Cómo sabemos que es de Jaime ?
16. ¿ Por qué le ha pedido la pluma Jaime a José ?
17. ¿ De qué tierra son los Rodríguez-MacKenna ?
18. ¿ Es Irlanda la tierra de O'Higgins ?
19. ¿ Qué país es ?
20. ¿ Quién es Bernardo O'Higgins ?
21. ¿ Hay muchos nombres « extranjeros » en Chile ?
22. ¿ Qué quiere decir un nombre extranjero en la América Latina ?
23. ¿ En qué país de la América Latina se encuentran muchos nombres italianos ?
24. ¿ Qué nombres extranjeros se encuentran en Inglaterra ?

3. *Ask questions that will get the following answers:*

1. Para mí el invierno es una estación como las otras.
2. Hay hielo y nieve sólo en el invierno.
3. Uno puede romperse la cabeza cuando hay hielo en la calle.
4. Me gusta más el calor que el frío.
5. A mí me gustan todas las estaciones del año.
6. Para mí el clima ideal es el del norte.
7. La vida del trópico es muy agradable.
8. Yo siempre paso el invierno en el sur.
9. No, no tengo pluma fuente.
10. No le quiero prestar mi pluma a Jaime porque se la lleva consigo.
11. No me explico por qué lo hace.
12. José le quiere enseñar unas fotografías a Luis.
13. Son fotografías de su hermana.

14. Creo que están debajo de esos libros.
15. No, mi pluma no lleva mi nombre.
16. Los Rodríguez-MacKenna son de Chile.
17. Es un personaje famoso en la historia chilena.
18. Mi padre es español y mi madre es escocesa.
19. Las personas de Chile se llaman chilenos.
20. Sí, es de Irlanda mi mamá.

4. *After hearing again the* LISTENING-IN *Section of* UNIT 8, *give answers to the following questions based directly on it:*

1. ¿ Cuántas estaciones tiene el año en el país de Manuel ?
2. ¿ Cuáles son las dos estaciones ?
3. ¿ Qué tiempo hace en el invierno ?
4. ¿ Cómo es el verano ?
5. ¿ Por qué nos parece raro eso ?
6. ¿ Cómo es la primavera aquí ?
7. ¿ Cómo es el otoño ?
8. ¿ Qué cree la gente de cada país ?
9. ¿ Qué decimos nosotros del frío ?
10. ¿ Cómo es la vida del trópico ?
11. ¿ Por qué vive más felíz la gente del trópico ?
12. ¿ Qué viaje va a hacer el inglés ?
13. ¿ Dónde quiere pasar el invierno, Manuel ?
14. ¿ Por qué ?
15. ¿ Qué pasa cuando Antonio usa una pluma fuente ?
16. ¿ Tiene pluma ahora Antonio ?
17. ¿ Cuántas plumas tiene Luis ?
18. ¿ Qué pluma le quiere prestar a su amigo ?
19. ¿ Dónde está la pluma en este momento ?
20. ¿ Qué van a ver los amigos ?

II. WRITING SPANISH.

The following sentences are variations on the content of the BASIC DIALOGUES *of* UNIT 8. *Write them out in Spanish.*

1. For us there's nothing like the climate of the south.
2. I agree with you. I don't like [the] snow.
3. [The] spring and [the] summer are the ideal seasons.

4. [The] winter too — the winter in (*use* **de**) the tropics.

5. Joe says [that] he doesn't feel very strong today.

6. Jim's (a) good fellow, but he always talks nonsense.

7. Remember what Dick says.

8. I can't explain it. — Neither (can) I.

9. It seems as though they do that on purpose.

10. What name does the pen have (on it)? (*use* **llevar**)

11. What country are the Carmonas from?

12. Do you know Paul Aguilar? — I don't have the pleasure, nor do I want to have it.

13. I'm not asking him for the car again.

14. O'Higgins a Chilean name? It can't be!

15. Are there many Chileans in this country?

16. To me it seems very funny.

17. Where are the pictures? — Look for them (over) there.

18. [The] foreign names seem strange.

19. Is it the same for you as for me?

20. We're going to take a trip through the tropics.

21. She's married to (*use* **con**) a Scot.

22. One of these days I'm going to take a trip.

23. By the way, are your parents from Ireland?

24. Why do you ask me that?

25. This is the last time I('ll) lend it to you.

26. They say that the people of the tropics live very happily.

27. You say [that the] work is good for the health? Nonsense!

28. Why do you complain about everything?

29. With me it's just the opposite.

30. Why do you stay in the south?

31. This is the last summer I('ll) spend here.

32. Every time I lend him something he takes it away with him.

33. What does this mean? — It doesn't mean anything.

34. The pictures are under some books.

35. I'm not going to show them to her.

D. REVIEW OF UNIT 9

I. SPEAKING SPANISH.

1. *Review* SECTION A *of* UNIT 9 *just as you did for* UNITS 6–8.

2. *Give answers to the following questions:*

1. ¿ Qué día empiezan las vacaciones para nosotros?

2. ¿ Cuántos días de vacaciones vamos a tener?

3. ¿ Dónde piensa usted pasar las vacaciones?

4. ¿ Piensa usted salir de aquí en seguida?

5. ¿ Qué le gusta a usted hacer cuando hace buen tiempo?

6. ¿ Prefiere usted estudiar al aire libre?

7. ¿ Por qué es difícil estudiar en el cuarto de Federico?

8. ¿ En qué piso está el cuarto?

9. ¿ Cómo es el cuarto de usted?

10. ¿ En qué piso estamos ahora?

11. ¿ Cuántos pisos tiene la casa donde usted vive?

12. ¿ Por qué va a ser difícil desocupar el cuarto?

13. ¿ De quién es el par de zapatos blancos que encuentran?

14. ¿ Cuántas raquetas de tenis encuentran?

15. ¿ Dónde están las raquetas?

16. ¿ De quién son?

17. ¿ Cómo van a dividir sus corbatas?

18. ¿ Qué le pide Juana a María?

19. ¿ Qué le pregunta Juana a María?

20. ¿ A dónde va Juana esta noche?

21. ¿ Con quién va a salir?

22. ¿ Por qué no puede decírselo a su amiga?

23. ¿ Va a salir con el novio de su amiga?

24. ¿ Qué vestido se va a poner Juana?

25. ¿ Qué cartera va a llevar?

3. *Ask questions that will get the following answers:*

1. Las vacaciones empiezan la semana próxima.

2. Vamos a tener diez días de vacaciones.

3. Son las vacaciones de primavera.

4. En el verano tenemos tres meses de vacaciones.

5. Las clases terminan a principios del mes.

6. Este verano voy a hacer un viaje a México.

7. No, es la segunda vez que voy a México.

8. No, no quiero ir a otro país, porque me gusta más México.

9. El cuarto donde yo vivo está en el tercer piso.

10. El cuarto es pequeño y no entra mucha luz.

11. No me pongo los zapatos blancos porque no están limpios.

12. Mi raqueta de tenis está detrás de la puerta.

13. Esa chica es la novia de Roberto.

14. Usted no la ha visto antes porque no vive aquí.

15. Sí, son míos esos dos libros.

16. Sí, es tuya esta corbata.

17. Mi novia no tiene buen gusto para escoger corbatas.

18. No, yo no ayudo a mi novia a comprar sombreros.

19. Lo siento mucho, Enrique, pero no me gusta dar consejos a mis amigos.

20. No me puedo poner el vestido blanco porque no está limpio.

4. *After hearing again the* LISTENING-IN *Section of* UNIT 9, *give answers to the following questions based directly on it:*

1. ¿ Quiénes hablan en esta conversación ?

2. ¿ De qué están hablando ?

3. ¿ Qué dicen de los vestidos negros ?

4. ¿ Qué hace el novio de Leonor ?

5. ¿ Por qué usa sombrero Leonor ?

6. ¿ Por qué no le gusta a Gloria usar sombrero ?

7. ¿ Qué le pide Gloria a su amiga ?

8. ¿ Por qué necesita pedir prestada una raqueta ?

9. ¿ Dónde está la raqueta de Leonor ?

10. Si no está detrás de la puerta, ¿ dónde debe de estar ?

11. ¿ Qué va a hacer esta noche Leonor ?

12. ¿ Qué necesita ella ?

13. ¿ Tiene cartera blanca su amiga ?

14. ¿ Quién tiene dos carteras ?

15. ¿ Quiere Leonor llevar la cartera que le ofrece Gloria ?

II. WRITING SPANISH.

The following sentences are variations on the content of the BASIC DIALOGUES *of* UNIT 9. *Write them out in Spanish:*

1. Winter's getting close.

2. We can't study out doors any more.

3. When it's not good weather I shut myself in with a book.

4. There's (*use* entrar) a lot of light in this room.

5. First I do my work, and then I enjoy myself.

6. You're admirable. With me it's just the opposite.

7. Every time I study in this dark room I feel like sleeping.

8. Of course! What else do you expect ?

9. I think [that] Jim's room is on the third floor.

10. His room is small, but it's very clean.

11. To a certain extent it's your fault.

12. It's sunny today, thank the Lord.

13. Classes begin next month, but I don't know what day.

14. I plan to get out of here right away. And (how about) you ?

15. I'm going to leave soon.

16. I'm not going to stay a minute longer.

17. Everybody wears white shoes here, **even in** [the] winter.

18. It seems **very** strange to [the] foreigners.

19. I plan to go to Mexico at the beginning of next month.

20. Have you seen that there are three neckties of yours here ?

21. I'm not in the mood for thinking about details.

22. Whose is that tennis racquet [that's] behind the door ?

23. It must be Henry's. Let's take it out (*use* quitar) of there.

24. Have you noticed her **eyes** ?

25. It's impossible not to notice them.

26. Shall I put on my black dress or my blue (one) ? — Put on your white (one).

27. I take off my necktie when it's hot.

28. Then why don't you take off your hat too?
29. Who am I going out with? — It's a big secret!
30. Don't you want to make a good impression on the teacher?
31. Give me some advice, will you?

32. I always have a hard time moving out of a room.
33. I'll give them back to you tomorrow.
34. Anyway it's not going to be easy.
35. I think the best thing is to stay here.

SPANISH–ENGLISH VOCABULARY

FOR UNITS 6–9

A

abierto (*see* abrir)
abrir to open
abuelo, -la grandfather, grandmother
acá here
acercarse to approach, come near
acompañar to accompany
acordarse (acuerda-) to remember
acostarse (acuesta-) to lie down, go to bed
acuerdo accord, agreement
además besides
admirable admirable
afeitarse to shave
agosto August
ahí there
el aire libre open air
alguno (algún) some
alto loud; tall
allí there
antes before
apetito appetite
apurarse to hurry
así thus, so

B

bañarse to bathe
bastante rather, quite
blanco white
buscar to look for

C

cabeza head
la calle street
caray: qué caray *exclamation*
carta letter
cartera handbag
casarse to get married
casi almost
catorce fourteen
celebrar to celebrate
cerrar (cierra-) to shut, close
cierto certain, sure
cincuenta fifty
el cine movies
claro of course
el coche car
compañero companion
conmigo = con + mí
conozco (*see* conocer)
consejo advice
consigo = con + sí
contener (contiene-) to contain
contigo = con + ti
costar (cuesta-) to cost
cuál which
cuarenta forty
cuarto room
cuidado care
cultura culture
el cumpleaños birthday

CH

chica girl
chileno Chilean

D

debajo under
deber must, ought
defender (defiende-) to defend
demasiado too much
dentro within
derecha right (*opposite of* left)
derecho right
desocupar to vacate, move out of

el detalle detail
detrás behind
devolver (devuelve-) to return give back
di (*see* decir)
diez ten
diga- (*see* decir)
Dios God
divertirse (divierte-) to enjoy oneself
dividir to divide
doce twelve
doy (*see* dar)

E

ejemplo example
él *pronoun* he, him
ellos *pronoun* they, them
encanto delight
encerrar (encierra-) to enclose, confine
encontrar (encuentra-) to meet; to find
enseñar to show
entrar to enter, go in
entre *preposition* between
eres (*see* ser)
escocés, -esa Scots, Scottish
escoger to choose, pick
escribir to write
escuchar to listen
esperar to expect
la estación season
explicar to explain
extranjero foreign

F

famoso famous
el favor favour

feliz happy
fijarse to notice
fortuna fortune
fotografía photograph, picture
fuerte strong

G

gracioso funny
gusto taste

H

hasta even
hielo ice
historia history

I

idea idea
ideal ideal
importancia importance
imposible impossible
la impresión impression
inspirar to inspire
invitar to invite
italiano Italian
izquierda left

J

joven young
julio July
juntar to assemble, collect
juntos together

L

le *3rd person pronoun*
leer to read
libro book
limpio clean
lo *article* the
luego later
la luz light

LL

llevar to carry, take

M

madre mother
mañana morning

el martes Tuesday
mejor best
merecer to deserve
merezco (*see* merecer)
el mes month
mí *pronoun* me
mío (mi) *possessive* my, mine
mismo same
modo way
momento moment
mundo world

N

nada nothing
negro black
ni nor
el nombre name
el norte north
nos *pronoun* us, *etc.*
nosotros *pronoun* we, us
noventa ninety
novio, -ia boy-friend, girl-friend
nuestro *possessive* our, ours
nueve nine
nunca never

O

ocupar to occupy, take up
ochenta eighty
ofender to offend
ofrecer to offer
ofrezco (*see* ofrecer)
oiga- (*see* oír)
oír to hear
ojo eye
olvidar to forget
once eleven
oscuro dark
oye- (*see* oír)

P

el par pair
parecer to seem
pasar to pass, spend; to happen
paseo drive
paso step
peor worse
pequeño small, little
persona person

el personaje personage, figure
piso floor
pluma fuente fountain pen
pobre poor
poco little, few
pon (*see* poner)
poner to put
pongo (*see* poner)
posible possible
precisamente precisely, exactly
preguntar to ask
preparar to prepare
presentar to present, introduce
prestar to lend
prima cousin
principio beginning
pronto soon
propósito: a propósito by the
    way; on purpose
próximo next
puerta door
pues well
punto point

Q

quedarse to stay, remain
quejarse to complain
quitar to remove, take off

R

raqueta racquet
raro rare, strange
regalo gift, present
el reloj watch
romper to break
rubio blond

S

salga- (*see* salir)
la salud health
sea- (*see* ser)
secreto secret
seguida: en seguida at once,
    immediately
seguir (sigue-) to follow, come
    next
seguro sure
sentir (siente-) to regret, be sorry
el septiembre September
serio serious
sesenta sixty

setenta seventy
si if
sí *reflexive 3rd person pronoun*
siempre always
sin *preposition* without
el sol sun
solo alone
soltero bachelor
superior superior
sur south
suyo (su) *3rd person possessive*

T

tampoco neither
tan so
tarde late
la tarde afternoon
te *pronoun* you, *etc.*
temprano early

ten (*see* tener)
el tenis tennis
ti *pronoun* you
tierra land
todavía yet
tonterías nonsense
trabalenguas tongue-twister
trece thirteen
treinta thirty
trópico tropics
tuyo (tu) *possessive* you, yours

U

último last
útil useful

V

varios various, several

vaya- (*see* ir)
ve (*see* ir)
veinte twenty
ven (*see* venir)
veo (*see* ver)
verdad true
vestido dress
vestir (viste-) to dress
el viaje trip
vida life
viejo old
visita visit
visto (*see* ver)
vivir to live
volver (vuelve-) to return, go
  back, come back

Z

zapato shoe

Visiting a Hospital.   Quarrelling with Your Friends.   Using Numbers and Dates.

Forms and Use of the Preterite Tense: Regular Verbs; **-ir** Verbs; **dar**, **ser,** and **ir**.

A. BASIC DIALOGUES
1. "I had an argument with my girl."

ENGLISH MEANING	AIDS TO LISTENING	SPANISH SPELLING

Record Side 4, after first spiral.

STEVE:

(you) went	fuíste	fuiste
yesterday	ayér	ayer
Where did you go yesterday afternoon ?	¿ a-dónde fuíste ayér por-la-tárde ?	¿ A dónde fuiste ayer por la tarde ?
(I) went	fuí	fuí
(I) found	enkontré	encontré
I went to look for you at your house and didn't find you.	fuí a-buskár-te a-tu-kása i-no-t'enkontré.	Fuí a buscarte a tu casa y no te encontré.

FRANK:

somebody, someone	álgien	alguien
the hospital	el-ospitál	el hospital
I went to see somebody [that's] at the hospital.	fuí a-bér a-álgien k'está en-el-ospitál.	Fuí a ver a alguien que está en el hospital.

STEVE:

sick, ill	enférma	enferma
Either that person's very sick or he's a very good friend of yours.	o-está mui-enférma ésa persóna o-eş-mui-amígo túyo.	O está muy enferma esa persona o es muy amigo tuyo.

FRANK:

Why do you say that ?	¿ por-ké díθes éso ?	¿ Por qué dices eso ?

STEVE:

Because I know you.	por-ke-te-konóθko.	Porque te conozco.[1]*
You don't like either hospitals or visiting.	a-tí no-te-gústan ni-los-ospitáleş ni-laş-bisítas.	A ti no te gustan [2] ni los hospitales ni las visitas.[3]

FRANK:

to be mistaken	ekibokár-se	equivocarse

* The raised figures in this and succeeding units refer to GRAMMATICAL NOTES which immediately follow BASIC DIALOGUES.

ENGLISH MEANING	AIDS TO LISTENING	SPANISH SPELLING
(That's) not true. You're mistaken.	no-éṣ berdád. estás ekibokádo.	No es verdad.⁴ Estás equivocado.

STEVE:

| You mean you like to pay calls? | ¿ kiéreṣ deθír ke-te-gústa aθér bisítas ? | Quieres decir que te gusta hacer visitas ? |

FRANK:

| to be a question | tratár-se | tratarse |
| Nó. I mean it's not a question of either a sick person or a good friend. | nó. kiéró deθír ke-no-se-tráta ni-de-una-persóna mui--enférma ni-de-um-buén amígo. | No. Quiero decir que no se trata ni de una persona muy enferma ni de un buen amigo. |

STEVE:

| Explain yourself, then. | esplíka-te pues. | Explícate, pues. |

FRANK:

| a relative | um-pariénte | un pariente |
| It's a question of a relative of mine. | se-tráta de-um-pariénte mío. | Se trata de un pariente mío. |

STEVE:

to imagine	imajinár	imaginar
to worry, to be concerned	preokupár-se	preocuparse
Neither (can) I imagine you being concerned about a relative.	tampóko te-imajíno preokupándo-te por-um--pariénte.	Tampoco te imagino preocupándote por un pariente.

FRANK:

an opinion	una-opinión	una opinión
high	álta	alta
You have a very high opinion of me, don't you?	tiénes una-opinión mui-álta de--mí, ¿ berdád ?	Tienes una opinión muy alta de mi, ¿ verdad ?⁴

STEVE:

I know you pretty well.	te-konóθko mui-bién.	Te conozco muy bien.
to grow (up)	kreθér	crecer
(we) grew (up)	kreθímos	crecimos
Remember we grew up together.	akuérda-te ke-kreθímos júntos.	Acuérdate que crecimos juntos.

FRANK:

| my character | mi-karákter | mi carácter |
| If you don't like my character, you can look for another friend. | si-no-te-gústa mi-karákter, puédeṣ buskár-te ótro amígo. | Si no te gusta ² mi carácter, puedes buscarte otro amigo. |

STEVE:

(it) was not	no-fué	no fué
a criticism	una-krítika	una crítica
a description	una-deskripθión	una descripción

ENGLISH MEANING	AIDS TO LISTENING	SPANISH SPELLING
(That) wasn't a criticism, it was (just) a description of your character.	no-fué una-krítika: fué una--deskripθión de-tu-karákter.	No fué una crítica; fué una descripción de tu carácter.

FRANK:

You and your descriptions!	¡ tú kon-tuş-deskripθiónes!	¡ Tú con tus descripciones!

STEVE:

in (a) bad mood	de-mál umór	de mal humor
I see you're in a bad mood today.	béo k'estáş de-mál umór ói.	Veo que estás de mal humor hoy.
That's not *my* fault.	yó no-téngo la-kúlpa de-éso.	Yo no tengo la culpa de eso.

FRANK:

I'm not in a good mood.	no-estói de-buén umór.	No estoy de buen humor.
(I) slept	dormí	dormí
last night	anóche	anoche
I didn't sleep much last night.	dormí póko anóche.	Dormí poco anoche.

STEVE:

(it) happened	pasó	pasó
What happened?	¿ ke pasó?	¿ Qué pasó?
(you) went to bed	te-akostáste	te acostaste
What time did you go to bed?	¿ a-ké óra te-akostáste?	¿ A qué hora te acostaste?

FRANK:

(I) went to bed	me-akosté	me acosté
I went to bed around ten thirty, but I didn't get to sleep until pretty late.	me-akosté komo-a-laş-diéθ i-média, pero-no-me-dormí asta-mui-tárde.	Me acosté como a las diez y media, pero no me dormí hasta muy tarde.

STEVE:

Are you worried about something?	¿ estás preokupádo por-álgo?	¿ Estás preocupado por algo?

FRANK:

I never worry about anything, you know that very well.	yó núnka me-preokúpo por--náda, yá lo-sábes.	Yo nunca me preocupo por nada, ya lo sabes.

STEVE:

Yes, I'm the one that worries about things.	sí, el-ke-se-preokúpa por-las--kósas soi-yó.	Sí, el que se preocupa por las cosas soy yo.

FRANK:

(I) went out	salí	salí
I went out with Rosita last night.	salí kon-rrosíta anóche.	Salí con Rosita anoche.

STEVE:

(you) had a good time	se-dibirtiéron	se divirtieron
Didn't you have a good time?	¿ no-se-dibirtiéron?	¿ No se divirtieron?

[114]

ENGLISH MEANING	AIDS TO LISTENING	SPANISH SPELLING
So you slept very badly.	de-módo ke-dormíste mui-mál.	De modo que dormiste muy mal.
(she) slept	durmió	durmió
I imagine Rosita slept poorly too.	me-imajíno ke-rrosíta durmió mál también.	Me imagino que Rosita durmió mal también.

FRANK:

I'm not going to set foot in a hospital again.	no-buélbo a-ponér pié en-un--ospitál.	No vuelvo a poner pie en un hospital.

STEVE:

Nor go out with Rosita?	¿ ni-a-salír kon-rrosíta?	¿ Ni a salir con Rosita?

FRANK:

No.	tampóko.	Tampoco.

2. "We've got numbers today."

HENRY:

What time is it?	¿ ke-óra és?	¿ Qué hora es?

TOM:

to stop	dejár	dejar
jokes	brómas	bromas
Stop joking, fellow.	¡ déja-te de-brómas, ómbre.	Déjate de bromas, hombre.
the date	la-fécha	la fecha
Today it's about numbers and dates.	ói se-tráta de-números i-féchas.	Hoy se trata de números [5] y fechas. [6]

HENRY:

I'm still having fun with the (business) of "quarter past four, quarter to four."	todabía me-dibiérto kon-lo-de--las-kuátro i-kuárto, las--kuátro menos-kuárto.	Todavía me divierto con lo de « las cuatro y cuarto, las cuatro menos cuarto. »

TOM:

Forget it.	¡ olbída-lo.	Olvídalo.
an ache, a pain	un-dolór	un dolor
It looks as though there are some more headaches here.	akí paréθe ke-ai-máṣ dolóreṣ de-kaβéθa.	Aquí parece que hay más dolores de cabeza.

HENRY:

(a) hundred	θiénto	ciento
"(A) hundred pages, (a) hundred (and) ten pages."	θiém pájinas — θiénto dieθ pájinas.	« Cien páginas, ciento diez páginas. »
two hundred	dosθiéntos	doscientos
"Two hundred men, two hundred women."	dosθiéntos ómbres — dosθiéntaṣ mujéres.	« Doscientos hombres, doscientas mujeres. »
Hurray for the women!	¡ bíban laṣ-mujéres!	¡ Vivan las mujeres!

ENGLISH MEANING	AIDS TO LISTENING	SPANISH SPELLING
Tom:		
"Two hundred men and women."	dosθiéntos ómbres i-mujéres.	« Doscientos hombres y mujeres.»
Hurray for the men!	¡ bíƀan los-ómbres!	¡ Vivan los hombres!
Henry:		
four hundred	kuatroθiéntos	cuatrocientos
five hundred	kiniéntos	quinientos
"Four, four hundred; five, five hundred."	kuátro, kuatroθiéntos. θínko, kiniéntos.	« Cuatro, cuatrocientos; cinco, quinientos. »
(they) were mistaken	se-ekiƀokáron	se equivocaron
I think they made a mistake.	kréo ke-s'ekiƀokáron.	Creo que se equivocaron.
Tom:		
seven hundred	seteθiéntos	setecientos
nine hundred	noƀeθiéntos	novecientos
"Seven, seven hundred; nine, nine hundred." Looks as though they didn't.	siéte, seteθiéntos. nuéƀe, noƀeθiéntos. paréθe ke-nó:	« Siete, setecientos; nueve, novecientos. » Parece que no.
Henry:		
necessary	neθesárias	necesarias
These complications don't seem to me necessary.	éstas komplikaθióneş no-me--paréθen neθesárias.	Estas complicaciones no me parecen necesarias.
to discover	deskuƀrír	descubrir
(they) discovered	deskuƀriéron	descubrieron
(one) thousand	míl	mil
"America was discovered in fourteen ninety-two."	deskuƀriéron l'américa en-míl kuatroθiéntoş noƀénta i-dós.	« Deṣcubrieron la América en mil cuatrocientos noventa y dos. »
Tom:		
the independence	la independénθia	la independencia
the United States	los-estáđos uníđos	los Estados Unidos
"Seventeen seventy-six — the independence of the United States."	míl seteθiéntos seténta i-séis — la-independénθia đe-los--estáđos uníđos.	« Mil setecientos setenta y seis — la independencia de los Estados Unidos. »

GRAMMATICAL NOTES

1. Some Verb Forms. In the verb **conocer,** and in most verbs with the final shape **-ecer,** the root ends in the consonant combination **-zc-** in the 1st-person singular of the straight present and in the command-forms, thus:

con**ocer**: con**ozco**: con**ozca**-
ofr**ecer**: ofr**ezco**: ofr**ezca**-
mer**ecer**: mer**ezco**: mer**ezca**-
par**ecer**: par**ezco**: par**ezca**-

2. Comparative Usage: Liking, etc. Spanish has no exact equivalent of the English verb *to like*. In order to express this idea Spanish most commonly uses **gustar,** which means basically *to please*. The construction is therefore the reverse of the English, in that the "thing liked" is the subject of the verb, and the "person liking" is its indirect object. The person-number of **gustar** is of course determined by that of the subject ("thing liked"), which usually follows the verb. Compare the two examples in this unit with the following from earlier dialogues:

No me **gustan** las películas románticas.
A mí no me **gusta** el invierno.
Me gusta más el frío que el calor.
Además le **gustan** las mujeres elegantes.

Spanish also frequently uses **parecer,** *to seem* in this same construction as the equivalent of English *think*. With **¿ Qué le pareció a Rosita ?** compare **¿ No te parece ?**, *Don't you think (so)?*

3. Comparative Usage: Definite Article. Spanish, unlike English, uses the definite article before nouns when they designate the ENTIRE CLASS of things named, or the thing named AS A WHOLE. With **los hospitales** and **las visitas** as classes of things, compare the nouns with articles in the following sentences:

¿ Para qué sirven **los hermanos** (BROTHERS AS A CLASS) entonces ?
Los hombres (MEN AS A CLASS) no se fijan en esos detalles.
No me gustan **las películas románticas** (ROMANTIC MOVIES AS A CLASS OF MOVIES).
Dicen que **los países fríos** (COLD COUNTRIES AS A CLASS OF COUNTRIES) tienen una cultura superior.
Además le gustan **las mujeres elegantes** (SMART WOMEN AS A CLASS OF WOMEN).
Me gusta más **el frío** (COLD IN GENERAL) que **el calor** (HEAT IN GENERAL).
Pero **el trabajo** (WORK IN GENERAL) ocupa demasiado tiempo.
Sólo sé que es una cosa que **la gente** (PEOPLE IN GENERAL) no entiende muy bien.

4. Verdad. The word **verdad** is a (feminine) noun meaning *truth*. In addition to its frequent occurrence in the phrase **ser verdad,** *to be true*, it is used by itself, with interrogative intonation, after a statement which the speaker expects the other person to confirm or deny. In the following examples, note that **verdad** thus acts as the equivalent of all the numerous English verbal phrases used for this purpose:

Jaime vive a la derecha, **¿ verdad ?** (*doesn't he ?*)
Pasas todo el día trabajando, **¿ verdad ?** (*don't you ?*)
Se juntan muchas cosas en un año, **¿ verdad ?** (*don't they ?*)
Tienes una opinión muy alta de mí, **¿ verdad ?** (*don't you ?*)
Saliste con Rosita anoche, **¿ verdad ?** (*didn't you ?*)

5. Number words. The Spanish words for two-digit numbers were illustrated in UNIT 6 (**ochenta y cinco, sesenta y dos,** etc.). These compound phrases are used for 16 through 19, **quince** being the last single word in the teens. 16–19, and the compounds of 20, are WRITTEN as single words: **dieciséis** (not **diez y seis**), **diecisiete, dieciocho, diecinueve; veintiuno** (not **veinte y uno**), **veintidós, veintitrés,** etc.

The words **ciento** and **mil** never have the indefinite article before them (compare English *a hundred, one thousand,* etc.). They show no gender agreement. The word **ciento** is shortened to **cien** when it directly precedes a noun. The compound number-words for 200 and up do show gender agreement (MASC. **-os,** FEM. **-as**).

6. Year dates. The formula for numbers of

three or four digits is illustrated by the year-date **mil cuatrocientos noventa y dos** (1492). In year- dates the hundred-digit has the masculine form (agreeing with **años** understood).

B. STUDY

Review SECTION A, *covering up the English.*

C. LISTENING IN

1. *Review* SECTION A, *repeating the Spanish and giving the English.*

2. *Listen in as (1) Isabel tells about a book she read, and (2) Paco tells how he didn't sleep well:* *Record Side 4, after first spiral.*

(*1*)

ISABEL: Anoche leí un libro de trescientas cincuenta páginas.

ELENA: La felicito. Yo nunca leo. ¿Qué libro leyó?

ISABEL: Un libro que se llama *Juana María.* Se trata de una mujer y de dos hombres que se pelearon por ella.

ELENA: Una mujer muy hermosa, me imagino.

ISABEL: ¡Claro!

ELENA: ¿Y qué pasó?

ISABEL: Bueno, un día el primo de Juana María la visitó, y los dos salieron a dar una vuelta. El novio de Juana María, de nombre Alejandro, los vió juntos, y no conociendo al primo se enojó y se peleó con él.

ELENA: ¿Alejandro no le pidió ninguna explicación a Juana María?

ISABEL: No le pidió ninguna explicación, y en seguida se fué de viaje.

ELENA: A mí me parece que Alejandro se portó muy mal. ¿Y cómo terminó la historia?

ISABEL: Después de varios meses alguien le escribió a Alejandro la verdad. Volvió en seguida, olvidaron todo y se casaron.

ELENA: Es una historia muy mala. No sé por qué la leyó usted.

ISABEL: Ni yo tampoco.

(*2*) (*Not recorded*)

PACO: Anoche dormí muy mal.

NACHO: ¿Qué te pasó?

PACO: No sé. Creo que trabajé demasiado ayer.

NACHO: Te doy un consejo. No trabajes demasiado. Es muy malo. ¿A qué hora te acostaste?

PACO: Me acosté temprano pero no me dormí hasta muy tarde.

NACHO: Me imagino que estás muy cansado hoy.

PACO: Estoy muy cansado. Soñé con unas cosas muy raras.

NACHO: ¿Con qué soñaste?

PACO: Ya no me acuerdo de los detalles.

NACHO: Entonces olvidemos todo eso y vamos a divertirnos.

PACO: Buena idea. Vamos.

D. GRAMMATICAL ANALYSIS
VERBS: THE PAST TENSE

The Spanish verb, like the English verb, occurs in two tenses — present and past. English has just one past-tense form for each of its verbs (for example *walk: walked; take: took; bring: brought*). In Spanish, on the other hand, every verb has two sets of forms in the past tense, called the PRETERITE forms and the IMPERFECT forms. We will first analyze some of the preterite forms and observe their use, reserving for a later unit our study of the imperfect forms and of the distinctions which these two sets of past-tense forms serve to express.

[120]

1. FORMS OF THE PRETERITE PAST.

(1) **Regular Verbs.** The following models show the preterite past forms of the regular verbs:

TYPE I: EX. **invitar**

	SING.	PLU.
1ST	invité	invitamos
2ND	invitaste	
3RD	invitó	invitaron

TYPE II: EX. **entender**

	SING.	PLU.
1ST	entendí	entendimos
2ND	entendiste	
3RD	entendió	entendieron

In these past-tense forms, two of the person-number endings are different from those which appear in the present tense: the 2nd-singular ending is **-ste** instead of **-s**, and the 3rd-plural ending is **-ron** instead of **-n**. These special person-number endings occur ONLY IN THE PRETERITE PAST FORMS of the Spanish verb.

Apart from the special person-number endings in two of the forms, the distinctive sign of the preterite past is the STRESSED TYPE-VOWEL. In TYPE I verbs (-ar) the type-vowel is **-a-** (as we would expect); in TYPE II verbs (either **-er** or **-ir**) it is **-i-** in the 1st and 2nd-person forms, and the diphthong **-ie-** in the 3rd-person forms.

Finally we note the following replacements of the type-vowel in forms having no person-number ending:

TYPE I

1ST SING. -a- replaced by -é (invita-: invité)
3RD SING. -a- replaced by -ó (invita-: invitó)

TYPE II

3RD SING. -(i)e- replaced by -(i)ó (entendie-: entendió)

(2) **-ir Verbs with Unstressed Root-Vowel Alternation.** In -ir verbs like **sentir** and **dormir**, the unstressed root-vowels alternate between **-e-** and **-i-** or between **-o-** and **-u-** as follows in the preterite past forms:

1ST-2ND: sentí- (sentí, sentimos; sentiste)
3RD: sintió, sintieron

| 1ST-2ND: | preferí- | divertí- |
| 3RD: | prefirió, prefirieron | divirtió, divirtieron |

| 1ST-2ND: | pedí- | serví- |
| 3RD: | pidió, pidieron | sirvió, sirvieron |

| 1ST-2ND: | seguí- | dormí- |
| 3RD: | siguió, siguieron | durmió, durmieron |

Thus **-e-** and **-o-** occur in the forms where the type-vowel is **-i-** (as in the general form), while **-i-** and **-u-** occur in the forms where the type-vowel is the diphthong **-ió** or **-ié-**.

(3) **Preterite Past of dar.** The verb **dar**, normally TYPE I, is a TYPE II verb in the preterite past and thus has the following forms:

1ST-2ND: dí- (dí, dimos; diste)
3RD: dié- (dió, dieron)

(4) **Preterite Past of ser and ir.** The verbs **ser** and **ir** are identical in their preterite past forms, which are:

1ST-2ND: fuí- (fuí, fuimos; fuiste)
3RD: fué- (fué, fueron)

In the 3rd person, the type-vowel diphthong is reduced to **-é-** after the root **fu-**, and is not replaced by the usual **-ó** in the singular.

2. FUNCTION OF THE PRETERITE PAST.

In the following sentences from the BASIC DIALOGUES of this unit the verbs are in the preterite past:

> Fuí a buscarte a tu casa y no te **encontré**.
> Acuérdate que **crecimos** juntos.
> No **fué** una crítica; **fué** una descripción de tu carácter.
> ¿ Qué **pasó** ? ¿ A qué hora te **acostaste** ?
> **Salí** con Rosita anoche.
> ¿ No se **divirtieron** ? — No. Nos **peleamos**.
> ¿ No le **diste** ninguna explicación ?
> Cuando por fin me **dormí**, **soñé** con hospitales.
> Creo que se **equivocaron**.
> **Descubrieron** la América en 1492.
> ¡ Eso lo **entendí** yo desde el primer día !

The term "preterite" means "over with," "gone by." In all these sentences the speaker is reporting an action which took place IN THE PAST — that is, at a time prior to the moment at which he is talking about it. Furthermore, in every case the past action is recorded AS A WHOLE; in other words the beginning, the course and the ending of the action are all equally in view, with no one of these phases singled out for more emphasis than another. The whole is presented simply as a

"happening" or "incident" which took place, in the recent or remote past.

It is the function of the Spanish preterite past to represent such WHOLE past happenings, and it will be helpful to have this idea in mind when we come to analyze, later, the contrasting function of the "imperfect" past.

E. GRAMMATICAL DRILLS

1. PRETERITE PAST TENSE.

A. *As you say the following sentences aloud, supply the proper person-number form of the preterite past tense of the verb in parentheses. Then give the English.*

EXAMPLE:

José (hablar) de muchas cosas.

MODEL:

José **habló** de muchas cosas.
Joseph talked about a lot of things.

1. Mis padres (llamarme) por teléfono.
2. (Ser) imposible terminar la carta.
3. Tú (tomar) mi sombrero, ¿ verdad ?
4. Parece que él y yo (equivocarse).
5. Nosotros sólo (aprender) las dos primeras páginas.
6. ¿ Dónde (comprar) usted esos zapatos ?
7. Mis amigos (descansar) un poco antes de salir.
8. Mi mamá (ayudarme) a hacer el trabajo.
9. ¿ Con quién (comer) ustedes anoche ?
10. Su padre (darle) un consejo muy útil.
11. ¿ Dónde (estudiar) tú el español ?
12. Hoy nosotros (imitar) al profesor dos horas.
13. ¿ A qué hora (levantarse) tu compañero ?
14. Yo (terminar) la primera parte esta mañana.
15. Anoche yo (conocer) a la señorita Móntez.
16. Mi compañero (dormir) toda la noche.
17. Estoy cansado. (Dormir) mal anoche.
18. Yo (empezar) aquel libro el año pasado.

19. ¿ (Entender) usted al profesor ?
20. Juana y yo (esperarte) media hora en esta esquina.
21. ¿ A dónde (ir) tus amigos ?
22. Hoy yo (llegar) tarde a la clase.
23. Yo (pedirle) un favor a mi primo.
24. Mi hermana (tratar) de escribir una carta en español.
25. ¿ (Oír) usted el radio esta tarde ?
26. Yo no (acordarme) del nombre de ese señor.
27. Los niños (volver) a casa a las once.
28. Jorge (acompañarme) al centro.
29. ¿ Cómo (olvidar) tú la cita ?
30. Roberto (afeitarse) en dos minutos.
31. ¿ Por qué (cerrar) usted los ojos ?
32. Mi novia y yo (divertirnos) mucho en la fiesta.
33. Eduardo (pedirme) prestada la pluma.
34. Los estudiantes no (leer) la lección.
35. ¿ (Divertirse) ustedes durante las vacaciones ?
36. ¿ Cuántas cartas (escribir) tú ayer ?
37. ¿ (Fijarse) usted en el sombrero de esa muchacha ?
38. ¿ De qué (quejarse) ese estudiante ?
39. Yo (buscar) el libro en el cuarto de Jaime.
40. El profesor no (explicar) muy bien la lección.
41. Yo (acercarme) a la casa para verla mejor.
42. ¿ Tú (devolverle) esas cosas a Pedro ?
43. La señora (encerrarse) en su cuarto.
44. Yo (vestirme) en cinco minutos.
45. Rosita (preferir) quedarse en casa, no sé por qué.
46. Enrique no (creerme).
47. Todas las muchachas (vestirse) de blanco.

48. Pablo y Anita (casarse) en el año cuarenta y tres.
49. Mis vacaciones no (ser) muy agradables.
50. Mamá y yo (salir) temprano.

B. *Using the sentences that follow, ask a question using the preterite past of the verb in parentheses. Then phrase an answer in which the same verb is used, being careful to change the person-number form if the sense so requires.*

EXAMPLE:

¿ Dónde (aprender) usted el español ?

MODEL:

Q. — ¿ Dónde **aprendió** usted el español ?
A. — Lo **aprendí** en Barcelona.

1. ¿ A quién (invitar) usted a la fiesta ?
2. ¿ A qué hora (acostarte) anoche ?
3. ¿ Cuándo (bañarte) la última vez ?
4. ¿ Dónde (encontrar) usted el libro por fin ?
5. ¿ (Enseñarle) usted las fotografías a Luisa ?
6. ¿ Qué (preguntarte) esa señorita ?
7. ¿ Qué (prestarle) usted a su amigo ?

8. ¿ Cuánto tiempo (quedarse) ustedes en España ?
9. ¿ Quién (romperse) la cabeza ?
10. ¿ Por qué (enojarse) usted ?
11. ¿ Qué clase de corbata (escoger) tú ?
12. ¿ (Ofenderte) porque no te llamé por teléfono ?
13. ¿ (Quitarte) el sombrero antes de entrar ?
14. ¿ (Costar) mucho esos zapatos tuyos ?
15. ¿ En qué parte del país (crecer) usted ?
16. ¿ Dónde (comprar) usted su coche ?
17. ¿ En qué año (descubrir) la América ?
18. ¿ Quiénes (pelearse) y por qué ?

2. YEAR DATES.

Say the Spanish for the following year-dates:

1776	1620
1812	1319
1238	1478
1914	1939
1866	1193
1085	1850
1588	1727
1948	1945

F. STUDY

1. *Review* SECTION A, *with the Spanish covered.*   **2.** *Prepare the* CONVERSATIONS.

G. CONVERSATIONS

1. *Reproduce the* BASIC DIALOGUES *in Spanish.*
2. *Using the* BASIC DIALOGUES *as your model, develop conversations such as:*

(*a*) Telling about the bad day you had yesterday (or whenever it was): a visit to a hospital, a fight with your girl-friend or boy-friend, little sleep, bad dreams, bad humour next day, etc.

(*b*) Quizzing each other on dates; asking your conversation partner in what year (¿ **En qué año** ...?) he did this or that. (Never mind if it's a trivial thing like shaving or going into town — you're practising dates.)

A. BASIC DIALOGUES

"So you're from Peru! Won't you help me with my Spanish lesson?"

ENGLISH MEANING	AIDS TO LISTENING	SPANISH SPELLING

Record Side 4, after second spiral.

GIRL:

You're South American, aren't you?	ustéd es-sudamerikáno, ¿ berdád ?	Usted es sudamericano, ¿ verdad ?

SEÑOR:

the order	la-órden	la orden
At your service, Miss.	a-sus-órdenes señoríta.	A sus órdenes, señorita.

GIRL:

What country are you from?	¿ de-ké país es-ustéd ?	¿ De qué país es usted ?

SEÑOR:

I'm from Peru.	soi-del-perú.	Soy del Perú.

GIRL:

Are you (an) Inca?	¿ es-ustéd ínka ?	¿ Es usted inca ?

SEÑOR:

Indian blood	sángre índia	sangre india
I have a little Indian blood, yes.	téngo um-póko de-sángre índia, sí:	Tengo un poco de sangre india, sí.
But the Indians of my country aren't called Incas any more.	pero-yá no-se-łáman ínkaş los--índioş de-mi-tiérra.	Pero ya [1] no se llaman incas los indios de mi tierra.

GIRL:

Then what are they called?	¿ kómo se-łáman entónθes.	¿ Cómo se llaman, entonces ?

SEÑOR:

Well, Indians.	pues-índios.	Pues, indios.

GIRL:

Are there many Indians in Peru?	¿ ai-múchos índios en-el-perú ?	¿ Hay muchos indios en el Perú ?

SEÑOR:

Yes indeed!	¡ kómo nó señoríta.	¡ Cómo no, señorita !
a million	un-miłón	un millón
We have more than a million Indians.	tenémoş máş de-un-miłón de--índios.	Tenemos más de un millón de indios.[2]

ENGLISH MEANING	AIDS TO LISTENING	SPANISH SPELLING
GIRL:		
Holy smoke!	¡ ké karái!	¡ Qué caray!
to laugh	rreír (rríe-)	reír (ríe-)
What are you laughing at?	¿ de-ké se-rríe ustéd, señór.	¿ De qué se ríe usted, señor?
SEÑOR:		
to pardon, to excuse	perdonár	perdonar
amusement	gráθia	gracia
Excuse me, Miss, but it amuses me to hear you say "Qué caray!"	¡ perdónc-me señoríta, pero-me--áθe gráθia oír-la deθír ké karái.	Perdóneme, señorita, pero me hace gracia oírla decir « ¡ Qué caray! »
GIRL:		
Isn't it said?	¿ no-se-díθe?	¿ No se dice?
to pronounce	pronunθiár	pronunciar
(Or) did I pronounce it wrong?	¿ lo-pronunθié mál?	¿ Lo pronuncié mal?
SEÑOR:		
very much	muchísimo	muchísimo
You pronounced it very well, and it's said a great deal.	lo-pronunθió mui-ƀién, i-se-díθe muchísimo.	Lo pronunció muy bien, y se dice muchísimo.
But usually only men say it.	pero-en-jenerál sólo lo-díθen los--ómbres.	Pero en general sólo lo dicen los hombres.
GIRL:		
an expression	una-espresión	una expresión
Is it not a nice expression?	¿ es-una-espresión mála?	¿ Es una expresión mala?
SEÑOR:		
to assure	asegurár	asegurar
It hasn't anything bad (about it), I assure you.	no-tiéne náda de-málo, le--asegúro.	No tiene nada de malo, le aseguro.
Where did you learn it?	¿ dónde lo-aprendió?	¿ Dónde lo aprendió?
GIRL:		
My Spanish teacher always says it.	siémpre lo-díθe mi-profesór d'españól.	Siempre lo dice mi profesor de español.
to teach	enseñár	enseñar
Here they teach us that you have to imitate the teacher in everything.	akí nos enséñan ke-ái ke-imitár al-profesór en-tódo.	Aquí nos enseñan que hay que imitar al [3] profesor en todo.
SEÑOR:		
dangerous	peligróso	peligroso
That's (all) very well, but it seems to me slightly dangerous.	éso está mui-ƀién, pero-me--paréθe um-póko peligróso.	Eso está muy bien, pero me parece un poco peligroso.
GIRL:		
I don't think (so).	no-me-paréθe:	No me parece.

[125]

ENGLISH MEANING	AIDS TO LISTENING	SPANISH SPELLING
thoroughly	a-fóndo	a fondo
the language	el-idióma	el idioma
All our teachers know the spoken language thoroughly.	tódoş nuéstros profesóres konóθen a-fóndo el-idióma abládo.	Todos nuestros profesores conocen a fondo el idioma hablado.

SEÑOR:

your enthusiasm	su-entusiáşmo	su entusiasmo
I congratulate you on your enthusiasm.	la-feliθíto por-su-entusiáşmo, señoríta.	La felicito por su entusiasmo, señorita.

GIRL:

Did you ever study a foreign language?	¿ estudió ustéd algúna béθ un--idióma estranjéro ?	¿ Estudió usted alguna vez un idioma extranjero ?

SEÑOR:

many years ago	aθe-múchos áños	hace muchos años
Yes, I studied English many years ago.	sí, estudié el-inglés aθe-múchos áños.	Sí, estudié el inglés hace muchos años.

GIRL·

In Lima?	¿ en-líma ?	¿ En Lima ?

SEÑOR:

a little town	um-puéblo chikíto	un pueblo chiquito
No, in a little town.	nó: en-um-puéblo chikíto.	No, en un pueblo chiquito.
I imitated the teacher too.	yó también imité al-profesór.	Yo también imité al [3] profesor.

GIRL:

You (did) too?	¿ ustéd también ?	¿ Usted también ?

SEÑOR:

Peruvian accent	aθénto peruáno	acento peruano
Yes, and I learned to speak English with (a) Peruvian accent.	sí, i-aprendí 'ablár inglés kon--aθénto peruáno.	Sí, y aprendí a hablar inglés [4] con acento peruano.

GIRL:

How funny!	¡ ké graθióso!	¡ Qué gracioso !

SEÑOR:

the interest	el-interés	el interés
to visit	bisitár	visitar
I'm interested in visiting your Spanish class one of these days.	téngo interés em-bisitár su-kláse d'español un-día de-éstos.	Tengo interés en visitar su clase de español un día de éstos.
It's been a pleasure . . .	e-tenído múcho gústo . . .	He tenido mucho gusto . . .

GIRL:

Oh, don't go away so soon!	¡ no-se-báya ustéd tam-prónto, señór.	¡ No se vaya usted tan pronto, señor !

to decide	deθidír	decidir
questions	pregúntas	preguntas

ENGLISH MEANING	AIDS TO LISTENING	SPANISH SPELLING
When I began to talk with you a few minutes ago, I decided to ask you some questions.	kuando-empeθé 'aƀlár kon--ustéd aθe-unoṣ-minútos, deθidí aθér-le algúnas pregúntas.	Cuando empecé a hablar con usted hace unos minutos, decidí hacerle algunas preguntas.

SEÑOR:

(you) did	íθo	hizo
You did well, Miss.	íθo ustéd ƀién señoríta.	Hizo usted bien, señorita.
about the people	soƀre-el-puéƀlo	sobre el pueblo
Do you want to ask me questions about the Peruvian people ?	¿ kiére aθér-me pregúntas soƀr'el--puéƀlo peruáno ?	¿ Quiere hacerme preguntas sobre el pueblo peruano ?

GIRL:

| No, about the Spanish language. | nó, soƀr'el-idióma españól. | No, sobre el idioma español. |

SEÑOR:

| General questions, or on tomorrow's lesson ? | ¿ pregúntas jeneráles —o-soƀre--la-leksión de-mañána. | ¿ Preguntas generales, o sobre la lección de mañana ? |

GIRL:

(you) could	púdo	pudo
to guess	adiƀinár	adivinar
How could you guess ?	¿ kómo púdo ustéd adiƀinár-lo.	¿ Cómo pudo usted adivinarlo ?

SEÑOR:

| Let's see. What are the questions ? | a-ƀér. ¿kuáles son-las--pregúntas ? | A ver. ¿Cuáles son las preguntas ? |

GIRL:

a little moment	un-momentíto	un momentito
Wait a second.	¡ espére un-momentíto.	Espere un momentito.
(I) put	púse	puse
the paper	el-papél	el papel
Where did I put the paper ?	¿ dónde púse el-papél.	¿ Dónde puse el papel ?
Oh, here it is.	á, akí está.	Ah, aquí está.

SEÑOR:

(you) came	bíno	vino
I see that you came prepared.	béo ke-ƀíno ustéd preparáda.	Veo que vino usted preparada.

GIRL:

some sentences	unas-fráses	unas frases
the following verbs	loṣ-ƀérbos sigiéntes	los verbos siguientes
I've got to write some sentences with the following verbs.	téngo k'eskriƀír unas-fráses kon--loṣ-ƀérbos sigiéntes.	Tengo que escribir unas frases con los verbos siguientes.
The first (one) is	el-priméro es	El primero es
"to bring: brought "	traér, tráje	« traer: traje »

SEÑOR:

to swim	nadár	nadar
the suit	el-tráje	el traje

[127]

ENGLISH MEANING	AIDS TO LISTENING	SPANISH SPELLING
Put "I can't swim because I didn't bring (a) suit."	pónga, no-puédo nadár por-ke--no-tráje tráje.	Ponga « No puedo nadar porque no traje traje. »
GIRL:		
How funny you are!	¡ Qué gracioso es usted !	¡ ké graθióso es-ustéd !
SEÑOR:		
a joke	un-chíste	un chiste
(That)'s an old joke in Spanish.	es-un-chíste mui-biéjo en--espñól.	Es un chiste muy viejo en español.
GIRL:		
Now with	aóra kon-	Ahora con
"say: said"	deθír, dijéron	« decir: dijeron »
SEÑOR:		
"They told me the picture's no good."	me-dijéron ke-la-pelíkula no--eṣ-buéna.	« Me dijeron que la película no es buena. »
This isn't a hard job.	no-eṣ-difíθil éste trabájo.	No es difícil este trabajo.
GIRL:		
Not for you.	para-ustéd nó.	Para usted no.
Now with	aóra kon-	Ahora con
"have: had"	tenér, túbo	« tener: tuvo »
SEÑOR:		
"John didn't have time to shave."	juán no-túbo tiémpo par'afei-társe.	« Juan no tuvo tiempo para afeitarse. »
GIRL:		
Fine! There are only three left.	· mui-bién ! sólo kédan trés.	¡ Muy bien ! Sólo quedan tres.
"be: was"	estár: estúbo	« estar: estuvo »
SEÑOR:		
"The party was very good."	estúbo mui-buéna la-fiésta.	« Estuvo muy buena la fiesta. »
GIRL:		
"know: knew"	sabér, supímos	« saber: supimos »
SEÑOR:		
"We didn't find it out till last night."	no-lo-supímos ast'anóche.	« No lo supimos hasta anoche. »
GIRL:		
"want: wanted"	kerér, kisíste	« querer: quisiste »
SEÑOR:		
"You wouldn't believe me."	tú no-kisíste kreér-me.	« Tú no quisiste creerme. »
What's next?	¿ ké síge?	¿ Qué sigue ?
GIRL:		
That's all.	éso es-tódo:	Eso es todo.
Thanks a million.	un-milón de-gráθias.	Un millón de gracias.

ENGLISH MEANING	AIDS TO LISTENING	SPANISH SPELLING
SEÑOR:		
Not at all, Miss.	no-ái de-ké, señoríta.	No hay de qué, señorita.
I'm always at your service.	estói siémpre a-sus-órdenes.	Estoy siempre a sus órdenes.
GIRL:		
Tell me, sir, why does Spanish have such queer verbs?	¡ díga-me, señór. ¿ por-ké tiéne bérbos tan-rráros el-españól.	Dígame, señor, ¿ por qué tiene verbos tan raros el español?
SEÑOR:		
I don't know.	no-sé.	No sé.
perhaps	tal-béθ	tal vez
Perhaps so as to be like English.	tal-béθ para-sér komo-el-in--glés.	Tal vez para ser como el inglés.
GIRL:		
a pleasure	um-plaθér	un placer
It's been a great pleasure to talk with you, sir.	a-sído um-plaθér mui-gránde ablár kon-ustéd, señór.	Ha sido un placer muy grande hablar con usted, señor.
I've learned a lot.	e-aprendído múcho.	He aprendido mucho.
SEÑOR:		
Thank you, Miss.	gráθias señoríta.	Gracias, señorita.
I took pleasure in talking with you.	túbe múcho gústo en-ablár kon--ustéd.	Tuve mucho gusto en hablar con usted.

GRAMMATICAL NOTES

1. ya.

The Spanish word **ya** basically means *already* or *by now*, as illustrated in the following sentences:

> **Ya** hemos aprendido mucho.
> **Ya** me acuerdo que son suyas.
> **Ya** veo su casa.
> **Ya** es tarde.
> Me cartera negra **ya** está vieja.

Used before a negative word, **ya** is the normal word for expressing *any more, any longer:*

> Pero **ya no** se llaman incas los indios de mi tierra.
> **Ya no** tengo sueño.
> **Ya no** tengo cabeza para estudiar.
> Creo que **ya no** vuelve a pedírtela.

Used with a verb of believing or knowing, **ya** serves merely to intensify the force of the verb, as in **¡ Ya lo creo !**, *I should say so !*

As seen in all these examples, **ya** is very frequently placed before the verb.

2. millón.

The Spanish word for *million* does not go directly with a noun, as do the words for the lesser numbers. The word **millón** is itself a noun of quantity, and another noun following it is preceded by **de**. (Compare English nouns of quantity like *a ton of coal, an acre of land*.)

3. DIRECT OBJECTS: NOUNS DESIGNATING PERSONS.

When a Spanish noun designating a specific person is the direct object of a verb, it is preceded by the preposition **a**. In this function the **a** has no equivalent meaning (such as *to*) in English. Compare the following sentences from earlier units:

> Sí, es fácil imitar **a la profesora.**
> Después voy a ver **a unos amigos españoles.**
> Quiero presentarle **a mi amigo Marcelo Sánchez.**

[129]

As in the two examples in this unit (**imitar al profesor**), the "contraction" **al** occurs whenever the preposition **a** precedes the masculine singular article **el.** Note this same contraction in other types of phrase, such as **al contrario, ir al cine, al aire libre.**

4. COMPARATIVE USAGE: DEFINITE ARTICLE.

Spanish, unlike English, generally uses the (masculine) definite article before the name of a language. With **Yo estudié el inglés hace muchos años,** compare:

> Usted habla muy bien **el español.**
> ¿ Cuánto tiempo necesita uno para aprender **el español** ?
> **El inglés** es más fácil.

However, when the name of the language directly follows a form of **hablar,** the article is normally not used:

> Es muy simpático, pero no **habla inglés.**
> Los españoles también **hablan español.**
> Aprendí a **hablar inglés** con acento peruano.

Note also non-use of the article in noun phrases with **de: la lección de español, mi profesor de español, su clase de español.**

B. STUDY

Review SECTION A, *covering up the English.*

C. LISTENING IN

1. *Review* SECTION A, *repeating the Spanish and giving the English.*

2. *Listen in as Joaquín tells Mario how he helps a friend with his Spanish lessons:*

Record Side 4, after second spiral.

JOAQUÍN: Hace dos días vino a verme un amigo.
MARIO: ¿ Por qué vino a verte ?
JOAQUÍN: Me trajo un trabajo de español. No pudo hacerlo él solo.
MARIO: ¿ No es inteligente ?
JOAQUÍN: Sí, es inteligente, pero dice que le gustan mis explicaciones del idioma.
MARIO: ¿ Por qué no le hizo preguntas a su profesor ?
JOAQUÍN: Dijo que su profesor no habla bien el inglés, y que por eso sus explicaciones son difíciles de entender.
MARIO: ¿ Qué clase de trabajo tuvo que preparar ?
JOAQUÍN: Tuvo que escribir frases con unos verbos.
MARIO: ¿ Cuándo empezó tu amigo a estudiar el español ?
JOAQUÍN: Empezó a estudiarlo hace algunos meses.

MARIO: ¿ Quién hizo el trabajo por fin, tú o él ?
JOAQUÍN: Lo hicimos los dos.
MARIO: ¿ Cómo pronuncia el español ?
JOAQUÍN: Lo pronuncia bastante bien, pero tiene un poco de acento inglés. Algunas palabras le son difíciles de pronunciar, pero sabe a fondo lo que ha estudiado.
MARIO: ¿ Qué son esos papeles ?
JOAQUÍN: Son unos papeles que olvidó mi amigo.
MARIO: Vamos a ver qué dicen. Ah, son unas frases en español. Aquí dice: « No lo supimos hasta anoche. » y « Tú no quisiste creerme. » Aquí hay otra frase que dice: « Mi abuela puso la pluma fuente en su cartera. »
JOAQUÍN: Son frases tontas, ¿ verdad ?
MARIO: La última sí.
JOAQUÍN: ¿ Quieres ir a la playa a nadar ahora ?
MARIO: No puedo ir a nadar porque no traje traje.
JOAQUÍN: ¿ En serio ?
MARIO: En serio. No traje.
JOAQUÍN: Yo te puedo prestar uno.
MARIO: Tu traje es demasiado chico para mí.
JOAQUÍN: Póntelo de todos modos. Quiero reírme.

D. GRAMMATICAL ANALYSIS
VERBS: THE PAST TENSE

We continue our study of the Spanish preterite past tense by observing the way it is formed in a certain group of verbs.

FORMS OF THE PRETERITE PAST.

(*1*) **Root-Changing Verbs.** A number of commonly used Spanish verbs of TYPE II have preterite past forms characterized by a changed root, as well as by a set of endings partially different from those of regular verbs. They are illustrated by the following two models:

	poner	
	SING.	PLU.
1ST:	**puse**	**pusimos**
2ND:	**pusiste**	
3RD:	**puso**	**pusieron**

	decir	
	SING.	PLU.
1ST:	**dije**	**dijimos**
2ND:	**dijiste**	
3RD:	**dijo**	**dijeron**

In verbs which have this kind of preterite past, the root is not only different in shape from the verb's normal root (**pon-: pus-; dec-: dij-**), but it is also STRESSED in the 1st and 3rd singular.

In the 3rd plural, the type-vowel diphthong is reduced to **-é-** after any root ending in **-j-**.

Ten verbs with the above kind of preterite past are listed below, together with their preterite roots. With each is given a sentence from the BASIC DIALOGUE of this unit containing a corresponding form:

decir: dij-
Me **dijeron** que la película no es buena.
estar: estuv-
Estuvo muy buena la fiesta.
hacer: hic-
Hizo usted bien, señorita.
poder: pud-
¿ Cómo **pudo** usted adivinarlo ?
poner: pus-
¿ Dónde **puse** el papel ?
querer: quis-
Tú no **quisiste** creerme.
saber: sup-
No lo **supimos** hasta anoche.
tener: tuv-
Juan no **tuvo** tiempo para afeitarse.
traer: traj-
No puedo nadar porque no **traje** traje.
venir: vin-
Veo que **vino** usted preparada.

(Like the regular verb **dar,** the verb **estar** is a TYPE II verb in the preterite past tense.)

E. GRAMMATICAL DRILLS

1. PRETERITE PAST TENSE OF ROOT-CHANGING VERBS.

As you say the following sentences aloud, supply the proper person-number form of the preterite past tense of the verb in parentheses. Then give the English.

EXAMPLE:

Juan no (hacer) su trabajo.

MODEL:

Juan no **hizo** su trabajo.
John didn't do his work.

1. ¿ Qué (decir) tus padres ?
2. Yo (saberlo) hace cinco días.
3. ¿ En qué año (hacer) ustedes el viaje ?
4. ¿ (Traer) usted su traje ?
5. Mis abuelos (estar) aquí de visita.
6. El extranjero (tener) mucho interés en visitar la clase.
7. Aquel señor no (querer) esperar.
8. ¿ Te acuerdas de cuándo (estar) aquí ese chileno ?
9. ¿ Qué (decirle) Paco a su novia ?
10. El muchacho trató, pero no (poder) pronunciar la palabra.

[131]

11. La señorita (querer) reír pero no (hacerlo).
12. Tú no (tener) la culpa de eso.
13. ¿Cómo (poder) usted adivinarlo?
14. Ayer (venir) a verme unos amigos.
15. Carmen (poner) las fotografías en su cartera.
16. ¿Tú (traerme) un regalo?
17. Nosotros no (saberlo) a tiempo.
18. Yo (venir) esta mañana, a ver qué le pasa a Carlos.

19. ¿Cuándo (estar) tú en Barcelona?
20. Lo siento, pero Luis y yo no (tener) tiempo para terminar.

2. REVIEW OF PRETERITE PAST TENSE OF REGULAR VERBS.

Go back over DRILL 1 *of* UNIT 11.

F. STUDY

1. *Review* SECTION A, *with the Spanish covered.* **2.** *Prepare the* CONVERSATIONS.

G. CONVERSATIONS

1. *Reproduce the* BASIC DIALOGUES *in Spanish.*

2. *Using the* BASIC DIALOGUES *as your model, develop conversations such as:*

(*a*) Talking with someone from a Spanish-speaking country, and telling him about the way you're learning his language. How did he learn yours?

(*b*) Questions-and-answers with your conversation partner about past events, working in the verbs **tener, venir, poder, poner, querer, decir, hacer, saber, traer, estar.**

Shopping. Colour. Size. Price. Falling Asleep.
Verbs: Forms and uses of the Imperfect. Spanish Imperfect for English
Past Progressive.

A. BASIC DIALOGUES

I. "I'll go shopping with you, but don't let me buy anything."

ENGLISH MEANING	AIDS TO LISTENING	SPANISH SPELLING

Note: This and Unit 14 are not recorded.

BETTY:

hello	óla	hola
Hello, Carmen! Where are you going?	¡ óla kármen. ¿ a-dónde bás?	¡ Hola, Carmen! ¿ A dónde vas?

CARMEN:

To town to get a pair of shoes.	al-θéntro a-buskár um-pár de--θapátos.	Al centro a buscar [1] un par de zapatos.
Want to go with me?	¿ kiéres akompañár-me?	¿ Quieres acompañarme?

BETTY:

do me the favour	áθ-me el-fabór	hazme [2] el favor
to allow, to let	dejár	dejar
I'll be glad to, but please don't let me buy anything.	kon-múcho gústo, pero-áθ-me el-fabór de-no-dejár-me komprár náda.	Con mucho gusto, pero hazme el favor de no dejarme comprar nada.

CARMEN:

Why?	¿ por-ké, mujér.	¿ Por qué, mujer?

BETTY:

the place	el-lugár	el lugar
the money	el-dinéro	el dinero
In (the) first place because I haven't got (any) money.	em-primér lugár por-ke-no--téngo dinéro.	En primer lugar porque no tengo dinero.
And then you know what happens when I go into town with anybody.	i-luégo tú sábeṣ lo-ke-pása kuando-akompáño a-álgien al-θéntro.	Y luego tú sabes lo que pasa cuando acompaño a alguien al centro.

CARMEN:

What happens?	¿ ké pása.	¿ Qué pasa?

BETTY:

to finish, to end	akabár	acabar
I always end up buying something.	siémpre akábo komprándo álgo.	Siempre acabo comprando algo.

ENGLISH MEANING	AIDS TO LISTENING	SPANISH SPELLING

CARMEN:

that weakness — ésa debilidád — esa debilidad

I didn't know you had that weakness. — no-sabía ke-tenías ésa debilidád. — No sabía que tenías esa debilidad.

BETTY:

I know it all right. — yó sí lo-sé. — Yo sí lo sé.

what kind — ké kláse — qué clase

What kind of shoes are you looking for? — ¿ ké kláse de-θapátoṣ búskas. — ¿ Qué clase de zapatos buscas ? [1]

CARMEN:

the week — la-semána — la semana

while — miéntras — mientras

to go, to walk — andár — andar

principal, main — prinθipál — principal

Three weeks ago, while I was walking along High Street, I saw an awfully pretty pair of shoes. — aθe-trés semánas, mientras--andába por-la-káĺe prinθipál, bí um-pár de-θapátoṣ múi bonítos. — Hace tres semanas,[3] mientras andaba por la calle principal, ví un par de zapatos muy bonitos.

BETTY:

a reaction — una-rreakθión — una reacción

quick, fast — rrápida — rápida

Three weeks ago? What a lightening reaction! — ¿ aθe-trés semánas? ¡ ké rreakθión mas-rrápida ! — ¿ Hace tres semanas ? [4] ¡ Qué reacción más rápida !

CARMEN:

I get out of work at five, and I haven't had time to go into town. — sálgo del-trabájo a-las-θínko, i--no-e-teníɗo tiémpo para-ír al-θéntro. — Salgo del trabajo a las cinco, y no he tenido tiempo para ir al centro.

BETTY:

You used to get out at four, didn't you? — ántes salías a-las-kuátro, ¿ berdáɗ ? — Antes salías a las cuatro, ¿ verdad ?

CARMEN:

Yes, but not any more. — sí, pero-yá nó. — Sí, pero ya no.

BETTY:

What shop did you see them in? — ¿ en-ké tiénda los-bíste? — ¿ En qué tienda los viste ?

CARMEN:

modern — modérna — moderna

In that modern shop in High Street. — en-ésa tiénda modérna k'está en-la-káĺe prinθipál. — En esa tienda moderna que está en la calle principal.

BETTY:

outside — afuéra — afuera

to look at — mirár — mirar

the (show) window — el-eskaparáte — el escaparate

ENGLISH MEANING	AIDS TO LISTENING	SPANISH SPELLING
I('ll) stay outside here (and) look at the window.	yó me-kédo akí afuéra a-mirár el-eskaparáte.	Yo me quedo aquí afuera a mirar [1] el escaparate.
CARMEN:		
Don't be like that!	¡ no-séas así !	¡ No seas así !
new	nuébos	nuevos
Come in with me and help me pick out my new shoes.	¡ éntra kon-mígo i-ayúda-me a- -eskojér mis-θapátoṣ nuébos.	Entra conmigo y ayúdame a escoger mis zapatos nuevos.
CLERK:		
Were you looking for something ?	¿ buskában álgo, señorítas.	¿ Buscaban [1] algo, señoritas ?
CARMEN:		
high heel	takón álto	tacón alto
Yes. About three weeks ago I saw a pair of high-heeled shoes in the window.	sí. aθe-unas-trés semánas, bí en-el-eskaparáte um-pár de- -θapátoṣ de-takón álto.	Sí. Hace unas tres semanas,[3] ví en el escaparate un par de zapatos de tacón alto.
CLERK:		
As high as this ?	¿ tan-álto komo-éste ?	¿ Tan alto como éste ?
CARMEN:		
more low	maṣ-bájo	más bajo
No, a little (bit) lower.	nó, um-póko maṣ-bájo.	No, un poco más bajo.
CLERK:		
the colour	el-kolór	el color
(they) were	éran	eran
the price	el-préθio	el precio
What colour were they and what was the price ?	¿ de-ké kolór éran i-kuál éra el-préθio.	¿ De qué color eran y cuál era el precio ?
CARMEN:		
pound	líbra	libra
They were black, and I think they cost two pounds ten.	éran négros, i-kréo ke-kostában dóṣ líbraṣ diéθ.	Eran negros, y creo que costaban dos libras diez.
CLERK:		
to sit down	sentár-se (siénta-)	sentarse (sienta-)
Oh yes. Sit down, please.	á sí. ¡ siénten-se, señorítas.	Ah sí. Siéntense, señoritas.
green	bérde	verde
red	rrójo	rojo
We only have a few pairs left, in green and red.	sólo nos-kédan unos-kuántos páres em-bérde i-en-rrójo.	Sólo nos quedan unos cuantos pares en verde y en rojo.
What size do you wear ?	¿ ké número úsa ?	¿ Qué número usa ?
CARMEN:		
Five and a half.	θínko i-médio.	Cinco y medio.

[135]

ENGLISH MEANING	AIDS TO LISTENING	SPANISH SPELLING
CLERK:		
I'm very sorry, Miss.	lo-siénto múcho, señoríta.	Lo siento mucho, señorita.
These four and a halfs are the largest we have.	éste pár de-kuátro i-médio es-el-maş-gránde ke-tenémos.	Este par de cuatro y medio es el más grande que tenemos.
to try	probár (prueba-)	probar (prueba-)
Do you wish to try them on?	¿ kiére probár-se-los ?	¿ Quiere probárselos ?
CARMEN:		
surely	segúra ménte	seguramente
to fit	entrár	entrar
Yes, but they're bound not to fit me.	sí, pero-segúra ménte no-me--bán a-entrár.	Sí, pero seguramente no me van a entrar.
short	kórto	corto
See? Look how short it is!	¿ bé ustéd ? ¡ Míre ké kórto me--kéda.	¿ Ve usted ? Mire qué corto me queda.
to hurt	lastimár	lastimar
It hurts my foot	me-lastíma el-pié.	Me lastima el pie.
CLERK:		
I'm very sorry.	lo-siénto múcho, señoríta.	Lo siento mucho, señorita.
BETTY:		
pity, shame	lástima	lástima
What (a) shame! Those are awfully pretty shoes.	¡ ké lástima ! son-mui-bonítos ésos θapátos.	¡ Qué lástima ! Son muy bonitos esos zapatos.
What size did you say they were?	¿ ké número díjo ustéd ke-éran ?	¿ Qué número dijo usted que eran ?
CLERK:		
Four and a half.	kuátro i-médio.	Cuatro y medio.
BETTY:		
exactly, just	eksákta ménte	exactamente
Just the size I wear.	eksákta ménte el-número ke-úso yó.	Exactamente el número que uso yo.
(Will) you let me try them on?	¿ me-déja probár-los ?	¿ Me deja probarlos ?
CLERK:		
With pleasure.	kon-tódo gústo, señoríta.	Con todo [4] gusto, señorita.
They fit you very well.	le-kédan mui-ḅién.	Le quedan muy bien.
made	échos	hechos
Those shoes were made for you.	ésos θapátos fuéron échos para--ustéd.	Esos zapatos fueron hechos para usted.
BETTY:		
You're right. They fit very well.	tiéne rraθón. me-kédan mui--ḅién.	Tiene razón. Me quedan muy bien.
comfortable	kómodos	cómodos

Whether you head for Potosí, Cuzco, La Habana, Montevideo, Santiago, or Madrid, you'll find *Spanish* is an "Open, Sesame" to the hearts and affection of the interesting, and lovable peoples who inhabit the Spanish-speaking world. That world — in the Caribbean, in Spain, or in the tremendous continent of South America — is one of sharp, startling contrast in everything: geography, economy, industry, and customs. The couple, above, are taking a look at "Napoleon's Hat" as they enter the Straits of Magellan on their way round South America. Below, a plane lands high in the Andes of Peru while a llama pack train skirts the field. Notice the packs on the llamas. Burden them with an ounce more than their normal load, and they will calmly lie down until the load is lightened.

People who know romantic, impressive Guatemala City (right), claim that it has the ideal climate in all the world — a year-round temperature between 45 and 85 degrees — never too cold and never too hot. La Habana (below), is the impressive capital of Cuba. On the opposite page is pictured Columbus Park (the *Parque de Colon*) in the great metropolis of Buenos Aires, far to the south.

Madrid, the city, is like Spain, the nation, a spot where old and new are harmoniously blended with striking effect. Above is seen the *Gran Via*, of the Capital.

ENGLISH MEANING	AIDS TO LISTENING	SPANISH SPELLING
They're smart and comfortable at the (same) time.	son-elegántes i-kómodos a-la--béθ.	Son elegantes y cómodos a la vez.
Look, I('ll) take them.	¡ mire ustéd, me-loṣ-Iébo.	Mire usted, me los llevo.

BETTY:

| I expected it! I knew it! | me-lo-esperába . . . lo-sabía . . . | ¡ Me lo esperaba! ¡ Lo sabía! |

CARMEN:

| What? | ¿ ké kósa. | ¿ Qué cosa? |

BETTY:

(I) went	íba	iba
That I was going to buy something.	ke-íba a-komprár álgo.	Que iba a comprar algo.
And I didn't need them.	i-no-loṣ-neθesitába.	Y no los necesitaba.

2. "I fell asleep in class today."

MARTHA:

| I fell asleep in history class today. | ói me-dormí en-la-kláse de--istória. | Hoy me dormí en la clase de historia. |
| I'd never done that (before). | núnka abía écho éso. | Nunca había hecho eso. |

LOLA:

without doubt	sin-dúda	sin duda
a period	una-époka	una época
tranquil, quiet	trankíla	tranquila
No doubt you were studying a quiet period.	sin-dúda estában estudiándo una-époka trankíla.	Sin duda estaban estudiando una época tranquila.

MARTHA:

| the war | la-gérra | la guerra |
| Yes, the Hundred Years' War, no[thing] less. | sí, la-gérra de-los-θién áños, náda ménos. | Sí, la Guerra de los Cien Años, nada menos. |

LOLA:

| interesting | interesánte | interesante |
| Wasn't it interesting? | ¿ no-éra interesánte? | ¿ No era interesante? |

MARTHA:

| Yes, it was! | ¡ sí, kómo nó. | ¡ Sí, cómo no! |

LOLA:

| to bore | aburrír | aburrir |
| Then what do you do in the classes that bore you? | ¿ entónθes ké áθes en-las-kláses ke-te-abúrren. | ¿ Entonces qué haces en las clases que te aburren? |

MARTHA:

| I just couldn't keep my eyes open. | es-ke-no-podía tenér los-ójos abiértos. | Es que no podía tener los ojos abiertos. |

ENGLISH MEANING	AIDS TO LISTENING	SPANISH SPELLING

LOLA:
Poor girl!   ¡ poḇreθíta !   ¡ Pobrecita !

MARTHA:
to pay attention   ponér atenθión   poner atención
above all   soḇre-tódo   sobre todo
I wanted to pay attention to what the professor was saying, especially since I hadn't read to-day's lesson.   kería ponér atenθión a-lo-ke--deθía el-profesór, soḇre-tódo por-ke-no-aḇía leído la--lekθión de-ói.   Quería poner atención a lo que decía el profesor, sobre todo [4] porque no había leído la lección de hoy.

LOLA:
But you couldn't?   ¿ pero-no-podías ?   ¿ Pero no podías ?

MARTHA:
to resist   rresistír   resistir
There wasn't any way to resist sleep.   no-aḇía módo de-rresistír al--suéño.   No había modo de resistir al sueño.
I had got up at seven.   me-aḇía leḇantádo a-las-siéte.   Me había levantado a las siete.

LOLA:
And it was raining, too.   i-estáḇa l̇obiéndo tambіén.   Y estaba lloviendo también.
the noise, the sound   el-rruído   el ruido
the rain   la-l̇úḇia   la lluvia
The sound of rain makes (you) sleepy.   el-rruído de-la-l̇úḇia dá suéño.   El ruido de la lluvia da sueño.

MARTHA:
his monotonous voice   su-ḇóθ monótona   su voz monótona
I was following the professor's explanation, but his monotonous voice put me to sleep.   estáḇa sigiéndo la-esplikaθión del-profesór, pero-su-ḇóθ monótona me-íθo dormír.   Estaba siguiendo [5] la explicación del profesor, pero su voz monótona me hizo dormir.

LOLA:
to wake up   despertár (despiérta-)   despertar (despierta-)
Who woke you up?   ¿ kién te-despertó.   ¿ Quién te despertó ?

MARTHA:
neighbour   ḇeθíno   vecino
I don't know. My neighbour was sleeping too.   no-sé. mi-ḇeθíno estáḇa durmiéndo tambіén.   No sé. Mi vecino estaba durmiendo [5] también.

LOLA:
Didn't the professor say anything?   ¿ no-díjo náda el-profesór ?   ¿ No dijo nada el profesor ?

MARTHA:
absolute   absolúto   absoluto
the goodness, the kindness   la-ḇondád   la bondad
Absolutely (nothing). He had the   en-absolúto. túḇo la-ḇondád   En absoluto. Tuvo la bondad

ENGLISH MEANING	AIDS TO LISTENING	SPANISH SPELLING
kindness to let me sleep the whole hour.	de-dejár-me dormír tóda la--óra.	de dejarme dormir toda la hora.[4]

LOLA:
How do you feel now?   ¿ kómo te-siéntes aóra.   ¿ Cómo te sientes ahora ?

MARTHA:

awake   despiérta   despierta
(Wide) awake and rested, thank you.   despiérta i-deskansáda, gráθias: Despierta y descansada, gracias.

LOLA:

a cup of coffee   una-táθa de-kafé   una taza de café
(Shall) we go (and) have a cup of coffee ?   ¿ bámos a-tomár una-táθa de--kafé ?   ¿ Vamos a tomar una taza de café ?

MARTHA:

the library   la-bibliotéka   la biblioteca
I can't. I'm going to the library to read.   no-puédo. bói a-la-bibliotéka a-leér.   No puedo. Voy a la biblioteca a leer.

LOLA:

to leave   dejár   dejar
Leave it till later.   ¡ déja-lo para-después.   Déjalo para después.

MARTHA:

much curiosity   múcha kuriosidád   mucha curiosidad
I'm very curious to know who fought a hundred years, and why.   téngo múcha kuriosidád por--sabér kiénes se-peleáron θién áños i-por-ké.   Tengo mucha curiosidad por saber quiénes se pelearon cien años y por qué.

GRAMMATICAL NOTES

1. COMPARATIVE USAGE: looking, listening, waiting, asking.

The Spanish verbs **mirar**, **escuchar**, **esperar** and **pedir** are different from the corresponding English verbs in that they may take a DIRECT OBJECT, while *look, listen, wait, ask* never do. When followed by a direct object, **mirar** = *look at,* **escuchar** = *listen to,* **esperar** = *wait for,* **pedir** = *ask for.* Similarly **buscar**, which means basically *to seek* and always takes a direct object, is the commonest equivalent of English *look for.* In addition to the examples of **buscar** and **mirar** with direct objects in this unit, note the following sentences from earlier units:

Búscalas por allí.
Si no te gusta mi carácter, puedes **buscarte** otro amigo.
Escuche esto: « Es la una pero son las dos ».
¿ **Me espera** un momento ?
¿ Por qué te **pide** la pluma ?

2. FORMS OF hacer.

Irregular forms of the verb **hacer** are the one-syllable imperative **haz,** and the completive form (participle) **hecho.**

3. SPANISH hace = ENGLISH ago.

The Spanish equivalent for English *ago* after a time-expression is the verb-form **hace,** used in this pattern as a "preposition" and placed BEFORE the expression of time. In addition to the examples in this unit you saw two in the last unit:

> Estudié el inglés **hace muchos años.**
> Cuando empecé a hablar con usted **hace unos minutos,** decidí hacerle algunas preguntas.

4. SPANISH **todo = all, whole, every,** etc.

When **todo** accompanies a noun, the phrase does not necessarily contain the definite article (**con todo gusto, en todas partes, de todos modos**). When the article IS present, however, **todo** always PRECEDES it; compare English *all the . . .* but *the whole . . .* :

> **Todas las** (*all the*) tiendas están cerradas.
> **Todas las** (*all the*) estaciones tienen algo bueno.
> Tuvo la bondad de dejarme dormir **toda la** (*the whole*) hora.
> Pasas **todo el** (*the whole*) día trabajando, ¿ verdad ?

A Spanish PLURAL phrase with **todo + DEFINITE ARTICLE** is often the same as an English SINGULAR phrase with "*every*":

> No me levanto a la misma hora **todos los días** (*every day*).
> Yo tengo que levantarme a las seis y media **todas las mañanas** (*every morning*).

Either the masculine plural **todos** or the phrase **todo el mundo,** literally, *all the world,* expresses the idea of "*everybody*":

> Casi **todos** se han casado.
> Poco a poco se va casando **todo el mundo.**

The genderless singular form **todo** expresses the idea of "*everything*":

> Este señor se fija en **todo.**
> Nos enseñan que hay que imitar al profesor en **todo.**
> . . . sobre **todo** porque no había leído la lección de hoy.

5. VERBS: PROGRESSIVE FORMS.

The forms **siguiendo** and **durmiendo** illustrate the root-vowel alternation whereby, in certain **-ir** verbs, only **i** and **u** occur before the stressed type-vowel diphthong **-ié-**. We described this type of root-vowel alternation in connection with forms of the preterite past (UNIT 11). Here are the progressive forms of some other verbs of the group:

decir:	diciendo
servir:	sirviendo
pedir:	pidiendo
venir:	viniendo
divertir:	divirtiendo
preferir:	prefiriendo

B. STUDY

Review SECTION A, *covering up the English.*

C. LISTENING IN

1. *Review* SECTION A, *repeating the Spanish and giving the English.*

2. *Listen in* as Lola and Juana talk (among other things) about Juana's new shoes:*

LOLA: Estaba haciendo mucho calor anoche, ¿ verdad ?

JUANA: Sí, hasta que empezó a llover hacía mucho calor.

LOLA: Me gusta escuchar la lluvia. Vivo en el último piso de mi casa y la oigo muy bien.

JUANA: Yo me desperté con el ruido de la lluvia. Eran como las tres de la mañana. No volví a dormirme hasta muy tarde.

LOLA: ¿ Cómo te sientes hoy ?

JUANA: Tengo mucho sueño. No puedo tener los ojos abiertos. Tengo que dormir como trece horas esta noche.

LOLA: Es imposible dormir trece horas.

JUANA: Yo a veces duermo catorce o quince horas.

LOLA: ¿ Qué tienes en el pie derecho ?

* These conversations are not recorded as Units 1–12 cover the vocabulary and pronunciation of all Units 1–14.

JUANA: Son estos zapatos nuevos. Me lastiman los pies.

LOLA: ¡ Qué lástima ! ¿ No te quedan bien ?

JUANA: No. Son muy cortos.

LOLA: ¿ Por qué los compraste entonces ?

JUANA: Porque no tenían otros zapatos verdes.

LOLA: Es una tontería comprar zapatos que lastiman los pies.

JUANA: Nunca había hecho eso. Y no lo vuelvo a hacer tampoco.

LOLA: ¿ Cuándo los compraste ?

JUANA: Los compré hace unos cuantos días.

LOLA: ¿ Tenían de esos zapatos en otros colores ?

JUANA: Los tenían en rojo y en negro.

LOLA: Yo no uso tacones tan altos como tú.

JUANA: También los tenían con el tacón un poco más bajo.

LOLA: ¿ En qué tienda los encontraste ?

JUANA: En esa tienda de zapatos moderna que está en la calle principal.

LOLA: ¿ De qué precio eran ?

JUANA: Me costaron dos libras.

LOLA: Es mucho dinero, sobre todo cuando te lastiman los pies.

JUANA: Estoy aburrida. ¿ Quieres ir al cine ?

LOLA: ¿ Qué película quieres ver ? Ya he visto dos esta semana.

JUANA: Sin duda has visto ésta también.

LOLA: ¿ Cuál es ?

JUANA: Es la que están dando en el centro. Es una película de guerra.

LOLA: Prefiero una película más tranquila. Además, tú tienes mucho sueño. Dejemos el cine para otro día.

JUANA: Tienes razón. No quiero dormirme en el cine.

D. GRAMMATICAL ANALYSIS

VERBS: THE PAST TENSE

We are now ready to analyze (*1*) the set of past-tense forms which Spanish has in addition to the preterite past — namely, the IMPERFECT past forms; and (*2*) the function of the IMPERFECT past as contrasted with that of the PRETERITE past.

1. FORMS OF THE IMPERFECT PAST.

(*1*) **Model Imperfects.** The following models show the imperfect past forms of Spanish verbs:

TYPE I: EX. **estar**

	SING.	PLU.
1ST	estaba	estábamos
2ND	estabas	
3RD	estaba	estaban

TYPE II: EX. **decir**

	SING.	PLU.
1ST	decía	decíamos
2ND	decías	
3RD	decía	decían

In these past-tense forms, the person-number endings (**-s, -mos, -n**) are the same as for the present tense, with none in the 1st and 3rd singular.

The distinctive sign of the imperfect past consists of two syllables, of which the first is the stressed type-vowel: TYPE I **-aba-**, TYPE II **-ía-**.

(*2*) **Irregular Imperfects.** Only three Spanish verbs have imperfect past forms which do not conform to the above pattern. They are:

ver: **veía-**
ir: **iba-**
ser: **era-**

Ver has here the alternate root **ve-**, the same as in the 1st singular of the straight present and in the command-forms (compare **veo, vea-**); **ir** has the **-b-** of TYPE I verbs; **ser** has a wholly irregular shape.

2. FUNCTION OF THE IMPERFECT PAST.

In the following sentences from the BASIC DIALOGUES of this unit the verbs are in the imperfect past:

No **sabía** que **tenías** esa debilidad.
¿ **Buscaban** algo, señoritas ?

Eran negros y creo que **costaban** trece cincuenta.
¡ Me lo **esperaba** ! ¡ Lo **sabía** !
. . . Que **iba** a comprar algo.
Y no los **necesitaba.**
Me **había** levantado a las siete.
Sin duda **estaban** estudiando una época tranquila.
Quería poner atención a lo que **decía** el profesor.
¿ Pero no **podías** ?

The term "imperfect" means "not finished." In all these sentences the speaker is referring back to an action which was taking place IN THE PAST; however, he is not recording the action AS A WHOLE, with its beginning and its course and its ending all equally in view — which he would be doing if he used the preterite past. Instead, he is looking back INTO THE COURSE of the action and is disregarding both its beginning and its ending. Furthermore, he is recording this action as a prevailing CIRCUMSTANCE — that is, as a descriptive or explanatory BACKGROUND for the central HAPPENING about which and around which he is talking.

Occasionally the central happening and a background circumstance are both recorded in a single utterance, as in the sentence **Mientras andaba por la calle principal** (background circumstance), **ví un par de zapatos muy bonitos** (central happening). There occur, however, many utterances in which only circumstances are mentioned and the central happening is somewhere else in the context of the conversation.

Comparative Usage

(*1*) **English Progressive Past — Spanish Simple Imperfect.** English very often records the circumstances forming the background of a central happening by using a PROGRESSIVE PHRASE in the past tense, while the Spanish equivalent may be merely the imperfect past:

While I was going down High Street . . .
Mientras **andaba** por la calle central . . .

Were you looking for something?
¿ **Buscaban** algo, señoritas ?

. . . that I was going to buy something.
. . . que **iba** a comprar algo.

I wanted to pay attention to what the professor was saying.
Quería poner atención a lo que **decía** el profesor.

Of course when Spanish does use a progressive phrase to represent a background circumstance in the past, the verb **estar** is in the imperfect:

And it was raining, too.
Y **estaba lloviendo** también.

On the other hand, English avoids the progressive phrase with some verbs, using only the simple past tense and therefore not formally distinguishing between circumstances and happenings. Among such verbs are *was, had* (including completive phrases), *knew, wanted:*

What colour were they and what was the price ?
¿ De qué color **eran** y cuál **era** el precio ?

There was no way to resist sleep.
No **había** modo de resistir al sueño.

I didn't know you had that weakness.
No **sabía** que **tenías** esa debilidad.

I expected it ! I knew it !
¡ Me lo **esperaba** ! ¡ Lo **sabía** !

I wanted to pay attention to what the professor was saying.
Quería poner atención a lo que **decía** el profesor.

Therefore in cases where the Spanish verbs **saber** or **querer,** for example, are used in the PRETERITE past to report a happening, English uses some other verb altogether:

No lo **supimos** haste anoche.
We didn't find it out until last night.

Tú no **quisiste** creerme.
You wouldn't believe me.

(*2*) **English *used to* — Spanish Simple Imperfect.** English uses a verbal phrase with *used to* to denote a background circumstance consisting of a HABITUALLY RECURRING action. Habitual past action is conveyed in Spanish merely by the imperfect past when accompanied by such adverbial expressions as **antes, siempre, todos los días,** etc.

You used to get out at four, didn't you?
Antes salías a las cuatro, ¿ verdad ?

E. GRAMMATICAL DRILLS

1. THE IMPERFECT PAST.

A. *As you read the following sentences aloud, supply the missing form of the verb in parentheses, putting it in the proper person-number of the imperfect past tense. Then give the English.*

EXAMPLE:

(querer) ¿ Qué —— usted ?

MODEL:

¿ Qué **quería** usted ?
What did you want ?

1. (buscar) ¿ A quién —— usted ayer ?
2. (tener) ¿ Cuántas páginas —— el libro ?
3. (llamarse) ¿ Cómo —— el señor ?
4. (estar) ¿ Quién —— en el teléfono ?
5. (ser) ¿ —— de usted el coche que ví ?
6. (decir) Mi abuelo siempre —— eso.
7. (querer) Y tú ¿ qué —— preguntarme ?
8. (gustarme) Antes —— dar una vuelta después de comer.
9. (ir) Juana —— a hacerlo pero no tuvo tiempo.
10. (verte) Yo no —— de donde estaba.
11. (ser) ¿ Qué hora —— cuando llegaste ?
12. (haber) ¿ —— mucha gente en la fiesta ?

B. *Take each of the following verbal phrases and make with it a full sentence beginning with* **Antes mi hermano y yo . . .**, *in which you tell what you and he used to do:*

EXAMPLE:

hablar español

MODEL:

Antes mi hermano y yo **hablábamos** español.
My brother and I used to speak Spanish.

1. estudiar juntos
2. levantarse temprano
3. llegar a tiempo
4. entender inglés
5. trabajar juntos pero ya no
6. comer a las doce
7. acostarse tarde
8. vivir en Londres

C. *Take each of the following verbal phrases and make a full sentence beginning with* **Tú** *and ending with* **todos los días, ¿ verdad ?** *in which you indicate what your friend used to do every day.*

EXAMPLE:

comer aquí

MODEL:

Tú **comías** aquí todos los días, ¿ verdad ?
You used to eat here every day, didn't you?

1. usar ese sombrero
2. venir a mi casa
3. escuchar el radio
4. olvidarlo
5. volver a casa
6. acompañarme
7. nunca acordarse de hacerlo
8. afeitarse
9. tener clase
10. ir a verla

2. IMPERFECT PAST: PROGRESSIVE PHRASES

Taking each of the verbal phrases that follow, and ending each sentence with . . . **cuando te ví ?**, *use the imperfect past of* **estar** *with the progressive form to ask your friend about what he was doing when you saw him.*

EXAMPLE:

qué . . . hacer

MODEL:

¿ Qué **estabas** haciendo cuando te ví ?
What were you doing when I saw you?

1. qué . . . mirar
2. a quién . . . buscar
3. por qué . . . pelearse
4. qué . . . decir
5. a quién . . . llamar

6. a quién . . . seguir
7. de qué . . . reírse
8. qué . . . tratar de hacer
9. qué . . . escuchar
10. a quién . . . esperar
11. qué . . . escribir
12. de qué . . . quejarse

3. IMPERFECT PAST: COMPLETIVE PHRASES.

Taking each of the verbal phrases that follow, and beginning with **Yo no** *and ending with* **todavía,** *make sentences using the imperfect past of* **haber** *with the completive form to tell what you hadn't done yet.*

EXAMPLE:

buscarlo

MODEL:

Yo no **lo había buscado** todavía.
I hadn't looked for it yet.

1. aprenderlo
2. verla
3. entenderlo
4. pedírselo
5. preguntárselo
6. oír nada
7. nadar aquí
8. comprarlos
9. hacer nada
10. trabajar allí
11. conocerlas
12. explicárselo
13. leer el libro
14. escribir la carta

4. IMPERFECT OR PRETERITE PAST?

As you read the following sentences aloud, choose the appropriate one of the two past-tense forms in parentheses. Then give the English.

EXAMPLE:

María siempre (pasaba — pasó) por nuestra casa.

MODEL:

María siempre **pasaba** por nuestra casa.
Mary always used to go by our house.

1. Esos muchachos (venían — vinieron) a verme dos veces ayer.
2. Antes (me aburría — me aburrió) su voz monótona pero ya no.
3. Jaime (me compraba — me compró) un par de zapatos muy bonitos.
4. Cuando (éramos — fuimos) niños, visitábamos a los abuelos todos los veranos.
5. Yo no estaba aquí cuando (llegaba — llegó) la carta.
6. Pablo no (iba — fué) con nosotros porque ya (era — fué) tarde.
7. Me dijeron que (iban — fueron) a tomar una taza de café.
8. Esta mañana (me despertaba — me desperté) a las diez.
9. El señor me dijo que no (sabía — supo) el nombre de la calle.
10. Cuando yo (era — fuí) estudiante, nunca (ponía — puse) atención a lo que (decía — dijo) el profesor.
11. ¿ (Era — Fué) alta la señorita que (venía — vino) ?
12. Anoche Lola (veía — vió) un sombrero muy bonito.
13. Estos zapatos (me lastimaban — me lastimaron) cuando (eran — fueron) nuevos.
14. Antes nunca (escuchábamos — escuchamos) el radio pero ahora nos gusta.
15. No (habíamos — hubimos) comido y por eso (teníamos — tuvimos) mucha hambre.
16. Leonor no (me perdonaba — me perdonó) por lo que le dije.
17. ¿ No (se ofendía — se ofendió) tu novia cuando la dejaste en su casa ?
18. El hombre no (se quitaba — se quitó) el sombrero cuando entró.
19. Pedro (salía — salió) de la casa cuando yo lo ví.
20. (Estábamos — Estuvimos) estudiando cuando nos llamaron.

F. STUDY

1. *Review* SECTION A, *with the Spanish covered.* **2.** *Prepare the* CONVERSATIONS.

G. CONVERSATIONS

1. *Reproduce the* BASIC DIALOGUES *in Spanish.*

2. *Using the* BASIC DIALOGUES *as your model develop conversations such as:*

(*a*) Going shopping with a friend; getting into a conversation with a clerk; discussing prices, colors, size and fit. You can be buying a suit, a dress, a tie, a hat, or shoes.

(*b*) Telling about how you fell asleep in class the other day, and what happened.

The Days of the Week. North American and South American Pharmacies.

Passive Phrases: **Ser** and the Completive Form of the Verb; the Reflexive; the Third-Person Plural Form of the Verb.

Negative words: **nada, nadie, nunca, ninguno, ni, tampoco.**

A. BASIC DIALOGUES

1. "Let's learn the days of the week."

ENGLISH MEANING	AIDS TO LISTENING	SPANISH SPELLING

Note: This Unit is not recorded.

BILL:

What do you think of the idea of studying together?

¿ ké te-paréθe la-idéa d'estudiár júntos?

¿ Qué te parece la idea de estudiar juntos?

HENRY:

advantages
in dialogue form

bentájas
en-fórma de-diálogo

ventajas
en forma de diálogo

It has some advantages, since the sentences are presented in dialogue form.

tiéne algúnas bentájas, yá ke--se-preséntan las-fráses en--fórma de-diálogo.

Tiene algunas ventajas, ya que se presentan las frases en forma de diálogo.

BILL:

the danger
mad

el-peligro
lóko

el peligro
loco

And you can study out loud without the danger of people thinking you're mad.

i-se-puéde estudiár em-bóθ álta sim-peligro de-pasár por-lóko.

Y se puede[1] estudiar en voz alta sin peligro de pasar por loco.

HENRY:

That's right.

es-θiérto.

Es cierto.

At my house they think I talk to myself because I read the dialogues out loud.

en-mi-kása kréen ke-áblo sólo por-ke-léo los-diálogos em-bóθ álta.

En mi casa creen que hablo solo porque leo los diálogos en voz alta.

BILL:

What's today's lesson?

¿ kuál es-la-lekθión de-ói?

¿ Cuál es la lección de hoy?

HENRY:

The days of the week.

los-días de-la-semána.

Los días de la semana.

BILL:

The following expressions are used:

se-úsan las-sigiéntes espresiónes.

Se usan las siguientes expresiones:

"Eight days or one week";
"Fifteen days or two weeks."

ócho días o-úna semána.
kínθe días o-dós semánas.

« Ocho días o una semana »;
« Quince días o dos semanas.»

[146]

ENGLISH MEANING	AIDS TO LISTENING	SPANISH SPELLING

HENRY:
Does (that) mean they have one more day than we (do)? — ¿ kiére deθír ke-tiénen ún día más ke-nosótros? — ¿ Quiere decir que tienen un día más que nosotros?

BILL:
I don't get it. — yó no-lo-entiéndo. — Yo no lo entiendo.
useless — inútil — inútil
It's no use asking the teacher. — es-inútil preguntár-se-lo al--profesór. — Es inútil preguntárselo al profesor.

nobody, no one — nádie — nadie
He never explains anything to anybody. — él núnka l'esplíka náda a-nádie. — Él nunca le explica nada a nadie.

HENRY:
an idiom — un-modíşmo — un modismo
He always answers "It's an idiom." — siémpre kontésta es-un--modíşmo. — Siempre contesta « Es un modismo. »

BILL:
to count — kontár (kuénta-) — contar (cuenta-)
Well, let's count the days. — buéno, ¡ bámos a-kontár loş-días. — Bueno, vamos a contar los días.
truly, really — de-béras — de veras
(Let's) see if they've really got one more day than we (have). — a-bér si-de-béras tiénen ún día más ke-nosótros. — A ver si de veras tienen un día más que nosotros.

HENRY:
Monday — lúnes — lunes
Sunday, one. Monday, two. — domíngo, úno. lúnes, dós. — Domingo, uno. Lunes, dos.

BILL:
Wednesday — miérkoles — miércoles
Tuesday, three. Wednesday, four. — mártes, trés. miérkoles, kuátro. — Martes, tres. Miércoles, cuatro.

HENRY:
Thursday — juebes — jueves
Friday — biérnes — viernes
Thursday, five. Friday, six. — juébes, θínko. biérnes, séis. — Jueves, cinco. Viernes, seis.

BILL:
Saturday, seven. Sunday, eight. — sábado, siéte. domíngo, ócho. — Sábado, siete. Domingo, ocho.

HENRY:
Sunday we counted already. — el-domíngo yá lo-kontámos. — El domingo [2] ya lo contamos.

BILL:
Then it's an idiom! — entónθes es-un-modíşmo. — ¡ Entonces es un modismo !

HENRY:
the mass, the church service — la-mísa — la misa
"(On) Sundays we go to church." — loş-domíngos se-bá a-mísa. — « Los domingos [2] se va [1] a misa.»

ENGLISH MEANING	AIDS TO LISTENING	SPANISH SPELLING

BILL:

"We go back to work every Monday." | se-búelbe al-trabájo tódoş loş--lúnes. | « Se vuelve [1] al trabajo todos los lunes.»

HENRY:

the rest, the others | loş-demás | los demás
"The other days we look forward to Saturday." | loş-demáş días s'espéra el--sábado. | « Los demás días se espera [1] el sábado. »

BILL:

this author | éste autór | este autor
to kill | matár | matar
This author kills me with his ideas. | éste autór me-máta kon-sus--idéas. | Este autor me mata con sus ideas.

a humourist | un-umorísta | un humorista
He thinks he's (a) humourist. | se-krée umorísta. | Se cree humorista.[3]

HENRY:

Here it says "one day yes, another no." | akí díθe ún día sí, ótro nó. | Aquí dice « un día sí, otro no. »
What's that? | ¿ ké es-éso ? | ¿ Qué es eso ?

BILL:

(That) means "every two days" or "every other day." | kiére deθír káda dóş días. | Quiere decir « cada dos días. »

HENRY:

"Tomorrow, day after tomorrow." | mañána, pasádo mañána. | « Mañana, pasado mañana. »

BILL:

"Yesterday, day before yesterday." | ayér, anteayér. | « Ayer, anteayer. »

HENRY:

past, last | pasádo | pasado
"Last Friday, next Friday." | el-biérnes pasádo, el-biérnes próksimo. | « El viernes pasado, el viernes próximo. » [2]

BILL:

"Today is Tuesday, tomorrow is Wednesday." | ói eş-mártes, mañána eş--miérkoles. | « Hoy es martes, mañana es miércoles. » [2]

HENRY:

"Next week is the coming week." | la-semána próksima eş-la--semána ke-biéne. | « La semana próxima [2] es la semana que viene. »

BILL:

I've got (a) headache. | téngo dolór de-kabéθa. | Tengo dolor [3] de cabeza.

HENRY:

Where does it say that? | ¿ dónde díθe éso? | ¿ Dónde dice eso ?

[148]

ENGLISH MEANING	AIDS TO LISTENING	SPANISH SPELLING
BILL:		
I'm saying it to you.	te-lo-estói diθiéndo yó.	Te lo estoy diciendo yo.
HENRY:		
to review, to go over	rrepasár	repasar
Don't you want to go over the lesson (again)?	¿ no-kiéres rrepasár la-leksión?	¿ No quieres repasar la lección?
BILL:		
We('ll) do it tomorrow morning.	lo-aθémoş mañána por-la--mañána.	Lo hacemos mañana por la mañana.[4]

2. The North American "Drugstore".

JULIO:		
a pharmacy	una-farmáθia	una farmacia
North American	norteamerikána	norteamericana
To a foreigner there's nothing so interesting as a North American "drugstore".	para-un-estranjéro no-ái náda tan-interesánte komo--una-farmáθia norteamerikána.	Para un extranjero no hay nada tan interesante como una farmacia norteamericana.
BOB:		
What's interesting about it?	¿ ké tiéne de-interesánte?	¿ Qué tiene de interesante?
JULIO:		
Haven't you ever been abroad?	¿ núnka a-estádo ustéd en-el--estranjéro?	¿ Nunca ha estado usted en el extranjero?
BOB:		
No, never.	nó, núnka.	No, nunca.
JULIO:		
a great difference	una-grán diferénθia	una gran diferencia [5]
There's a great difference between the pharmacies there and those of other countries.	ái una-grán diferénθia entre--las-farmáθias alí i-laş-de--ótros países.	Hay una gran diferencia entre las farmacias de allí y las de otros países.
BOB:		
What are yours like?	¿ kómo son-laş-de-ustédes?	¿ Cómo son las de ustedes?
JULIO:		
Ours are like the English (ones).	laş-nuéstras son-kómo-las--inglésas.	Las nuestras son cómo las inglesas.
to sell	bendér	vender
medicines	mediθínas	medicinas
Only medicines and things like that are sold (in them).	sólo se-bénden mediθínas i--kósas así.	Sólo se venden medicinas y cosas así.

ENGLISH MEANING	AIDS TO LISTENING	SPANISH SPELLING

BOB:

the pharmacist	el-farmaθéutiko	el farmacéutico
to earn	ganár	ganar
The pharmacist earns his living making up medicines, as he should.	el-farmaθéutiko se-gana la-bída preparándo mediθínas, komo- -debe.	El farmacéutico se gana la vida preparando medicinas, como debe.
What impression did you get the first time you went into an American drugstore?	¿ké impresión túbo ustéd la- -priméra béθ k'entró en-una- -farmáθia amerikána?	¿Qué impresión tuvo usted la primera vez que entró en una farmacia americana?

JULIO:

I couldn't imagine what kind of (a) shop it was.	no-púde imajinár-me ké kláse de-tiénda éra.	No pude imaginarme qué clase de tienda [3] era.
newspapers	periódikos	periódicos
sweets	dúlθes	dulces
I saw newspapers, books, sweets . . . everything.	bí periódikos — líbros — dúlθes — bí de-tódo.	Ví periódicos, libros, dulces . . . ví de todo.
only	úniko	único
to be lacking	faltár	faltar
About the only (thing) lacking was clothes.	kási lo-úniko ke-faltába éra rrópa.	Casi lo único que faltaba era ropa.

BOB:

Then it can be said that the North American "drugstore" is a general store in which medicines also are sold.	entonθes se-puéde deθír ke-la- -farmáθia norteamerikána es-una-tienda jenerál donde- -también se-benden medi- θínas.	Entonces se puede decir que la farmacia norteamericana es una tienda general donde también se venden medicinas.

JULIO:

said	dícho	dicho
Well said.	bien dícho.	Bien dicho.
the lunch	el-almuerθo	el almuerzo
cheap	baráto	barato
The lunches that are served are good, cheap, and quick.	los-almuérθos ke-se-sírben som- -buénos, barátos i-rrápidos.	Los almuerzos que se sirven son buenos, baratos y rápidos.

ENGLISH MEANING	AIDS TO LISTENING	SPANISH SPELLING

BOB:

Tell me, what sort of books are sold (there)? ¡dígame, ¿ ké kláse de-líbros se-bénden ? Dígame, ¿ qué clase de libros se venden ?

JULIO:

There are some for every taste. los-ái para-todoş loş-gústos. Los hay para todos los gustos.

   this little book   éste libríto   este librito

   to entitle   titular   titular

   brief, short   brebe   breve

Look at this little book entitled *Short History of Culture.* ¡ míre éste libríto tituládo brebe istória de-la-kultúra. Mire este librito titulado *Breve Historia de la Cultura.*

   (it) was written   fué eskríto   fué escrito

It was written by a well-known author. fué eskríto por-un-autór mui--konoθído. Fué escrito por un autor muy conocido.

And it cost only twenty-five cents. i-sólo kostába beinti-θinko θentábos. Y sólo costaba veinticinco centavos.

GRAMMATICAL NOTES

1. SUBJECTLESS REFLEXIVE VERBS.

Spanish often uses a subjectless reflexive verb in the 3rd singular to indicate action by someone unspecified — that is, "*people in general.*" As in the present examples, English for this purpose sometimes uses such subjects as *we, you,* etc. in the non-specific meaning of "*a person*" or "*one.*" (Spanish **uno** is less formal than English *one* in this same sense; you have seen it used earlier, for example in **¿ Por qué trabaja uno tanto ?**, *Why does a person work so much?*)

2. WEEK-DAYS, ETC.

All the Spanish names of the week-days are masculine. The five which end in **-es** have the same form for both singular and plural. Unlike English, Spanish week-day nouns are preceded by the definite article in all cases except after **ser** in phrases telling what day it is (**Hoy es sábado,** etc.). Spanish uses nothing corresponding to English *on* before week-day words: *on Monday* = **el lunes;** *on Fridays* = **los viernes,** etc.

As with the week-day words, Spanish also uses the definite article with **semana** in designating *next week, last week.*

3. COMPARATIVE USAGE: INDEFINITE ARTICLE.

There are numerous situations in which English uses an indefinite article (*a, an*) but Spanish does not. Three occur in this unit. Although it is not worth our while to classify and analyze all cases, we bring together as typical all those which have appeared in previous units:

> Tenemos **casa** (*a house*) en Londres.
> Jorge dice que es **cuestión** (*a question*) de psicología.
> Treinta minutos son **media hora** (*half an hour*).
> Cuarenta y cinco minutos son **tres cuartos de hora** (*three quarters of an hour*).
> ¡ No tengo **reloj** (*a watch*)!
> Si no te gusta mi carácter, puedes buscarte **otro** (*an-other*) amigo.
> ¿ Es usted **inca** (*an Inca*) ?
> Aprendí a hablar inglés **con acento peruano** (*a Peruvian accent*).
> No puede nadar porque no traje **traje** (*a suit*).

4. Tomorrow morning, ETC.

The phrase **mañana por la mañana,** literally, *tomorrow in the morning*, shows the pattern used in Spanish for designating "a part of a day within a day." Thus also *yesterday afternoon* = **ayer por la tarde;** *Thursday night* = **el jueves por la noche,** etc.

5. Grande.

The adjective **grande** has the shortened form **gran** IN THE SINGULAR when it precedes the noun it accompanies.

6. VERB FORMS.

The verbs **decir** and **escribir** have irregular completive forms: decir: **dicho;** escribir: **escrito.**

B. STUDY

Review SECTION A, *covering up the English.*

C. LISTENING IN

1. *Review* SECTION A, *repeating the Spanish and giving the English.*

2. *Alfredo tells Rodolfo about their friend Jaime's trip to Caracas.*

ALFREDO: El otro día ví a un amigo tuyo.

RODOLFO: ¿ Quién era ?

ALFREDO: Jaime García.

RODOLFO: ¿ Qué te dijo Jaime ?

ALFREDO: Me dijo que había pasado ocho días en Caracas.

RODOLFO: ¿ Cuándo estuvo en Caracas ?

ALFREDO: Hace quince días.

RODOLFO: Yo también estaba en Caracas en esos días. No lo ví en ninguna parte.

ALFREDO: ¿ No te dijo Jaime que iba a hacer el viaje ?

RODOLFO: No me había dicho nada. ¿ Qué día salió para Caracas ?

ALFREDO: A principios del mes, el día dos. Fué a casa de unos parientes.

RODOLFO: Por eso no lo ví, entonces. Sus parientes viven lejos del centro.

ALFREDO: Dice que se divirtió mucho.

RODOLFO: ¿ Qué hizo ?

ALFREDO: Salió de aquí el miércoles por la noche y llegó allá el jueves a las seis de la mañana. En el viaje conoció a una señorita inglesa que visitaba Venezuela por primera vez.

RODOLFO: ¡ Qué suerte ! ¿ Hablaba español la señorita ?

ALFREDO: Hablaba muy poco. Pero era una ventaja porque Jaime prefería hablar inglés.

RODOLFO: Como era extranjera la señorita, me imagino que Jaime quiso acompañarla por la ciudad.

ALFREDO: Fué precisamente lo que pasó. El viernes fueron a nadar, y el sábado fueron a una fiesta.

RODOLFO: ¿ Qué hicieron el domingo ?

ALFREDO: El domingo llovió y no pudieron ir a ninguna parte. Sóló que la señorita quiso ir a misa.

RODOLFO: ¿ La acompañó Jaime ?

ALFREDO: Sí, pero fué gracioso.

RODOLFO: ¿ Qué pasó?

ALFREDO: Fueron a oír una misa protestante, y

dice Jaime que por primera vez se sintió extranjero en su país.

D. GRAMMATICAL ANALYSIS

I. VERBS: PASSIVE PHRASES

The following two Spanish sentences illustrate the "passive voice" phrase, a verbal pattern common to both English and Spanish.

> Este librito **fué escrito** por un autor muy conocido.
> Esos zapatos **fueron hechos** para usted.

In Spanish the first verb of the passive phrase is **ser** (in the appropriate tense), and the completive form of the second verb agrees in gender and number with the subject.

The most frequent use of the passive phrase in Spanish is in sentences where mention is made of the "agent" (the "doer") of the action, for example **un autor muy conocido** in the first sentence above. Such a sentence is merely an alternative way of expressing a verbal action — that is, "x is acted upon by y," instead of "y acts upon x"; in other words the first sentence above is an alternative way of saying **Un autor muy conocido escribió este librito.**

Comparative Usage

(*1*) In many expressions where THE AGENT IS NOT MENTIONED, English uses a passive phrase but Spanish uses other patterns such as the following.

A. **Reflexive Verb with Subject.** When the subject of the sentence is some lifeless thing, Spanish very frequently uses a REFLEXIVE verb. The SUBJECT, which of course determines the person-number of the reflexive verb, is commonly placed AFTER THE VERB:

> *Only medicines and things like that are sold.*
> Sólo **se venden** medicinas y cosas así.

> *The following expressions are used.*
> **Se usan** las siguientes expresiones.

> *The sentences are presented in dialogue form.*
> **Se presentan** las frases en forma de diálogo.

> *Are foreign names found only in Chile?*
> ¿ Sólo en Chile **se encuentran** nombres extranjeros?

> *Isn't it said? — It's said a great deal.*
> ¿ No **se dice**? — **Se dice** muchísimo.

The reflexive verb is of course never understood literally here, since the subjects are things incapable of acting upon themselves.

B. **Reflexive Verb without Subject.** When the expression is subjectless, Spanish uses a reflexive verb in the 3rd singular:

> *It can be said that the North American "drugstore" . . .*
> **Se puede** decir que la farmacia norteamericana . . .

> *It can't be denied that American industry does wonders.*
> No **se puede** negar que la industria americana hace maravillas.

C. **3rd Plural Verb with Object.** Another frequent Spanish usage corresponding to the passive phrase in English is a verb in the 3rd plural with an OBJECT. The subject of the verb is understood as human, but unspecified, just as indefinite "they" often is in English:

> *America was discovered in 1492.*
> **Descubrieron** la América en 1492.

(*2*) English uses the same pattern as the passive phrase — that is, the verb *be* + completive form — to denote that the subject is in a certain state or condition. The Spanish equivalent in this case is **estar** + COMPLETIVE FORM AS ADJECTIVE, as in the following examples from early units:

> *The teacher is tired too.*
> La profesora también **está cansada.**

> *All the stores are closed.*
> Todas las tiendas **están cerradas.**

II. NEGATIVE WORDS

The following sentences illustrate the principal negative words used in Spanish:

El profesor **nunca** le explica **nada** a **nadie**.
No se trata **ni** de una persona muy enferma **ni** de un buen amigo.
¿ **No** le diste **ninguna** explicación?
¿ **Ni** a salir con Rosita? — **Tampoco**.

A Spanish negative sentence always has at least one negative word BEFORE THE VERB. Thus if a negative word (such as **nada**) comes later in the sentence, the verb is automatically preceded by **no**. On the other hand if some other negative word comes before the verb, **no** is not used.

Comparative Usage of Negative Words

Corresponding to each Spanish negative word, English has both a negative and a positive form, thus:

SPANISH	ENGLISH NEGATIVE FORM	ENGLISH POSITIVE FORM
nada	nothing	anything
nadie	nobody (no one)	anybody (anyone)
nunca	never	ever
ninguno	no (none)	any
ni	neither, nor	either, or
tampoco	neither	either

In an English negative sentence, only one negative form can occur. This may be either the *not* accompanying the verb, or a negative form elsewhere in the sentence, but not both. Hence any further word of this kind which may occur is in the POSITIVE form. With this principle in mind, observe the correspondences between English and Spanish in the following sentences:

For a foreigner there's **nothing** *so interesting as a North American "drugstore".*
Para un extranjero no hay **nada** tan interesante como una farmacia norteamericana.

But please don't let me buy **anything**.
Pero hazme el favor de no dejarme comprar **nada**.

He never explains **anything** *to* **anybody**.
Él nunca le explica **nada** a **nadie**.

Haven't you **ever** *been abroad?*
¿ **Nunca** ha estado usted en el extranjero?

Didn't you give her **any** *explanation?* — **None**.
¿ No le diste **ninguna** explicación? — **Ninguna**.

It's not a question of **either** *a very sick person or a good friend.*
No se trata **ni** de una persona muy enferma **ni** de un buen amigo.

Neither *do I.* (*or*) *I don't* **either**.
Ni yo **tampoco**.

In the frequent cases where English uses the word *any* without (any) emphasis, Spanish uses no corresponding word at all:

Don't you have **any** *brothers and sisters?*
¿ No tiene usted hermanos?

I haven't got **any** *white shoes.*
Yo no tengo zapatos blancos.

E. GRAMMATICAL DRILLS

1. PASSIVE PHRASES.

Re-express the sentences that follow using passive phrases, and give the English equivalents:

EXAMPLE:

Colón descubrió la América.

MODEL:

La América fué descubierta por Colón.

1. Un autor conocido escribió el libro.
2. El farmacéutico prepara las medicinas.
3. Los estudiantes pronuncian y aprenden los diálogos fácilmente.
4. Perdonaron al hombre después de dos días.
5. Van a dividir el país en cuatro partes.
6. Una persona conocida mató a la mujer.
7. Empezaron el trabajo hace cinco años.
8. Un vecino encontró al niño.

9. Terminaron el trabajo en 1947.
10. Mis amigos han traído todo esto.

2. REFLEXIVE VERBS.

Make the verbs in parentheses reflexive, using the present tense. In giving the English equivalents, use passive phrases or indefinite subjects.

EXAMPLE:

(hacer) ¿ Cómo —— eso?

MODEL:

¿ Cómo **se hace** eso?
How is that done? or *How do you do that?*

1. (pronunciar) ¿ Cómo —— su nombre?
2. (explicar) ¿ Cómo —— las dos cosas?
3. (decir) —— que no es bueno comer muchos dulces.
4. (hablar) ¿ —— español en esa tienda?
5. (abrir) ¿ Cómo —— esta puerta?
6. (decir) ¿ Cómo —— eso en español?
7. (poder) Esas cosas no —— decir.
8. (poder) ¿ Dónde —— comprar una raqueta de tenis?
9. (vender) ¿ En qué tienda —— regalos?
10. (encontrar) En una farmacia norteamericana —— muchas cosas.
11. (usar) No —— esas expresiones.
12. (celebrar) —— esa fecha con fiestas.
13. (hace) Eso nunca —— aquí.
14. (servir) No —— sándwiches en las farmacias sudamericanas.
15. (oír) No —— muy bien su voz.

3. DAYS OF THE WEEK.

Give the Spanish for each of the English sentences that follow, and then repeat it for all the other days of the week.

EXAMPLE:

Today is Monday, (etc.).

MODEL:

Hoy es lunes ... Hoy es martes ... Hoy es miércoles ... etc.

1. On Tuesday I went into the town (etc.).
2. I don't work on Wednesdays (etc.).
3. Tomorrow is Thursday (etc.).
4. He's getting here next Friday (etc.).
5. Saturday (etc.) is (a) holiday (**día de fiesta**).
6. Last Sunday (etc.) it rained.
7. Yesterday was Monday (etc.).
8. We see them every Tuesday (etc.).

4. NEGATIVE WORDS.

As you read the following sentences aloud, for the short blank before the verb supply **no** *if it is required, and for the long blank supply the appropriate negative word. Then give the English for the whole sentence.*

EXAMPLE:

— he dicho ——.

MODEL:

No he dicho **nada.**
I haven't said anything.

1. — hay —— (*nobody*) en el cuarto.
2. No, mamá, yo — tengo —— en el bolsillo.
3. ¿ De dónde vienes tú? — — vengo de —— parte.
4. ¿ Ese señor —— — llega a tiempo?
5. No, él — llega —— a tiempo.
6. Mi novia — me ofreció —— explicación.
7. —— — vino a la clase esta mañana.
8. ¿ — hay —— diferencia entre las dos palabras?
9. No, gracias, — quiero tomar —— ahora.
10. —— película — me ha gustado tanto como ésa.
11. Roberto — quiere ir, —— yo ——.
12. — conozco a —— en este pueblo.
13. ¿ —— — ha estado usted en la América Latina?
14. — tengo —— hermanos —— hermanas.
15. A —— — le gusta comer tanto como a Jorge.

F. STUDY

1. *Review* SECTION A, *with the Spanish covered.*   **2.** *Prepare the* CONVERSATIONS.

G. CONVERSATIONS

1. *Reproduce the* BASIC DIALOGUES *in Spanish.*

2. *Using the* BASIC DIALOGUES *as your model, develop conversations such as:*

(*a*) Discussing the days of the week, and what you do (or did, or used to do) on each day.

(*b*) Talking about a North American "drugstore" with a foreigner, and about pharmacies in his own country.

Review.

Unit Eleven. Unit Twelve. Unit Thirteen. Unit Fourteen.

UNIT
15

A. REVIEW OF UNIT 11

I. SPEAKING SPANISH.

1. *Review thoroughly* SECTION A *of* UNIT 11 *making sure you can say the English with the English text covered and the Spanish with the Spanish text covered.*

2. *Give answers to the following questions: (Any answer that makes sense is all right, provided it's in the form of a full sentence. It shouldn't be just* **Sí, No,** *or some other monosyllable. You don't need to confine yourself to the vocabulary of* UNIT 11; *use any words you know by now.)*

1. ¿ A dónde fué usted ayer por la tarde ?
2. ¿ A dónde fué Esteban (Steve) ayer por la tarde ?
3. ¿ Por qué no encontró a su amigo ?
4. ¿ Le gustan a Francisco (Frank) los hospitales ?
5. ¿ Le gustan a Francisco las visitas ?
6. ¿ Quién está en el hospital ?
7. ¿ Tiene usted muchos parientes ?
8. ¿ Dónde viven sus parientes ?
9. ¿ Por qué se conocen muy bien los dos amigos ?
10. ¿ Por qué está de mal humor Francisco ?
11. ¿ De qué humor está usted hoy ?
12. ¿ Cuándo está usted de mal humor ?
13. ¿ A qué hora se acostó Francisco anoche ?
14. ¿ A qué hora se durmió ?
15. ¿ A qué hora se acostó usted anoche ?
16. ¿ Con quién salió Francisco anoche ?
17. ¿ Por qué no se divirtieron Francisco y Rosita ?
18. ¿ Se pelea usted a veces con la gente ?
19. ¿ Con quién se pelea usted ?
20. ¿ Qué invitación le hizo Francisco a Rosita ?
21. ¿ Para qué día fué la invitación ?
22. ¿ La invitó antes o después de que se pelearon ?
23. ¿ Qué contestó Rosita ?
24. ¿ Qué pasó después ?
25. ¿ A qué hora la llevó Francisco a su casa ?
26. ¿ Qué hizo Rosita ?
27. ¿ Qué explicación le dió Francisco ?
28. ¿ Cómo se portó Francisco en la opinión de Esteban ?
29. ¿ Durmió bien Francisco ?
30. ¿ Con qué soñó ?
31. ¿ Qué cosas no vuelve a hacer Francisco ?
32. ¿ De qué se trata el segundo diálogo ?
33. ¿ En qué año descubrieron la América ?
34. ¿ Cuál fué el año de la independencia de los Estados Unidos ?
35. ¿ En qué año empezó la última guerra ?
36. ¿ En qué año terminó la guerra ?
37. ¿ En qué año llegó usted aquí ?
38. ¿ En qué año piensa usted salir de aquí ?

3. *Ask the questions that would get the following answers:*

1. Fuí a hacer una visita anoche.
2. Fuí a visitar a un pariente mío.
3. Vive lejos de mi casa este pariente.
4. Nunca he estado muy enfermo, gracias a Dios.
5. Sí, he estado en el hospital, pero sólo de visita.
6. Mi amigo va a salir del hospital dentro de dos semanas.
7. Sí, nos conocemos muy bien Rosita y yo.
8. El profesor no está de muy buen humor hoy.
9. Creo que es porque los muchachos no saben la lección.
10. Me acosté como a la una ayer.
11. No, a la una de la mañana.
12. No me pasó nada anoche. ¿ Por qué ?
13. No, no estoy preocupado; estoy enojado.
14. Estoy enojado porque vas a estar ocupada el sábado.

15. No, yo nunca me peleo con mis compañeros.
16. No, dormí mal anoche.
17. Sí, soñé con la clase de español.
18. No, yo nunca me duermo en la clase.
19. No, no tengo dolor de cabeza.
20. Cuando tengo dolor de cabeza me acuesto.
21. La fiesta es mañana.
22. No, hombre, nunca me equivoco cuando se trata de fiestas.

4. *After hearing again the* LISTENING-IN *Section of* UNIT 11, *give answers to the following questions based directly on it:*

(a)

1. ¿ Qué leyó Isabel anoche ?
2. ¿ Cuántas páginas tenía el libro ?
3. ¿ Cómo se llamaba el libro ?
4. ¿ De qué se trataba el libro ?
5. ¿ Cómo era Juana María ?
6. ¿ Quién visitó a Juana María un día ?
7. ¿ Qué hicieron Juana María y su primo ?
8. ¿ Quién era Alejandro ?
9. ¿ Por qué se enojó Alejandro ?
10. ¿ No le pidió ninguna explicación a Juana María ?
11. ¿ A dónde se fué Alejandro ?
12. ¿ Cómo terminó la historia ?
13. ¿ Es buena esta historia ?

(b)

14. ¿ Cómo durmió Paco anoche ?
15. ¿ Por qué durmió mal ?
16. ¿ Qué consejo le da Nacho a Paco ?
17. ¿ Cuándo se acostó Paco, y cuándo se durmió ?
18. ¿ Con qué cosas soñó ?

II. WRITING SPANISH.

The following sentences are variations on the content of the BASIC DIALOGUES *of* UNIT 11. *Write them out in Spanish. Parentheses around an English word mean that it isn't expressed in the Spanish version; brackets around a word not normally present in the English mean that it is expressed in the Spanish.*

1. Where did you meet your friend ?
2. Who did you go out with yesterday afternoon ?
3. I think [that] I was mistaken* yesterday.
4. Roberto and Jorge grew up together, didn't they ?
5. Somebody took away a book from my room yesterday.
6. I always make mistakes when I have to give dates.
7. Did you get angry when she said that ?
8. Of course I got angry, and we fought.
9. In what year did your parents go to the United States ?
10. Paco is in (a) bad mood; he has (a) headache.
11. I think he's worried about something.
12. No, he never worries about anything.
13. Girls always tell me [that] they're very busy.
14. Did you invite her to go to the beach ?
15. It seems that I always have bad luck.
16. She went into the house without saying anything.
17. He behaved very well this time. Can you believe it ?
18. They didn't give me any explanation.
19. I'm still learning the last lesson.
20. So you prefer to accept somebody else's invitation ? — Well, accept it !
21. He's in the hospital, but he's not very sick.
22. I won't set foot in that house again.
23. Don't you like my criticisms ?
24. It's better not to think of that.
25. How many pages did you read (*use 2nd person*) last night ?
26. I read two hundred and twenty-five pages.
27. What happened in 1550 ?
28. They say [that] that man is a hundred years old.
29. In what year was New Zealand discovered ?
30. There are three hundred and sixty-five days in a year.
31. I dreamed about you last night.

---

*How do you write the final consonant of the root of **equivocar** before the 1st singular preterite ending -é ?

32. Paul thinks [that] it's going to rain this afternoon.
33. To me it looks as though it isn't.

34. Congratulations! You arrived on time.
35. Can I offer you something?

B. REVIEW OF UNIT 12

I. SPEAKING SPANISH

1. *Review thoroughly* SECTION A *of* UNIT 12.

2. *Give answers to the following questions:*

1. ¿ De qué país es el señor?
2. ¿ De qué país es usted?
3. ¿ Qué sangre tiene el señor?
4. ¿ Hay indios en los Estados Unidos?
5. ¿ Tiene sangre india usted?
6. ¿ Cómo se llamaban antes los indios del Perú?
7. ¿ Cuántos indios hay en el Perú?
8. ¿ Hay tantos indios en los Estados Unidos como en el Perú?
9. ¿ De qué se ríe el señor?
10. ¿ Se usa mucho la expresión « ¡ Qué caray! »?
11. ¿ Cómo la pronunció la señorita?
12. ¿ Quiénes usan la expresión en general?
13. ¿ Es una expresión mala?
14. ¿ Dónde la aprendió la señorita?
15. ¿ Hay alguna expresión en español que le gusta a usted?
16. ¿ Qué les enseñan en la clase de español?
17. ¿ Cuándo estudió inglés el señor?
18. ¿ Lo estudió en Lima?
19. ¿ Vive usted en un pueblo chiquito?
20. ¿ Cómo aprendió a hablar inglés el señor?
21. ¿ Con qué acento habla usted español?
22. ¿ En qué tiene interés el señor?
23. ¿ Qué idea tuvo la señorita cuando conoció al señor?
24. ¿ Qué preguntas le quiere hacer al señor?
25. ¿ Qué trabajo tiene que hacer la señorita?

3. *Ask questions that will get the following answers:*

1. No, señor, soy norteamericano.
2. No, no soy indio.
3. No, no hay indios en el pueblo donde vivo.
4. Sí, hay algunos indios en los Estados Unidos.
5. No, la expresión « ¡ Qué caray! » no tiene nada de malo.
6. La aprendí en mi clase de español.
7. Me la enseñó el profesor.
8. Hay más de mil extranjeros en este pueblo.
9. Sí, yo conozco a fondo el idioma español.
10. Yo estudié la historia de América hace muchos años.
11. No, no te quiero hacer ninguna pregunta.
12. Tampoco quiero contestar a ninguna pregunta.
13. No puedo adivinar qué día es tu cumpleaños.
14. No me acuerdo dónde puse el papel.
15. Me lo trajeron esta mañana.
16. No lo hicimos porque no tuvimos tiempo.
17. Me lo dijo Paco anoche.
18. Lo supe ayer.
19. No quisieron acompañarnos porque era tarde.
20. No, no pude terminar hoy.

4. *After hearing again the* LISTENING-IN *Section of* UNIT 12, *give answers to the following questions based directly on it:*

1. ¿ Cuándo vino a verte el amigo?
2. ¿ Por qué vino a verte?
3. ¿ Por qué te trajo el trabajo de español?
4. ¿ No es un muchacho inteligente?
5. ¿ Por qué no le hizo preguntas a su profesor?
6. ¿ Qué clase de trabajo tuvo que preparar?
7. ¿ Cuándo empezó tu amigo a estudiar el español?
8. ¿ Quién hizo el trabajo por fin, tú o él?
9. ¿ Cómo pronuncia el español tu amigo?
10. ¿ Qué papeles son ésos?
11. ¿ Qué dicen los papeles?
12. ¿ Cómo son las frases?
13. ¿ Quieres ir a la playa a nadar ahora?
14. ¿ De qué me voy a reír?

II. WRITING SPANISH

The following sentences are variations on the content of the BASIC DIALOGUES *of* UNIT 12. *Write them out in Spanish.*

1. That word isn't used much.
2. What are those people laughing at?
3. I think they are laughing at us.
4. Are there as many Indians here as in Mexico?
5. Where did you learn to swim?
6. I don't know (how) to swim; to me it seems dangerous.
7. It seems so; but I assure you that it's neither dangerous nor hard.
8. Are the Indians of Peru Incas?
9. Several countries have more than a hundred thousand Indians.
10. I have a little Spanish blood.
11. Pardon me, sir. What country are you from?
12. Lima is in Peru, isn't it?
13. Only women use that expression.
14. I like to hear you speak Spanish; it amuses me.
15. Why do you always imitate the professor in everything?
16. I imitate him because I want to learn the expressions that he uses.
17. The professor knows the English language thoroughly.
18. How did you guess that?
19. He decided to ask me some questions.
20. I'm interested in knowing what he asked you.
21. Let's see. What were the questions?
22. I was very busy yesterday.
23. I have to answer [to] the following questions.
24. Where did I put my suit?
25. That's an old joke in English too.
26. They didn't have time to eat.
27. Why didn't you bring your sister?
28. What did Mrs. Rojas tell you?
29. There are only ten minutes left.
30. Your friends wouldn't wait.

C. REVIEW OF UNIT 13

I. SPEAKING SPANISH

1. *Review thoroughly* SECTION A *of* UNIT 13.

2. *Give answers to the following questions:*

1. ¿ Quiénes hablan en este diálogo?
2. ¿ A dónde va Carmen?
3. ¿ Qué favor le pide Betty a su amiga?
4. En primer lugar, ¿ por qué no quiere comprar nada Betty?
5. ¿ Qué debilidad tiene Betty?
6. ¿ Tiene usted la misma debilidad que Betty?
7. ¿ Cuándo vió los zapatos Carmen?
8. ¿ En qué tienda los vió?
9. ¿ Por qué no los compró antes?
10. ¿ Qué quiere hacer Betty cuando llegan a la tienda?
11. ¿ Qué clase de tacón tenían los zapatos que había visto Carmen?
12. ¿ Quiénes usan tacón alto?
13. ¿ De qué color eran los zapatos?
14. ¿ De qué color son los zapatos de usted?
15. ¿ Cuánto costaban?
16. ¿ Cuánto cuesta un buen par de zapatos hoy?
17. ¿ Les quedan muchos zapatos de los que busca Carmen?
18. ¿ En qué colores los tienen?
19. ¿ Qué número de zapato usa Carmen?
20. ¿ Qué número de zapato usa usted?
21. ¿ Los tienen en el número de Carmen?
22. ¿ Qué zapatos prueba Carmen?
23. ¿ Por qué hay que probar los zapatos antes de comprarlos?
24. ¿ Son cómodos los zapatos nuevos?
25. ¿ Cómo le queda el zapato que prueba?
26. ¿ Qué pregunta entonces Betty?
27. ¿ Qué número de zapato usa Betty?
28. ¿ Qué hace Betty?
29. ¿ Cómo le quedan los zapatos?
30. ¿ Cómo son los zapatos?

Contrast — sharp and unrelieved, mountain, plateau, jungle, delta, fertile plains and rugged slopes — marks the geography of the Spanish-speaking world. The photographs on this and succeeding pages give you some idea of the land and its methods of transportation. Above: An extended view of the Bolivian plateau high in the Andes. Below: Lake Atitlan in Guatemala; around it are twelve Indian villages, each named after one of the apostles.

Above: A modern steamer approaches the Chilean port of Arica. Below: A modern truck bogs down in the flooded jungle highways of Guatemala, miles to the north. The construction and maintenance of modern highways has in many regions been physically and economically impossible. In many such spots in Central and South America air travel has wrought miraculous changes.

Above: The train has stopped for the lunch break at the world's highest railway station at Galera Pass in central Peru. There, 15,680 feet above sea level, passengers take lunch from roadside vendors. Below: The motor-car, however, is much at home in all great cities. Here, cars are parked around San Martin Square in the heart of Lima.

And no matter where you travel, or how, remember: *¡Evite accidentes!* and always *¡Tome su derecha!* Above: A traffic policeman in Guatemala City. Below: Another kind of traffic problem in an ancient street in Cuzco. Notice the houses; they date back to the times of the Conquistadores. And they're built on cobblestone bases raised by the Incas long before Columbus.

TOME SU DERECHA

EVITE FLANCOS ACCIDENTES

31. ¿ Qué sabía Betty ?
32. ¿ Qué le pasó a Marta en la clase de historia ?
33. ¿ Se ha dormido usted en esta clase alguna vez ?
34. ¿ Qué estaban estudiando ?
35. ¿ A qué hora se había levantado Marta ?
36. ¿ Qué otras cosas le dieron sueño en la clase ?
37. ¿ Por qué no la despertó su vecino ?
38. ¿ Qué hizo el profesor ?
39. ¿ A dónde va Marta ahora ?
40. ¿ Qué va a leer ?

3. *Ask questions that will get the following answers:*

1. No puedo acompañarte al centro porque no tengo dinero.
2. Voy al centro a buscar un par de zapatos.
3. La única debilidad que tengo es la de comer demasiado.
4. La calle principal de este pueblo se llama High Street.
5. Sí, me gustan mucho las casas modernas.
6. Sí, tengo zapatos con tacón alto.
7. No los uso todos los días, porque no son muy cómodos.
8. No sé quién tiene ojos azules.
9. Estaba buscando mi libro. ¿ Lo has visto ?
10. José estaba trabajando cuando lo ví.
11. Era verde el vestido.
12. No, no estaba en casa cuando me llamaron.
13. No sabía que iban a llegar tarde.
14. No, no había estudiado el español antes de venir a esta clase.
15. Estaba durmiendo.
16. Antes vivíamos en aquella casa.
17. Yo no iba a ninguna parte.
18. Creo que era el señor López.

4. *After reading again the* LISTENING-IN *Section of* UNIT 13, *give answers to the following questions based directly on it:*

1. ¿ Qué tiempo hacía anoche ?
2. ¿ Llovió anoche ?
3. ¿ En qué piso vive Lola ?
4. ¿ Qué cosa oye bien Lola ?

5. ¿ Qué ruido despertó a Juana ?
6. ¿ Qué hora era ?
7. ¿ Cómo se siente Juana hoy ?
8. ¿ Cuántas horas quiere dormir ?
9. ¿ Qué tiene Juana en el pie derecho ?
10. ¿ Cómo le quedan los zapatos nuevos ?
11. ¿ Por qué los compró ?
12. ¿ Cuándo los compró ?
13. ¿ En qué otros colores los tenían ?
14. ¿ De qué precio eran ?
15. ¿ Cuántas películas ha visto Lola esta semana ?
16. ¿ Qué clase de película están dando en el centro ?
17. ¿ Por qué no van al cine las dos amigas ?

II. WRITING SPANISH.

The following sentences are variations on the content of the BASIC DIALOGUES *of* UNIT 13. *Write them out in Spanish.*

1. I didn't know [that] you were at home.
2. Where were you going yesterday when we saw you ?
3. They saw them two weeks ago.
4. The children were making a lot of noise.
5. What are you looking at ?
6. I'm not looking at anything. I'm looking for the library.
7. Close the door, will you ? — It's closed already.
8. Then do me the favour of not opening it.
9. There are lots of modern stores in High Street, aren't there ?
10. What kind of (an) accent do you have in Spanish ?
11. I have the best accent possible.
12. Don't let her buy anything.
13. They stayed outside to look at the people.
14. The dresses that were in the (show) window were very pretty.
15. Don't you like high-heeled shoes ? —Yes, but I don't wear them all the time.
16. I didn't know what time you got out of work.
17. Help me [to] look for my pen.

18. What colour were the hats?

19. I don't remember what colour they were.

20. Don't you want to try on the shoes [in order] to see if they fit you?

21. What size [of] shoe did you say you wore? — Four and a half.

22. Isn't it hard to find shoes of that size? — Yes, sometimes.

23. What street is the library on?

24. I didn't need those things that I bought.

25. No doubt you couldn't resist the price.

26. I was sleeping, but my neighbour woke me up.

27. I had never fallen asleep in class before.

28. What were you saying? I wasn't listening.

29. Keep your eyes open, and pay attention to what I tell you.

30. I'm bored. Let's go out.

31. I'm sorry, but I don't want to do anything now.

32. A monotonous voice makes (you) sleepy, doesn't it?

D. REVIEW OF UNIT 14

I. SPEAKING SPANISH.

1. *Review* SECTION A *of* UNIT 14.

2. *Give answers to the following questions:*

1. ¿ Por qué es una buena idea estudiar con otra persona?

2. ¿ Por qué pasa Enrique por loco en su casa?

3. ¿ Cuál es la lección de hoy?

4. ¿ Cuántos días tiene una semana?

5. ¿ Cuáles son los días de la semana?

6. ¿ Le gusta al profesor dar explicaciones?

7. ¿ Qué contesta el profesor cuando se las piden?

8. ¿ Qué se hace los domingos?

9. ¿ Qué se hace los lunes?

10. ¿ Qué se hace los demás días?

11. ¿ Va usted a misa los domingos?

12. ¿ Le gusta a usted el lunes? ¿ Por qué?

13. ¿ Qué día de la semana le gusta más, y por qué?

14. ¿ Qué piensa Guillermo del autor de este diálogo?

15. ¿ Qué día es hoy?

16. ¿ Qué día fué ayer?

17. ¿ Qué día es mañana?

18. ¿ Qué día fué anteayer?

19. ¿ Qué día es pasado mañana?

20. ¿ Qué hizo usted el viernes pasado?

21. ¿ Qué piensa usted hacer el viernes próximo?

22. ¿ Qué otra manera hay de decir « la semana que viene »?

23. ¿ Tiene usted dolor de cabeza?

24. ¿ Quiere repasar la lección?

25. ¿ Qué le parece interesante a un extranjero?

26. ¿ Ha estado usted en el extranjero?

27. ¿ En qué país ha estado usted?

28. ¿ Cuándo estuvo usted allá?

29. ¿ Por cuánto tiempo?

30. ¿ Quiere volver a ese país? ¿ Por qué?

31. ¿ Qué cosas se pueden comprar en una farmacia norteamericana?

32. ¿ Qué impresión tuvo Julio la primera vez que entró en una farmacia norteamericana?

33. ¿ Qué cosas se venden en las farmacias de otros países?

34. ¿ Qué cosas vió Julio en la farmacia norteamericana?

35. ¿ Qué cosa faltaba?

36. ¿ Se puede comer en una de esas farmacias?

37. ¿ Cómo son los almuerzos?

38. ¿ Qué clase de libros se venden en algunas farmacias norteamericanas?

39. ¿ Cuánto cuestan esos libritos?

3. *Ask questions that will get the following answers:*

1. Yo estudio en voz alta.

2. Vivo solo en el cuarto.

3. Sí, me pueden oír desde los otros cuartos.

4. Nada. ¿ Qué pueden decir?

5. Sí, se ríen a veces.

6. La lección de hoy se trata de los días de la semana.

7. Sólo nos quedan como cinco semanas de clase.

8. Sí, me cuesta mucho trabajo estudiar en estos días.

9. Sólo estudio cuando el tiempo está malo.

10. Cuando hace buen tiempo no puedo quedarme en la casa.

11. Salgo a divertirme.

12. No, no leo mucho.

13. Los únicos autores que conozco son autores extranjeros.

14. Ayer fué lunes.

15. Hoy es martes.

16. Pasado mañana es jueves.

17. Voy a descansar un poco. Tengo dolor de cabeza.

18. No, no quiero repasar la lección.

19. Comemos el almuerzo en la farmacia.

20. No, no me gusta comer mucho en el almuerzo.

21. No, no he visto el periódico de hoy.

22. No fué barato el traje; costó quince libras.

4. *After reading again the* LISTENING-IN *Section of* UNIT 14, *give answers to the following questions based directly on it:*

1. ¿A quién viste el otro día?
2. ¿Qué te dijo Jaime?
3. ¿Cuándo estuvo Jaime en Caracas?
4. ¿En qué país está Caracas?
5. ¿Tú viste a Jaime en Caracas?
6. ¿No te dijo Jaime que iba a hacer el viaje?
7. ¿Fué a un hotel en Caracas?
8. ¿Dónde viven sus parientes?
9. ¿Se divirtió mucho Jaime?
10. ¿Qué día salió de aquí?
11. ¿A qué hora llegó a Caracas?
12. ¿A quién conoció en el viaje?
13. ¿Había estado en Venezuela antes?
14. ¿Hablaba español la señorita inglesa?
15. ¿Por qué era esto una ventaja para Jaime?
16. ¿Qué quiso hacer Jaime?
17. ¿Qué hicieron el viernes?

18. ¿Qué día fueron a una fiesta?
19. ¿Qué tiempo hizo el domingo?
20. ¿A dónde fueron el domingo?
21. ¿Qué quiso hacer la señorita el domingo?
22. ¿La acompañó Jaime?
23. ¿Qué clase de misa oyeron?
24. ¿Qué reacción tuvo Jaime?

II. WRITING SPANISH.

The following sentences are variations on the content of the BASIC DIALOGUES *of* UNIT 14. *Write them out in Spanish:*

1. There is no one as interesting as he.
2. What's interesting about him?
3. The only thing lacking here is a newspaper.
4. Where are medicines made up?
5. There's a great difference between Spanish and English.
6. How do those people earn their living?
7. Do you like sweets? — Then put these in your pocket.
8. It's no use explaining anything to her.
9. I never give advice to anybody.
10. (Shall) we go to the beach on Saturday afternoon?
11. Are books cheap in your country?
12. By whom was that book written?
13. I always study my Spanish lesson out loud.
14. That poor man talks to himself all day.
15. Do you think he's mad?
16. It can be said that this life has some advantages.
17. Today it's a question of the days of the week.
18. They don't sell clothes in that shop.
19. We can't see them before tomorrow afternoon.
20. How do you say that in Spanish?
21. These new shoes are killing me!
22. Really? Then why don't you take them off?
23. In general I stay [at] home on Sundays.
24. What do you plan to do next Tuesday?
25. The same (thing) that I did last Tuesday: nothing.
26. Did you go to church last Sunday?

27. Day before yesterday was Wednesday, and
yesterday was Thursday.
28. So today is Friday, isn't it?

29. You're right. I was mistaken.
30. He goes home every two weeks.

SPANISH–ENGLISH VOCABULARY

FOR UNITS 11–14

A

absoluto absolute
aburrir to bore
acabar to finish
acento accent
aceptar to accept
adivinar to guess
afuera outside
alguien somebody, someone
almuerzo lunch
alto high
andar to walk, go
anoche last night
anteayer day before yesterday
asegurar to assure
la atención attention
el autor author
ayer yesterday

B

bajo low
barato cheap
biblioteca library
la bondad goodness, kindness
breve brief, short
broma joke

C

caballero gentleman
el café coffee
el carácter character
centavo cent
ciento (cien) hundred
la clase kind
el color colour
cómodo comfortable
conozco (*see* **conocer**)
contar (cuenta-) to count
contestar to answer, reply
corto short
crecer to grow
crítica criticism

cuantos: unos cuantos a few
cuatrocientos four hundred
la curiosidad curiosity

CH

chiquito little, tiny
el chiste joke, gag

D

la debilidad weakness
decidir to decide
dejar to stop, quit; to let, allow;
to leave
los demás rest, others
la descripción description
descubrir to discover
desde luego of course
despertar (despierta-) to wake
up
despierto awake
dí- (*see* **dar**)
diálogo dialogue
dicho (*see* **decir**)
diferencia difference
dij- (*see* **decir**)
dinero money
directamente directly
el dolor ache, pain
domingo Sunday
doscientos two hundred
duda doubt
los dulces sweets, candy

E

enfermo sick, ill
enojarse to get angry
enseñar to teach
entrar to fit
entusiasmo enthusiasm
época period
equivocarse to be mistaken

el escaparate show window
escrito (*see* **escribir**)
Estados Unidos United States
estuv- (*see* **estar**)
exactamente exactly
la explicación explanation
la expresión expression

F

faltar to be lacking
farmaceutico pharmacist
farmacia pharmacy
fecha date
felicitar to congratulate
el fin end
fondo: a fondo thoroughly
forma form
la frase sentence
fue-, fuí- (*see* **ser** *or* **ir**)

G

ganar to earn
gracia amusement
gran (*see* **grande**)
guerra war

H

haz (*see* **hacer**)
hecho (*see* **hacer**)
hic-, hizo (*see* **hacer**)
hola hello
el hospital hospital
el humor humour, mood
el humorista humorist

I

el idioma language
imaginar(se) to imagine
independencia independence
indio Indian

el interés interest
interesante interesting
inútil useless
la invitación invitation

J

el jueves Thursday

L

lástima shame, pity
lastimar to hurt
librito little book
loco mad
el lugar place
el lunes Monday

LL

lluvia rain

M

mal *adjective* (*see* malo)
mal *adverb* badly
matar to kill
medicina medicine
mientras while
el miércoles Wednesday
mil thousand
el millón million
mirar to look
misa mass, church service
moderno modern
modismo idiom
momentito little minute
monótono monotonous
muchísimo very much

N

nadar to swim
nadie nobody, no one
necesario necessary
norteamericano North American

novecientos nine hundred
nuevo new

O

ocupado busy
la opinión opinion
la orden order

P

palabra word
el papel paper
el pariente relative
pasado past, last
pelearse to fight
peligro danger
peligroso dangerous
perdonar to pardon
perfecto perfect
periódico newspaper
peruano Peruvian
el placer pleasure
playa beach
pobrecita poor thing
portarse to behave
precio price
pregunta question
preocuparse to worry, be concerned
principal principal, main
probar (prueba-) to try
pronunciar to pronounce
pud- (*see* poder)
pueblo town; people
pus- (*see* poner)

Q

quinientos five hundred
quis- (*see* querer)

R

rápido rapid, fast
la reacción reaction
reír (ríe-) to laugh

repasar to review
resistir to resist
rojo red
ruido noise

S

la sangre blood
seguramente surely
semana week
sentarse (sienta-) to sit down
setecientos seven hundred
siguiente following
sobre *preposition* on, above *etc.*
soñar (sueña-) to dream
sudamericano South American
la suerte luck
sup- (*see* saber)

T

el tacón heel
tal vez perhaps
taza cup
titular to entitle
traer to bring
traj- (*see* traer)
el traje suit
tranquilo tranquil, quiet
tratarse to be a question
tuv- (*see* tener)

U

único only

V

vender to sell
ventaja advantage
veras: de veras truly, really
verbo verb
verde green
el viernes Friday
vin- (*see* venir)
visitar to visit
la voz voice

Regular Verbs: with Root-vowel Alternation; with Variable Spelling of Root-final Consonant; with Root Ending in Vowel. Irregular Verbs. Personal Pronouns. Possessives.

GRAMMAR APPENDIX

REGULAR VERBS

TYPE I	ROOT	GENERAL (INFINITIVE)	PREDICTIVE STEM	PROGRESSIVE (GERUND)	COMPLETIVE (PAST PARTICIPLE)	IMPERATIVE
SAMPLE						SING. toma
tomar	tom-	tomar	tomar-	tomando	tomado	PLUR. tomad

	STEM	1ST SING.	2ND SING.	3RD SING.	1ST PLUR.	2ND PLUR.	3RD PLUR.
STRAIGHT PRESENT		-o	-a s	-a	-a mos	-á is	-a n
SUBJUNCTIVE PRESENT		-e	-e s	-e	-e mos	-é is	-e n
IMPERFECT PAST	tom-	-aba	-aba s	-aba	-ába mos	-aba is	-aba n
PRETERITE PAST		-é	-a ste	-ó	-a mos	-a steis	-a ron
SUBJUNCTIVE PAST		-ara	-ara s	-ara	-ára mos	-ara is	-ara n
PREDICTIVE PRESENT (*Future*)	tomar-	-é	-á s	-á	-c mos	-é is	-á n
PREDICTIVE PAST (*Conditional*)		-ía	-ía s	-ía	-ía mos	-ía is	-ía n

TYPE IIA	ROOT	GENERAL (INFINITIVE)	PREDICTIVE STEM	PROGRESSIVE (GERUND)	COMPLETIVE (PAST PARTICIPLE)	IMPERATIVE
SAMPLE						SING. come
comer	com-	comer	comer-	comiendo	comido	PLUR. comed

	STEM	1ST SING.	2ND SING.	3RD SING.	1ST PLUR.	2ND PLUR.	3RD PLUR.
STRAIGHT PRESENT		-o	-e s	-e	-e mos	-é is	-e n
SUBJUNCTIVE PRESENT		-a	-a s	-a	-a mos	-á is	-a n
IMPERFECT PAST	com-	-ía	-ía s	-ía	-ía mos	-ía is	-ía n
PRETERITE PAST		-í	-i ste	-ió	-i mos	-i steis	-ie ron
SUBJUNCTIVE PAST		-iera	-iera s	-iera	-iéra mos	-iera is	-iera n
PREDICTIVE PRESENT (*Future*)	comer-	-é	-á s	-á	-e mos	-é is	-á n
PREDICTIVE PAST (*Conditional*)		-ía	-ía s	-ía	-ía mos	-ía is	-ía n

[i]

| TYPE IIb
SAMPLE
vivir | ROOT

viv- | GENERAL
(INFINITIVE)
vivir | PREDICTIVE
STEM
vivir- | PROGRESSIVE
(GERUND)
viviendo | COMPLETIVE
(PAST PARTICIPLE)
vivido | IMPERATIVE
SING. **vive**
PLUR. **vivid** |

	STEM	1ST SING.	2ND SING.	3RD SING.	1ST PLUR.	2ND PLUR.	3RD PLUR.
STRAIGHT PRESENT	viv-	-o	-e s	-e	-i mos	-í s	-e n
SUBJUNCTIVE PRESENT		-a	-a s	-a	-a mos	-á is	-a n
IMPERFECT PAST		-ía	-ía s	-ía	-ía mos	-ía is	-ía n
PRETERITE PAST		-í	-i ste	-ió	-i mos	-i steis	-ie ron
SUBJUNCTIVE PAST		-iera	-iera s	-iera	-iéra mos	-iera is	-iera n
PREDICTIVE PRESENT (*Future*)	vivir-	-é	-á s	-á	-e mos	-é is	-á n
PREDICTIVE PAST (*Conditional*)		-ía	-ía s	-ía	-ía mos	-ía is	-ía n

REGULAR VERBS WITH ROOT–VOWEL ALTERNATION

TYPE I WITH ALTERNATION -e-/-ie-.   SAMPLE: **pensar** (**piensa-**).
ROOT: **pens-** and **piens-**, the latter occurring *when stressed*, in the following places only:

	ROOT	1ST SING.	2ND SING	3RD SING.	1ST PLUR.	2ND PLUR.	3RD PLUR.
STRAIGHT PRESENT	piens- pens-	-o	-a s	-a	-a mos	-á is	-a n
SUBJUNCTIVE PRESENT	piens- pens-	-e	-e s	-e	-e mos	-é is	-e n
IMPERATIVE SING. **piensa**, PLUR. **pensad**								

TYPE I WITH ALTERNATION -o-/-ue-.   SAMPLE: **contar** (**cuenta-**).
ROOT: **cont-** and **cuent-**, the latter occurring *when stressed* in the following places only:

	ROOT	1ST SING.	2ND SING.	3RD SING.	1ST PLUR.	2ND PLUR.	3RD PLUR.
STRAIGHT PRESENT	cuent- cont-	-o	-a s	-a	-a mos	-á is	-a n
SUBJUNCTIVE PRESENT	cuent- cont-	-e	-e s	-e	-e mos	-é is	-e n
IMPERATIVE SING. **cuenta**, PLUR. **contad**								

TYPE IIA WITH ALTERNATION -e-/-ie-. SAMPLE: perder (pierde-).
ROOT: **perd-** and **pierd-,** the latter occurring *when stressed*, in the following places only:

	ROOT	1ST SING.	2ND SING.	3RD SING.	1ST PLUR.	2ND PLUR.	3RD PLUR.
STRAIGHT PRESENT	pierd- perd-	-o	-e s	-e	-e mos	-é is	-e n
SUBJUNCTIVE PRESENT	pierd- perd-	-a	-a s	-a	-a mos	-á is	-a n
IMPERATIVE SING. pierde, PLUR. perded							

TYPE IIA WITH ALTERNATION -o-/-ue-. SAMPLE: volver (vuelve-).
ROOT: **volv-** and **vuelv-,** the latter occurring *when stressed*, in the following places only:

	ROOT	1ST SING.	2ND SING.	3RD SING.	1ST PLUR.	2ND PLUR.	3RD PLUR.
STRAIGHT PRESENT	vuelv- volv-	-o	-e s	-e	-e mos	-é is	-e n
SUBJUNCTIVE PRESENT	vuelv- volv-	-a	-a s	-a	-a mos	-á is	-a n
IMPERATIVE SING. vuelve, PLUR. volved							

TYPE IIB WITH ALTERNATION -e-/-ie-/-i-. SAMPLE: sentir (siente-).
ROOT: **sent-, sient-,** and **sint-. sient-** occurs *when stressed* — and **sint-** when unstressed and followed by -a-, -ió, or -ie- — in the following places only:

	ROOT	1ST SING.	2ND SING.	3RD SING.	1ST PLUR.	2ND PLUR.	3RD PLUR.
STRAIGHT PRESENT	sient- sent-	-o	-e s	-e	-i mos	-í s	-e n
SUBJUNCTIVE PRESENT	sient- sint-	-a	-a s	-a	-a mos	-á is	-a n
PRETERITE PAST	sent- sint-	-í	-i ste	-ió	-i mos	-i steis	-ie ron
SUBJUNCTIVE PAST	sint-	-iera	-iera s	-iera	-iéra mos	-iera is	-iera n
IMPERATIVE SING. siente, PLUR. sentid				PROGRESSIVE sintiendo			

TYPE IIB WITH ALTERNATION -o-/-ue-/-u-. SAMPLE: dormir (duerme-).
ROOT: dorm-, duerm-, and durm-. duerm- occurs *when stressed* — and durm- when unstressed and followed by -a-, -ió, or -ie- — in the following places only:

	ROOT	1ST SING.	2ND SING.	3RD SING.	1ST PLUR.	2ND PLUR.	3RD PLUR.
STRAIGHT PRESENT	duerm- dorm-	-o	-e s	-e	-i mos	-í s	-e n
SUBJUNCTIVE PRESENT	duerm- durm-	-a	-a s	-a	-a mos	-á is	-a n
PRETERITE PAST	dorm- durm-	-í	-i ste	-ió	-i mos	-i steis	-ie ron
SUBJUNCTIVE PAST	durm-	-iera	-iera s	-iera	-iéra mos	-iera is	-iera n
IMPERATIVE SING. duerme, PLUR. dormid				PROGRESSIVE durmiendo			

TYPE IIB WITH ALTERNATION -e-/-i-. SAMPLE: pedir (pide-).
ROOT: ped- and pid-, the latter occurring *when stressed* and when unstressed before -a-, -ió, or -ie-, in the following places only:

	ROOT	1ST SING.	2ND SING.	3RD SING.	1ST PLUR.	2ND PLUR.	3RD PLUR.
STRAIGHT PRESENT	pid- ped-	-o	-e s	-e	-i mos	-í s	-e n
SUBJUNCTIVE PRESENT	pid-	-a	-a s	-a	-a mos	-á is	-a n
PRETERITE PAST	ped- pid-	-í	-i ste	-ió	-i mos	-i steis	-ie ron
SUBJUNCTIVE PAST	pid-	-iera	-iera s	-iera	-iéra mos	-iera is	-iera n
IMPERATIVE SING. pide, PLUR. pedid				PROGRESSIVE pidiendo			

REGULAR VERBS WITH VARIABLE SPELLING OF ROOT-FINAL CONSONANT

TYPE I WITH ROOT-FINAL K-SOUND, WRITTEN c AND qu. SAMPLE: buscar.
ROOT-SPELLINGS: busc- and busqu-, the latter occurring before -e-, in the following places only:

	ROOT	1ST SING.	2ND SING.	3RD SING.	1ST PLUR.	2ND PLUR.	3RD PLUR.
SUBJUNCTIVE PRESENT	busqu-	-e	-e s	-e	-e mos	-é is	-e n
PRETERITE PAST	busqu- busc-	-é	-a ste	-ó	-a mos	-a steis	-a ron

TYPE I WITH ROOT-FINAL G-SOUND, WRITTEN g AND **gu**. SAMPLE: **llegar**.
ROOT-SPELLINGS: **lleg-** and **llegu-**, the latter occurring before **-e-**, in the following places only:

	ROOT	1ST SING.	2ND SING.	3RD SING.	1ST PLUR.	2ND PLUR.	3RD PLUR.
SUBJUNCTIVE PRESENT	llegu-	-e	-e s	-e	-e mos	-é is	-e n
PRETERITE PAST	llegu- lleg-	-é	-a ste	-ó	-a mos	-a steis	-a ron

TYPE I WITH ROOT-FINAL θ-SOUND, WRITTEN z AND c. SAMPLE: **empezar (empieza-)**.
ROOT-SPELLINGS: **empez- (empiez-)** and **empec- (empiec-)**, the latter occurring before **-e-**, in the following places only:

	ROOT	1ST SING.	2ND SING.	3RD SING.	1ST PLUR.	2ND PLUR.	3RD PLUR.
SUBJUNCTIVE PRESENT	empiec- empec-	-e	-e s	-e	-e mos	-é is	-e n
PRETERITE PAST	empec- empez-	-é	-a ste	-ó	-a mos	-a steis	-a ron

TYPE II WITH ROOT-FINAL G-SOUND, WRITTEN g AND **gu**. SAMPLE: **seguir (sigue-)**.
ROOT-SPELLINGS: **segu- (sigu-)** and **sig-**, the latter occurring before **-o** and **-a-**, in the following places only:

	ROOT	1ST SING.	2ND SING.	3RD SING.	1ST PLUR.	2ND PLUR.	3RD PLUR.
STRAIGHT PRESENT	sig- sigu- segu-	-o	-e s	-e	-i mos	-í s	-e n
SUBJUNCTIVE PRESENT	sig-	-a	-a s	-a	-a mos	-á is	-a n

TYPE II WITH ROOT-FINAL θ-SOUND, WRITTEN z AND c. SAMPLE: **convencer**.
ROOT-SPELLINGS: **convenc-** and **convenz-**, the latter occurring before **-o** and **-a-**, in the following places only:

	ROOT	1ST SING.	2ND SING.	3RD SING.	1ST PLUR.	2ND PLUR.	3RD PLUR.
STRAIGHT PRESENT	convenz- convenc-	-o	-e s	-e	-e mos	-é is	-e n
SUBJUNCTIVE PRESENT	convenz-	-a	-a s	-a	-a mos	-á is	-a n

[v]

TYPE II WITH ROOT-FINAL J-SOUND, WRITTEN **j** AND **g**. Sample: **escoger.**
ROOT-SPELLINGS: **escog-** and **escoj-**, the latter occurring before **-o** and **-a-**, in the following places only:

	ROOT	1ST SING.	2ND SING.	3RD SING.	1ST PLUR.	2ND PLUR.	3RD PLUR.
STRAIGHT PRESENT	escoj- escog-	-o	-e s	-e	-e mos	-é is	-e n
SUBJUNCTIVE PRESENT	escoj-	-a	-a s	-a	-a mos	-á is	-a n

REGULAR VERBS WITH ROOT ENDING IN VOWEL

TYPE IIA. SAMPLE: **leer.**
ROOT: **le-**, with following **-ió**, **-ie-** replaced by **-yó**, **-ye-**, and following **-i-** written with accent-mark.

	ROOT	1ST SING.	2ND SING.	3RD SING.	1ST PLUR.	2ND PLUR.	3RD PLUR.
PRETERITE PAST	le-	-í	-í ste	-yó	-í mos	-í steis	-ye ron
SUBJUNCTIVE PAST		-yera	-yera s	-yera	-yéra mos	-yera is	-yera n
PROGRESSIVE **leyendo**				COMPLETIVE **leído**			

TYPE IIB WITH ROOT-FINAL **-u**. SAMPLE: **construir.**
ROOTS: **constru-** and **construy-**, the latter occurring *when stressed*, and when unstressed before **-a-**. Following **-ió**, **-ie-** replaced by **-yó**, **-ye-**.

	ROOT	1ST SING.	2ND SING.	3RD SING.	1ST PLUR.	2ND PLUR.	3RD PLUR.
STRAIGHT PRESENT	construy- constru-	-o	-e s	-e	-i mos	-í s	-e n
SUBJUNCTIVE PRESENT	construy-	-a	-a s	-a	-a mos	-á is	-a n
PRETERITE PAST	constru-	-í	-i ste	-yó	-i mos	-i steis	-ye ron
SUBJUNCTIVE PAST		-yera	-yera s	-yera	-yéra mos	-yera is	-yera n
IMPERATIVE SING. **construye**, PLUR. **construid**				PROGRESSIVE **construyendo**			

IRREGULAR VERBS

(Tenses which are regular throughout all six person-numbers are not listed.)

andar PREDICTIVE STEM — PROGRESSIVE — COMPLETIVE — IMPERATIVE SING. **anda**
ROOTS: **and-, anduv-** **andar-** **andando** **andado** PLUR. **andad**

	STEM	1ST SING.	2ND SING.	3RD SING.	1ST PLUR.	2ND PLUR.	3RD PLUR.
PRETERITE PAST	anduv-	-e	-i ste	-o	-i mos	-i steis	-ie ron
SUBJUNCTIVE PAST		-iera	-iera s	-iera	-iéra mos	-iera is	-iera n

caer

	PREDICTIVE STEM	PROGRESSIVE	COMPLETIVE	IMPERATIVE
ROOTS: **ca-, caig-**	**caer-**	**cayendo**	**caído**	SING. **cae** PLUR. **caed**

	STEM	1ST SING.	2ND SING.	3RD SING.	1ST PLUR.	2ND PLUR.	3RD PLUR.
STRAIGHT PRESENT	caig- ca-	-o	-e s	-e	-e mos	-é is	-e n
SUBJUNCTIVE PRESENT	caig-	-a	-a s	-a	-a mos	-á is	-a n

conocer

	PREDICTIVE STEM	PROGRESSIVE	COMPLETIVE	IMPERATIVE
ROOTS: **conoc-, conozc-**	**conocer-**	**conociendo**	**conocido**	SING. **conoce** PLUR. **conoced**

	STEM	1ST SING.	2ND SING.	3RD SING.	1ST PLUR.	2ND PLUR.	3RD PLUR.
STRAIGHT PRESENT	conozc- conoc-	-o	-e s	-e	-e mos	-é is	-e n
SUBJUNCTIVE PRESENT	conozc-	-a	-a s	-a	-a mos	-á is	-a n

dar

	PREDICTIVE STEM	PROGRESSIVE	COMPLETIVE	IMPERATIVE
ROOT: **d-**	**dar-**	**dando**	**dado**	SING. **da** PLUR. **dad**

	STEM	1ST SING.	2ND SING.	3RD SING.	1ST PLUR.	2ND PLUR.	3RD PLUR.
STRAIGHT PRESENT		-oy	-a s	-a	-a mos	-a is	-a n
SUBJUNCTIVE PRESENT	d-	-é	-e s	-é	-e mos	-e is	-e n
PRETERITE PAST		-í	-i ste	-ió	-i mos	-i steis	-ie ron
SUBJUNCTIVE PAST		-iera	-iera s	-iera	-iéra mos	-iera is	-iera n

decir (dice-)

	PREDICTIVE STEM	PROGRESSIVE	COMPLETIVE	IMPERATIVE
ROOTS: **dec-, dic-, dig-,** **dij-, di**	**dir-**	**diciendo**	**dicho**	SING. **di** PLUR. **decid**

	STEM	1ST SING.	2ND SING.	3RD SING.	1ST PLUR.	2ND PLUR.	3RD PLUR.
STRAIGHT PRESENT	dig- dic- dec-	-o	-e s	-e	-i mos	-í s	-e n
SUBJUNCTIVE PRESENT	dig-	-a	-a s	-a	-a mos	-á is	-a n
PRETERITE PAST	dij-	-e	-i ste	-o	-i mos	-i steis	-e ron
SUBJUNCTIVE PAST	dij-	-era	-era s	-era	-éra mos	-era is	-era n
PREDICTIVE PRESENT	dir-	-é	-á s	-á	-e mos	-é is	-á n
PREDICTIVE PAST	dir-	-ía	-ía s	-ía	-ía mos	-ía is	-ía n

estar

	PREDICTIVE STEM	PROGRESSIVE	COMPLETIVE	IMPERATIVE
ROOTS: **est-, estuv-**	**estar-**	**estando**	**estado**	SING. **está** PLUR. **estad**

	STEM	1ST SING.	2ND SING.	3RD SING.	1ST PLUR.	2ND PLUR.	3RD PLUR.
STRAIGHT PRESENT	est-	-oy	-á s	-á	-a mos	-á is	-á n
SUBJUNCTIVE PRESENT	est-	-é	-é s	-é	-e mos	-é is	-é n
PRETERITE PAST	estuv-	-e	-i ste	-o	-i mos	-i steis	-ie ron
SUBJUNCTIVE PAST	estuv-	-iera	-iera s	-iera	-iéra mos	-iera is	-iera n

haber

	PREDICTIVE STEM	PROGRESSIVE	COMPLETIVE	IMPERATIVE
ROOTS: **hab-, h-, hay-, hub-**	**habr-**	**habiendo**	**habido**	*(none)*

	STEM	1ST SING.	2ND SING.	3RD SING.	1ST PLUR.	2ND PLUR.	3RD PLUR.
STRAIGHT PRESENT	h- hab-	-e	-a s	-a	-e mos	-é is	-a n
SUBJUNCTIVE PRESENT	hay-	-a	-a s	-a	-a mos	-á is	-a n
PRETERITE PAST	hub-	-e	-i ste	-o	-i mos	-i steis	-ie ron
SUBJUNCTIVE PAST	hub-	-iera	-iera s	-iera	-iéra mos	-iera is	-iera n
PREDICTIVE PRESENT	habr-	-é	-á s	-á	-e mos	-é is	-á n
PREDICTIVE PAST	habr-	-ía	-ía s	-ía	-ía mos	-ía is	-ía n

hacer

	PREDICTIVE STEM	PROGRESSIVE	COMPLETIVE	IMPERATIVE
ROOTS: **hac- (haz), hag-, hic- (hiz-)**	**har-**	**haciendo**	**hecho**	SING. **haz** PLUR. **haced**

	STEM	1ST SING.	2ND SING.	3RD SING.	1ST PLUR.	2ND PLUR.	3RD PLUR.
STRAIGHT PRESENT	hag- hac-	-o	-e s	-e	-e mos	-é is	-e n
SUBJUNCTIVE PRESENT	hag-	-a	-a s	-a	-a mos	-á is	-a n
PRETERITE PAST	hic- hiz-	-e	-i ste	-o	-i mos	-i steis	-ie ron
SUBJUNCTIVE PAST	hic-	-iera	-iera s	-iera	-iéra mos	-iera is	-iera n
PREDICTIVE PRESENT	har-	-é	-á s	-á	-e mos	-é is	-á n
PREDICTIVE PAST	har-	-ía	-ía s	-ía	-ía mos	-ía is	-ía n

ir

	PREDICTIVE STEM	PROGRESSIVE	COMPLETIVE	IMPERATIVE
ROOTS: *none*, **v-**, **vay-**, **fu-**	**ir-**	**yendo**	**ido**	SING. **ve** PLUR. **id**

	STEM	1ST SING.	2ND SING.	3RD SING.	1ST PLUR.	2ND PLUR.	3RD PLUR.
STRAIGHT PRESENT	v-	-oy	-a s	-a	-a mos	-a is	-a n
SUBJUNCTIVE PRESENT	vay-	-a	-a s	-a	-a mos	-á is	-a n
IMPERFECT PAST	*none*	iba	iba s	iba	íba mos	iba is	iba n
PRETERITE PAST	fu-	-í	-i ste	-é	-i mos	-i steis	-e ron
SUBJUNCTIVE PAST		-era	-era s	-era	-éra mos	-era is	-era n

jugar (juega-)

	PREDICTIVE STEM	PROGRESSIVE	COMPLETIVE	IMPERATIVE
ROOTS: **jug-** (**jugu-**), **jueg-** (**juegu-**)	**jugar-**	**jugando**	**jugado**	SING. **juega** PLUR. **jugad**

	STEM	1ST SING.	2ND SING.	3RD SING.	1ST PLUR.	2ND PLUR.	3RD PLUR.
STRAIGHT PRESENT	jueg- jug-	-o	-a s	-a	-a mos	-á is	-a n
SUBJUNCTIVE PRESENT	juegu- jugu-	-e	-e s	-e	-e mos	-é is	-e n

ofrecer

	PREDICTIVE STEM	PROGRESSIVE	COMPLETIVE	IMPERATIVE
ROOTS: **ofrec-**, **ofrezc-**	**ofrecer-**	**ofreciendo**	**ofrecido**	SING. **ofrece** PLUR. **ofreced**

	STEM	1ST SING.	2ND SING.	3RD SING.	1ST PLUR.	2ND PLUR.	3RD PLUR.
STRAIGHT PRESENT	ofrezc- ofrec-	-o	-e s	-e	-e mos	-é is	-e n
SUBJUNCTIVE PRESENT	ofrezc-	-a	-a s	-a	-a mos	-á is	-a n

LIKE ofrecer: merecer, parecer, aparecer, desaparecer, agradecer, crecer.

oír

	PREDICTIVE STEM	PROGRESSIVE	COMPLETIVE	IMPERATIVE
ROOTS: **o-**, **oy-**, **oig-**	**oir-**	**oyendo**	**oído**	SING. **oye** PLUR. **oíd**

	STEM	1ST SING.	2ND SING.	3RD SING.	1ST PLUR.	2ND PLUR.	3RD PLUR.
STRAIGHT PRESENT	oig- oy- o-	-o	-e s	-e	-í mos	-í s	-e n
SUBJUNCTIVE PRESENT	oig-	-a	-a s	-a	-a mos	-á is	-a n

poder (puede-)

	PREDICTIVE STEM	PROGRESSIVE	COMPLETIVE	IMPERATIVE
ROOTS: **pod-, pued-, pud-**	podr-	pudiendo	podido	(*none*)

	STEM	1ST SING.	2ND SING.	3RD SING.	1ST PLUR.	2ND PLUR.	3RD PLUR.
PRETERITE PAST	pud-	-e	-i ste	-o	-i mos	-i steis	-ie ron
SUBJUNCTIVE PAST		-iera	-iera s	-iera	-iéra mos	-iera is	-iera n
PREDICTIVE PRESENT	podr-	-é	-á s	-á	-e mos	-é is	-á n
PREDICTIVE PAST		-ía	-ía s	-ía	-ía mos	-ía is	-ía n

poner

	PREDICTIVE STEM	PROGRESSIVE	COMPLETIVE	IMPERATIVE
ROOTS: **pon-, pong-, pus-**	pondr-	poniendo	puesto	SING. **pon** PLUR. **poned**

	STEM	1ST SING.	2ND SING.	3RD SING.	1ST PLUR.	2ND PLUR.	3RD PLUR.
STRAIGHT PRESENT	pong- pon-	-o	-e s	-e	-e mos	-é is	-e n
SUBJUNCTIVE PRESENT	pong-	-a	-a s	-a	-a mos	-á is	-a n
PRETERITE PAST	pus-	-e	-i ste	-o	-i mos	-i steis	-ie ron
SUBJUNCTIVE PAST		-iera	-iera s	-iera	-iéra mos	-iera is	-iera n
PREDITIVE PRESENT	pondr-	-é	-á s	-á	-e mos	-é is	-á n
PREDICTIVE PAST		-ía	-ía s	-ía	-ía mos	-ía is	-ía n

LIKE **poner**: **proponer, suponer,** and all others having final shape **-poner.**

producir

	PREDICTIVE STEM	PROGRESSIVE	COMPLETIVE	IMPERATIVE
ROOTS: **produc-, produzc-, produj-**	producir-	produciendo	producido	SING. **produce** PLUR. **producid**

	STEM	1ST SING.	2ND SING.	3RD SING.	1ST PLUR.	2ND PLUR.	3RD PLUR.
STRAIGHT PRESENT	producz- produc-	-o	-e s	-e	-i mos	-í s	-e n
SUBJUNCTIVE PRESENT	produzc-	-a	-a s	-a	-a mos	-á is	-a n
PRETERITE PAST	produj-	-e	-i ste	-o	-i mos	-i steis	-e ron
SUBJUNCTIVE PAST		-era	-era s	-era	-éra mos	-era is	-era n

LIKE **producir**: all verbs having final shape **-ducir.**

[x]

querer (quiere-)

ROOTS: **quer-, quier-, quis-**

	PREDICTIVE STEM	PROGRESSIVE	COMPLETIVE	IMPERATIVE
	querr-	queriendo	querido	SING. **quiere** PLUR. **quered**

	STEM	1ST SING.	2ND SING.	3RD SING.	1ST PLUR.	2ND PLUR.	3RD PLUR.
PRETERITE PAST	quis-	-e	-i ste	-o	-i mos	-i steis	-ie ron
SUBJUNCTIVE PAST		-iera	-iera s	-iera	-iéra mos	-iera is	-iera n
PREDICTIVE PRESENT	querr-	-é	-á s	-á	-e mos	-é is	-á n
PREDICTIVE PAST		-ía	-ía s	-ía	-ía mos	-ía is	-ía n

reír (ríe-)

ROOTS: **re-, ri-(rí-)**

	PREDICTIVE STEM	PROGRESSIVE	COMPLETIVE	IMPERATIVE
	reir-	riendo	reído	SING. **ríe** PLUR. **reíd**

	STEM	1ST SING.	2ND SING.	3RD SING.	1ST PLUR.	2ND PLUR.	3RD PLUR.
STRAIGHT PRESENT	rí- re-	-o	-e s	-e	-í mos	-í s	-e n
SUBJUNCTIVE PRESENT	rí- ri-	-a	-a s	-a	-a mos	-a is	-a n
PRETERITE PAST	re- ri-	-í	-í ste	-ó	-í mos	-í steis	-e ron
SUBJUNCTIVE PAST	ri-	-era	-era s	-era	-éra mos	-era is	-era n

LIKE **reír**: sonreír.

saber

ROOTS: **sab-, s-, sep-, sup-**

	PREDICTIVE STEM	PROGRESSIVE	COMPLETIVE	IMPERATIVE
	sabr-	sabiendo	sabido	SING. **sabe** PLUR. **sabed**

	STEM	1ST SING.	2ND SING.	3RD SING.	1ST PLUR.	2ND PLUR.	3RD PLUR.
STRAIGHT PRESENT	s- sab-	-é	-e s	-e	-e mos	é is	-e n
SUBJUNCTIVE PRESENT	sep-	-a	-a s	-a	-a mos	-á is	-a n
PRETERITE PAST	sup-	-e	-i ste	-o	-i mos	-i steis	-ie ron
SUBJUNCTIVE PAST		-iera	-iera s	-iera	-iéra mos	-iera is	-iera n
PREDICTIVE PRESENT	sabr-	-é	-á s	-á	-e mos	-é is	-á n
PREDICTIVE PAST		-ía	-ía s	-ía	-ía mos	-ía is	-ía n

salir   PREDICTIVE STEM   PROGRESSIVE   COMPLETIVE   IMPERATIVE

ROOTS: **sal-, salg-**   **saldr-**   saliendo   salido   SING. **sal**   PLUR. **salid**

	STEM	1ST SING.	2ND SING.	3RD SING.	1ST PLUR.	2ND PLUR.	3RD PLUR.
STRAIGHT PRESENT	salg- sal-	-o	-e s	-e	-i mos	-í s	-e n
SUBJUNCTIVE PRESENT	salg-	-a	-a s	-a	-a mos	-á is	-a n
PREDICTIVE PRESENT	saldr-	-é	-á s	-á	-e mos	-é is	-á n
PREDICTIVE PAST		-ía	-ía s	-ía	-ía mos	-ía is	-ía n

ser   PREDICTIVE STEM   PROGRESSIVE   COMPLETIVE   IMPERATIVE

ROOTS: **s-, se-,** *none,* **fu-**   **ser-**   siendo   sido   SING. **sé**   PLUR. **sed**

	STEM	1ST SING.	2ND SING.	3RD SING.	1ST PLUR.	2ND PLUR.	3RD PLUR.
STRAIGHT PRESENT	s- *none*	-oy	ere s	es	-o mos	-o is	-o n
SUBJUNCTIVE PRESENT	se-	-a	-a s	-a	-a mos	-á is	-a n
IMPERFECT PAST	*none*	era	era s	era	éra mos	era is	era n
PRETERITE PAST	fu-	-í	-i ste	-é	-i mos	-i steis	-e ron
SUBJUNCTIVE PAST		-era	-era s	-era	-éra mos	-era is	-era n

tener (tiene-)   PREDICTIVE STEM   PROGRESSIVE   COMPLETIVE   IMPERATIVE

ROOTS: **ten-, tien-, teng-, tuv-**   **tendr-**   teniendo   tenido   SING. **ten**   PLUR. **tened**

	STEM	1ST SING.	2ND SING.	3RD SING.	1ST PLUR.	2ND PLUR.	3RD PLUR.
STRAIGHT PRESENT	teng- tien- ten-	-o	-e s	-e	-e mos	-é is	-e n
SUBJUNCTIVE PRESENT	teng-	-a	-a s	-a	-a mos	-á is	-a n
PRETERITE PAST	tuv-	-e	-i ste	-o	-i mos	-i steis	-ie ron
SUBJUNCTIVE PAST		-iera	-iera s	-iera	-iéra mos	-iera is	-iera n
PREDICTIVE PRESENT	tendr-	-é	-á s	-á	-e mos	-é is	-á n
PREDICTIVE PAST		-ía	-ía s	-ía	-ía mos	-ía is	-ía n

LIKE **tener**: **contener, detener,** and all others having the final shape **-tener.**

traer

	PREDICTIVE STEM	PROGRESSIVE	COMPLETIVE	IMPERATIVE
ROOTS: tra-, traig-, traj-	traer-	trayendo	traído	SING. **trae** PLUR. **traed**

	STEM	1ST SING.	2ND SING.	3RD SING.	1ST PLUR.	2ND PLUR.	3RD PLUR.
STRAIGHT PRESENT	traig- tra-	-o	-e s	-e	-e mos	-é is	-e n
SUBJUNCTIVE PRESENT	traig-	-a	-a s	-a	-a mos	-á is	-a n
PRETERITE PAST	traj-	-e	-i ste	-o	-i mos	-i steis	-e ron
SUBJUNCTIVE PAST		-era	-era s	-era	-éra mos	-era is	-era n

valer

	PREDICTIVE STEM	PROGRESSIVE	COMPLETIVE	IMPERATIVE
ROOTS: val-, valg-	valdr-	valiendo	valido	SING. **val** PLUR. **valed**

	STEM	1ST SING.	2ND SING.	3RD SING.	1ST PLUR.	2ND PLUR.	3RD PLUR.
STRAIGHT PRESENT	valg- val-	-o	-e s	-e	-e mos	-é is	-e n
SUBJUNCTIVE PRESENT	valg-	-a	-a s	-a	-a mos	-á is	-a n
PREDICTIVE PRESENT	valdr-	-é	-á s	-á	-e mos	-é is	-á n
PREDICTIVE PAST		-ía	-ía s	-ía	-ía mos	-ía is	-ía n

venir (viene-)

	PREDICTIVE STEM	PROGRESSIVE	COMPLETIVE	IMPERATIVE
ROOTS: ven-, vien-, veng-, vin-	vendr-	viniendo	venido	SING. **ven** PLUR. **venid**

	STEM	1ST SING.	2ND SING.	3RD SING.	1ST PLUR.	2ND PLUR.	3RD PLUR.
STRAIGHT PRESENT	veng- vien- ven-	-o	-e s	-e	-i mos	-í s	-e n
SUBJUNCTIVE PRESENT	veng-	-a	-a s	-a	-a mos	-á is	-a n
PRETERITE PAST	vin-	-e	-i ste	-o	-i mos	-i steis	-ie ron
SUBJUNCTIVE PAST		-iera	-iera s	-iera	-iéra mos	-iera is	-iera n
PREDICTIVE PRESENT	vendr-	-é	-á s	-á	-e mos	-é is	-á n
PREDICTIVE PAST		-ía	-ía s	-ía	-ía mos	-ía is	-ía n

LIKE **venir**: **convenir, intervenir** and all others having the final shape **-venir.**

ver

ROOTS: **v-, ve-**

	PREDICTIVE STEM	PROGRESSIVE	COMPLETIVE	IMPERATIVE
	ver-	**viendo**	**visto**	SING. **ve** PLUR. **ved**

	STEM	1ST SING.	2ND SING.	3RD SING.	1ST PLUR.	2ND PLUR.	3RD PLUR.
STRAIGHT PRESENT	ve- v-	-o	-e s	-e	-e mos	-e is	-e n
SUBJUNCTIVE PRESENT	ve-	-a	-a s	-a	-a mos	-á is	-a n
IMPERFECT PAST		-ía	-ías s	-ía	-ía mos	-ía is	-ía n

VERBS IRREGULAR ONLY IN COMPLETIVE FORM
(*Past Participle*)

abrir: **abierto**
cubrir: **cubierto**
descubrir: **descubierto**
devolver (devuelve-): **devuelto**

escribir: **escrito**
morir (muere-): **muerto**
romper: **roto**
volver (vuelve-): **vuelto**

PERSONAL PRONOUNS
VERB-OBJECT SERIES

	FUNCTION		SING.	PLUR.
1ST PERSON			me	nos
2ND PERSON			te	os
3RD PERSON	INDIRECT OBJECT		le	les
	DIRECT OBJECT	MASCULINE	lo *or* le	los *or* les
		FEMININE	la	las
		GENDERLESS	lo	
	REFLEXIVE OBJECT		se	

GRAMMAR APPENDIX

Supplementary Series

			Subject	Object
1st Person	Singular		yo	mí
	Plural	Masculine	nosotros	
		Feminine	nosotras	
2nd Person	Singular		tú	ti
	Plural	Masculine	vosotros	
		Feminine	vosotras	
3rd Person	Singular	Masculine	él	
		Feminine	ella	
		Genderless	ello	
		Courtesy Title	usted	
	Plural	Masculine	ellos	
		Feminine	ellas	
		Courtesy Title	ustedes	
Reflexive			*(none)*	sí

POSSESSIVES

Person-Number of Possessor	Full Forms				Shortened Forms	
	Sing.		Plur.		Sing.	Plur.
	Masc.	Fem.	Masc.	Fem.		
1st Sing.	mío	mía	míos	mías	mi	mis
1st Plur.	nuestro	nuestra	nuestros	nuestras	*(does not shorten)*	
2nd Sing.	tuyo	tuya	tuyos	tuyas	tu	tus
2nd Plur.	vuestro	vuestra	vuestros	vuestras	*(does not shorten)*	
3rd *(both)*	suyo	suya	suyos	suyas	su	sus

SPANISH–ENGLISH VOCABULARY

A

a *preposition* to, etc.
abajo downstairs
abandonar to abandon, desert
abierto (*see* abrir)
abrazar to embrace
abrazo embrace
el abril April
abrir to open
absoluto absolute
abuelo, -la grandfather, grandmother
aburrido boring
aburrir to bore
abuso abuse
acá here
acabar to finish
acento accent
aceptar to accept
acercarse to approach, come near
acompañar to accompany
aconsejar to advise
acordarse (acuerda-) to remember
acostarse (acuesta-) to lie down,
  go to bed
acostumbrarse to get accustomed, get used
la actividad activity
acuerdo accord, agreement
adelante forward
además besides
adiós good-bye
adivinar to guess
admirable admirable
admirar to admire
aeropuerto airport
afeitar to shave
aficionarse to become fond
afuera outside
agosto August
agradable pleasant, agreeable
agradecer to thank for
agua water
ahí there
ahora now
el aire libre open air
al = a + el

alabar to praise
alegrarse to be glad
alegre gay, merry
algo something
alguien somebody, someone
alguno (algún) some
almorzar (almuerza-) to have
  lunch
almuerzo lunch
alquilar to hire, rent
alto high; loud; tall
allá there
allí there
amable kind, agreeable
amigo, -ga friend
andar to walk, go
anoche last night
anteayer day before yesterday
antes before
antiguo ancient, old
anunciar to announce
añadir to add
año year
aparecer to appear
apellido last name
apenas hardly; as soon as
apetito appetite
apostar (apuesta-) to bet
apreciar to appreciate
aprender to learn
aprovechar to profit by, take
  advantage of
apurarse to hurry
apuro predicament
aquel, -lla, -llo (aquél, etc.)
  demonstrative that
aquí here
el árbol tree
el arte art
arreglar to arrange
arriba upstairs
el arroz rice
asegurar to assure
así thus, so
asomarse to appear
asombrar to amaze
asunto matter, subject
asustar to scare, frighten
la atención attention

atreverse to dare
aumentar to increase, gain
aun even
aunque although
el autobús bus
el autor author
avenida avenue
aventura adventure
el avión airplane
avisar to notify
ayer yesterday
ayudar to help
azul blue

B

bailar to dance
bajo low
el balcón balcony
bañar to bathe
barato cheap
barbaridad: qué barbaridad *exclamation*
bastante rather, quite
bastar to suffice, be enough
beca scholarship
biblioteca library
bien well
el bigote moustache
el billete bill
el bisté steak
blanco white
blando soft
boleto ticket
la bondad goodness, kindness
bonito pretty
botella bottle
bravo angry
brazo arm
breve brief, short
brindar to toast, drink to
broma joke
bueno (buen) good
buscar to look for

C

caballero gentleman
cabeza head

cabo end
cada each, every
caer to fall; to suit, appeal to
el café coffee
los calcetines socks
caliente hot, warm
el calor heat
callarse to be quiet, stop talking
la calle street
cama bed
cambiar to change
cambio change
camino road
campo country; field
cansar to tire
cantar to sing
la capacidad capacity, ability
el carácter character
característico characteristic
caramba *exclamation*
caray: qué caray *exclamation*
caro expensive
carta letter
cartera handbag
casa house
casarse to get married
casi almost
caso case
catorce fourteen
celebrar to celebrate
centavo cent
central central
centro centre
cerca near
cerrar (cierra-) to shut, close
científico scientific
ciento (cien) hundred
cierto certain, sure
cinco five
cincuenta fifty
el cine cinema
cita date
la ciudad city
claro clear; of course
la clase class; kind
el clima climate
el coche car
cola line, queue
colina hill
el color colour
comedia comedy
comer to eat
comida food; dinner

como like
cómo how
cómodo comfortable
compañero companion
compañía company
completo complete
la complicación complication
complicar to complicate
comprar to buy
común common
comunicarse to communicate, get in touch
con *preposition* with, etc.
conducta conduct, behaviour
confundir to confuse
conmigo = con + mí
conocer to know
conozca-, -zco (*see* conocer)
conque so
conseguir (consigue-) to obtain, get
consejo advice
consentir (consiente-) to consent, agree
consigo = con + sí
construir to construct, build
contacto contact
contar (cuenta-) to count; to relate, tell
contener (contiene-) to contain
contentarse to be satisfied
contento happy
contestar to answer, reply
contigo = con + ti
contrario contrary
convencer to convince
convenir (conviene-) to be worth while
corbata necktie
cortar to cut
cortesía politeness
corto short
correcto correct
corregir (corrige-) to correct
correr to run
corriente current
cosa thing
costar (cuesta-) to cost
la costumbre custom
crecer to grow
creer to believe, think
criada maid
crítica criticism

criticar to criticize
cruzar to cross
cuál which
cualquier any
cuando (cuándo) when
de vez en cuando from time to time
cuánto how much, how many
cuantos: unos cuantos a few
cuarenta forty
cuarto fourth; quarter; room
cuatro four
cuatrocientos four hundred
cuenta account
darse cuenta to realize
cuento story
cuerpo body
la cuestión question
cuidado care
cuidar to take care of
culpa fault
cultura culture
cultural cultural
el cumpleaños birthday
cuota quota, load
la curiosidad curiosity

CH

chica girl
chileno Chilean
chiquito little, tiny
el chiste joke, gag
el chofer driver, chauffeur

D

dama lady
dar to give
de *preposition* of, from, etc.
debajo under
deber must, ought
deberse to be due
débil weak
la debilidad weakness
decidir to decide
decir (dice-) to say
dedo finger
defender (defiende-) to defend
dejar to let, allow; to leave; to stop, quit
no dejar not to fail
del = de + el

delicado delicate
demás: los demás the rest, the others
demasiado too much
dentro within
derecha right (*opposite of left*)
derecho right
desaparecer to disappear
desayunarse to have breakfast
desayuno breakfast
descansar to rest
desconocido unknown
la descripción description
descubrir to discover
desde *preposition* from, etc.
   desde luego of course
desear to wish, desire
deseo desire
desocupar to vacate, move out of
despedirse (despide-) to take leave
despertar (despierta-) to wake up
despierto awake
después after
el detalle detail
detener (detiene-) to detain, hold up
detrás behind
devolver (devuelve-) to return, give back
di (*see* decir)
dí, di- (*see* dar)
el día day
diálogo dialogue
el diciembre December
dicho (*see* decir)
el diente tooth
diez ten
diferencia difference
difícil difficult, hard
la dificultad difficulty
diga-, -go (*see* decir)
dij- (*see* decir)
dinero money
Dios God
diplomático diplomatic
dir- (*see* decir)
la dirección direction
directo direct
discurso speech, talk
la discusión discussion
disgustar to displease

distancia distance
distinguir to distinguish
distinto different
divertido amusing, fun
divertirse (divierte-) to enjoy oneself
dividir to divide
doce twelve
doler (duele-) to ache, hurt
el dolor ache, pain
domingo Sunday
dónde where
dormir (duerme-) to sleep
dos two
doscientos two hundred
doy (*see* dar)
duda doubt
dudar to doubt
dueño owner, master
los dulces sweets
durante *preposition* during
durar to last
duro hard

E

echar to toss
la edad age
edificio building
educado: mal educado ill-mannered
ejemplo example
el *article* the
él *pronoun* he, him
elegante elegant
ella *pronoun* she, her
ellos, -as *pronoun* they, them
embargo: sin embargo however
empeñarse to insist, be anxious
empezar (empieza-) to begin, start
en *preposition* in, etc.
enamorarse to fall in love
encantar to delight
encanto delight
encargarse to take charge
encerrar (encierra-) to enclose, confine
encima on top
encontrar (encuentra-) to meet; to find
enemigo enemy
enero January

enfermo sick, ill
enojarse to get angry
enseñar to show; to teach
entender (entiende-) to understand
entero entire, whole
entonces then
entrar to enter, go in; to fit
entre *preposition* between, among
entregar to deliver
entusiasmo enthusiasm
época period
la equivocación mistake
equivocarse to be mistaken
eres (*see* ser)
el error mistake
es (*see* ser)
el escaparate show window
escapar(se) to escape
escena scene
escocés, -esa Scotch
escoger to choose, to pick
escribir to write
escrito (*see* escribir)
escuchar to listen
escuela school
ese, esa, eso (ése, etc.) *demonstrative* that
esfuerzo effort
español, -ola Spanish
especial special
especializarse to specialize
esperar to wait; to expect; to hope
esposa wife
esquina corner
la estación season; station
Estados Unidos United States
estar to be
este, esta, esto (éste, etc.) *demonstrative* this
estimar to esteem
el estudiante student
estudiar to study
estuv- (*see* estar)
evitar to avoid
exacto exact
exagerar to exaggerate
excelente excellent
la excursión excursion, tour
existir to exist
experiencia experience
la explicación explanation

explicar to explain
expresar to express
la expresión expression
extranjero foreign
extrañar to surprise; to miss

F

fácil easy
facilitar to facilitate, make easy
falta fail; lack
faltar to be lacking
fama reputation, fame
familia family
familiar family
famoso famous
farmaceutico pharmacist
farmacia pharmacy
el favor favor
febrero February
fecha date
felicitar to congratulate
feliz happy
fenomenal phenomenal
feo ugly
fiesta party
fijarse to notice
fijo fixed, set
el fin end
el final end
fino polite
firmar to sign
la flor flower
fondo: a fondo thoroughly
forma form
formal formal
formidable wonderful
fortuna fortune
fotografía photograph, picture
francés, -esa French
la frase sentence
frecuencia frequency
frente: en frente across, opposite
fresco cool
frío cold
frito fried
fué, fue- (see ser or ir)
fuí, fui- (see ser or ir)
fuera outside
fuerte strong
furioso furious

G

gana wish, desire
ganar to earn; to win
gastar to spend
gastos expenses
general general
la gente people
el gerente manager
gobierno government
el golpe blow
gracia amusement
gracias thanks
gracioso funny
gramatical grammatical
grande (gran) large, big
grave grave, serious
grupo group
guerra war
guía guide, guidebook
guitarra guitar
gustar to please
gusto pleasure; taste

H

ha- (see haber)
haber to have
el habitante inhabitant
hablar to speak, talk
habr- (see haber)
hacer to make; to do
haga-, -go (see hacer)
hambre hunger
har- (see hacer)
hasta preposition until, etc.
  adverb even
hay there is, there are
haz (see hacer)
he, hemos (see haber)
hemisferio hemisphere
hecho (see hacer)
hermano, -na brother, sister
hermoso beautiful
hic- (see hacer)
hielo ice
hijo, -ja son, daughter
hispano Hispanic, Spanish
historia history
hizo (see hacer)
hola hello
hombre man
hora hour

horrible horrible
el hospital hospital
el hotel hotel
hoy today
huevo egg
el humor humour, mood
el humorista humorist

I

idea idea
ideal ideal
el idioma language
iglesia church
igual equal
imaginar(se) to imagine
imaginario imaginary
imitar to imitate
impersonal impersonal
importancia importance
importante important
importar to matter
imposible impossible
la impresión impression
impresionar to impress
incorrecto incorrect
independencia independence
independiente independent
indicar to indicate, point
indio Indian
industria industry
la información information
ingenioso ingenious
inglés, -esa English
insistir to insist
inspirar to inspire
inteligente intelligent
intercambio interchange, exchange
el interés interest
interesante interesting
interesar to interest
internacional international
intervenir (interviene-) to intervene, interfere
interrumpir to interrupt
íntimo intimate
inútil useless
inventar to invent
invierno winter
la invitación invitation
invitar to invite
ir to go

italiano Italian
itinerario itinerary
izquierda left

J

el jamón ham
joven young
el jueves Thursday
jugar (juega-) to play
jugo juice
julio July
junio June
juntar to assemble, collect
juntos together

K

kilómetro kilometer

L

la, las *article* the
lado side
largo long
lástima shame, pity
lastimar to hurt
latino Latin
le *3rd-person pronoun*
la lección lesson
la leche milk
leer to read
lejos far
letra letter
levantarse to rise, get up
libra pound
libro book
limpio clean
lista menu
literatura literature
lo *article* the
lo *3rd-person pronoun*
loco mad
loro parrot
los *article* the
luego later
desde luego of course
el lugar place
el lunes Monday
la luz light

LL

llamar to call
llegar to arrive

lleno full
llevar to carry, take
llorar to weep, cry
llover (llueve-) to rain
lluvia rain

M

madre mother
magnífico magnificent, wonderful
mal *adjective* (*see* malo)
    adverb badly
malentendido misunderstanding
malo bad
malteado malted
mamá mother
mandar to order; to send
manera way, manner
la mano hand
manzana apple
mañana morning; tomorrow
el mar sea, ocean
maravilla marvel, wonder
marinero sailor
el martes Tuesday
marzo March
más more, most
matar to kill
materno maternal
mayo May
mayor larger, largest
me *pronoun* me, etc.
medicina medicine
médico doctor
medida measure, step
medio half
el mediodía noon
mejor better, best
memoria memory
la mención mention
menor smaller, smallest
menos less, least
mentira lie
merecer to deserve
merezca-, -zco (*see* merecer)
el mes month
mesa table
meterse to put oneself; to inter-
    fere, meddle
método method
mexicano Mexican
mi *possessive* my, etc.
mí *pronoun* me
miedo fear

mientras while
    mientras tanto meanwhile
el miércoles Wednesday
mil thousand
milagro miracle
el millón million
minuto minute
mío *possessive* my, mine
mirada look
mirar to look
misa mass, church service
mismo same
misterioso mysterious
la mitad half
moderno modern
modismo idiom
modo way
molestar to bother, annoy
momento moment
mono cute
monótono monotonous
el montón pile, heap
morir (muere-) to die
mosquito mosquito
mover (mueve-) to move
mozo waiter
muchacho, -cha boy, girl
mucho much, many
mujer woman
mundo world
museo museum
música music
muy very

N

nada nothing
nadar to swim
nadie nobody, no one
naranja orange
necesario necessary
la necesidad need
necesitar to need
negar (niega-) to deny
negocios business
negro black
nervioso nervous
ni nor
la nieve snow
ninguno (ningún) no, none
niño, -ña child
no no, not
la noche night
el nombre name

el **norte** north
norteamericano North American
nos *pronoun* us, etc.
nosotros, -tras *pronoun* we, us
notar to note, notice
noticias news
novecientos nine hundred
noventa ninety
el **noviembre** November
novio, -ia boy-friend, girl-friend
nuestro *possessive* our, ours
nueve nine
nuevo new
número number
numeroso numerous
nunca never

O

o or
el **octubre** October
ocupado busy
ocupar to occupy, take up
ocuparse to take care
ocurrir to occur
ochenta eighty
ocho eight
ofender to offend
oficina office
ofrecer to offer
ofrezca-, -zco (*see* **ofrecer**)
oiga-, -go (*see* **oír**)
oír to hear
ojalá *exclamation* I hope, I wish, etc.
ojo eye
olvidar to forget
omitir to omit
once eleven
la **opinión** opinion
la **oportunidad** opportunity, chance
opuesto opposite
la **orden** order
organizar to organize
oro gold
oscuro dark
otoño autumn, fall
otro other
oye- (*see* **oír**)

P

padre father
pagar to pay
página page

el **país** country
palabra word
el **pan** bread
papá Dad
papas potatoes
el **papel** paper; role
el **par** pair
para *preposition* for etc.
parar to stop
parecer to seem
el **pariente** relative
particular private
pasado past, last
pasar to pass, spend; to happen
paseo drive
paso step
el **pastel** pie
paterno paternal
la **paz** peace
pedir (pide-) to ask, ask for, order
pegar to hit
pelearse to fight
película movie, picture
peligro danger
peligroso dangerous
pelo hair
pena sorrow; trouble
pensar (piensa-) to think; to intend, plan
peor worse, worst
pequeño small, little
perder (pierde-) to lose
perdonar to pardon
perfecto perfect
periódico newspaper
permitir to permit, allow
pero but
persona person
el **personaje** personage, figure
peruano Peruvian
perro dog
pesado heavy
pesar: a pesar in spite
pico a little bit
el **pie** foot
piso floor
el **placer** pleasure
plata silver
playa beach
pluma fuente fountain pen
pobre poor
poco little, few

poder (puede-) to be able, can
podr- (*see* **poder**)
policía police
pon (*see* **poner**)
pondr- (*see* **poner**)
poner to put
ponerse to become
ponga-, -go (*see* **poner**)
por *preposition* by, etc.
porque because
portarse to behave
posible possible
practicar to practice
precio price
preciso precise, **exact**
preferir (prefiere-) to prefer
pregunta question
preguntar to ask
preguntarse to wonder
preocuparse to worry, be concerned
preparar to prepare
presentar to present, introduce
prestar to lend
primario primary
primavera spring
primero (primer) first
primo, -ma cousin
principal principal, **main**
principio beginning
prisa hurry
probable probable, likely
probar (prueba-) to try
el **problema** problem
producir to produce
profesor, -ora teacher, professor
prohibir to prohibit, forbid
prometer to promise
pronto soon
pronunciar to pronounce
propio own
proponer to propose, suggest
propósito: a propósito by the way; on purpose
proteger to protect
próximo next
psicología psychology
pud- (*see* **poder**)
pueblo town; people
puerta door
puerto port, waterfront
pues well
punto point

la puntualidad punctuality
pus- (*see* poner)

Q

que *conjunction* that
   preposition than, etc.
qué what
quedar(se) to stay, to remain
quejarse to complain
querer (quiere-) to want
querido dear
querr- (*see* querer)
queso cheese
qué va not at all
quién who
quince fifteen
quinientos five hundred
quis- (*see* querer)
quitar to remove, take off

R

rápido rapid, fast
raqueta racket
raro rare, strange
   raras veces seldom
rato while
la razón rightness; reason
razonable reasonable, sensible
la reacción reaction
la realidad reality
recado message
recibir to receive
recoger to pick up
recordar (recuerda-) to recall,
   remember
recuerdo memory
refrescos refreshments
regalo gift, present
regañar to scold, reprimand
regla rule
reír (ríe-) to laugh
la relación relation
el reloj watch
remediar to remedy
remedio remedy
repasar to review
reservar to reserve
resistir to resist
la responsabilidad responsibility
el restaurante restaurant
reunirse to meet, gather

revuelto scrambled
rico rich, delicious
río river
rojo red
romántico romantic
romper to break
ropa clothing, clothes
rubio blond
ruido noise

S

sábado Saturday
saber to know
sabr- (*see* saber)
sabroso delicious, flavorful
sacar to take out
sala room
saldr- (*see* salir)
salga-, -go (*see* salir)
salir to go out
la salud health
saludar to greet
saludo greeting
el sándwich sandwich
la sangre blood
santo, -ta saint
se *reflexive 3rd-person pronoun*
sé (*see* saber)
sea- (*see* ser)
seco dry
secreto secret
secundario secondary
la sed thirst
seguida: en seguida at once, immediately
seguir (sigue-) to follow, come
   next
segundo second
la seguridad sureness, certainty
seguro sure
seis six
semana week
sencillo simple
sentarse (sienta-) to sit down
sentir (siente-) to feel; to regret, be sorry
señor Mr., sir; gentleman
señora Mrs., madam; lady; wife
señorita Miss; young lady
el septiembre September
ser to be
serenata serenade

serio serious
servicio service
servidor, -ora servant
servir (sirve-) to serve
sesenta sixty
setecientos seven hundred
setenta seventy
si if
sí yes
sí *reflexive 3rd-person pronoun*
siempre always
siete seven
siglo century
siguiente following
simpático nice
sin *preposition* without
sino but
el sistema system
la situación situation
sobre *preposition* on, above, etc.
social social
el sol sun
solo alone
sólo only
soltero bachelor
sombrero hat
somos, son (*see* ser)
sonar (suena-) to sound
sonreír (sonríe-) to smile
soñar (sueña-) to dream
soy (*see* ser)
su *3rd-person possessive*
subir to go up, get on
suceder to happen
sudamericano South American
sueño sleepiness
la suerte luck
suficiente sufficient, enough
sup- (*see* saber)
superior superior
suponer to suppose, presume
el sur south
suyo *3rd-person possessive*

T

el tacón heel
tal: con tal provided
   qué tal how
   tal vez perhaps
también also, too
tampoco neither
tan so

tanto so much, so many
tardar to delay
tarde late
la tarde afternoon
el taxi taxi
taza cup
te *pronoun* you, etc.
teléfono telephone
el telegrama telegram
temer to fear
temprano early
ten (*see* **tener**)
tendr- (*see* **tener**)
tener (**tiene-**) to have
tenga-, -go (*see* **tener**)
el tenis tennis
tercero (**tercer**) third
el terminal terminal
terminar to finish
término term
ti *pronoun* you
tiempo time; weather
tienda store
tierra land
tío, tía uncle, aunt
tipo guy
titular to entitle
tocar to play
tocino bacon
todavía yet
todo all, whole
tomar to take; to drink.
tonterías nonsense
tonto fool
tostadas toast
trabajar to work
trabajo work
el trabalenguas tongue-twister
traer to bring
traj- (*see* **traer**)
el traje suit
tranquilo tranquil, quiet
el tranvía street car

tratar to try; to treat, to deal
tratarse to be a question
trato deal
trece thirteen
treinta thirty
el tren train
tres three
triste sad
tropezar (**tropieza-**) to meet up
trópico tropics
tu *possessive* your, etc.
tú *pronoun* you
el turista tourist
tuv- (*see* **tener**)
tuyo *possessive* your, yours

U

último last
único only
uno (**un**) one; *article* a, etc.
usar to use, wear
uso usage
usted you
útil useful

V

va- (*see* **ir**)
las vacaciones vacation
valer to be worth
el valor value
varios various, several
vaso glass
vaya- (*see* **ir**)
ve (*see* **ir**)
vea-, veo (*see* **ver**)
vecino neighbor
veinte twenty
ven (*see* **venir**)
vender to sell
venga-, -go (*see* **venir**)
venir (**viene-**) to come

ventaja advantage
ventana window
ver to see
verano summer
veras: de veras truly, really
verbo verb
la verdad truth
verde green
vestido dress
vestir (**viste-**) to dress
la vez time
en vez instead
viajar to travel
el viaje trip
vida life
viejo old
viento wind
el viernes Friday
vin- (*see* **venir**)
vino wine
visita visit
visitar to visit
vista sight
visto (*see* **ver**)
vivir to live
vivo alive
volar (**vuela-**) to fly
volver (**vuelve-**) to return, go
back, come back
voy (*see* **ir**)
la voz voice
vuelta walk
de vuelta back

Y

y and
ya already
yo *pronoun* I

Z

zapato shoe

ENGLISH–SPANISH VOCABULARY

A

a uno (un)
to abandon abandonar
ability (la) capacidad
able: to be able poder (puede-)[x]
absolute absoluto
abuse abuso
accent acento
to accept aceptar
to accompany acompañar
account cuenta
accustomed: to get accustomed
    acostumbrarse
ache (el) dolor
to ache doler (duele-)
across en frente
activity (la) actividad
to add añadir
admirable admirable
to admire admirar
advantage ventaja
    to take advantage of aprove-
    char
adventure aventura
advice consejo
to advise aconsejar
after después
afternoon (la) tarde
age (la) edad
to agree estar de acuerdo
    to agree to consentir (con-
    siente-) en
agreeable agradable; amable
air (el) aire
airplane (el) avión
airport aeropuerto
alive vivo
all todo
to allow dejar; permitir
almost casi
alone solo
already ya
also también
although aunque
always siempre
to amaze asombrar
amusement gracia
amusing divertido

ancient antiguo
and y
angry bravo
    to get angry enojarse
to announce anunciar
to annoy molestar
to answer contestar, contestar a
anxious: to be anxious to em
    peñarse en
any cualquier
to appeal to caer[vi–vii] bien a
to appear aparecer[ix]; asomarse
appetite apetito
apple manzana
to appreciate apreciar
to approach acercarse
April (el) abril
arm brazo
to arrange arreglar
to arrive llegar[v]
art (el) arte
to ask (inquire) preguntar; (request)
    pedir (pide-)
to assemble juntar
to assure asegurar
attention (la) atención
August agosto
aunt tía
author (el) autor
autumn otoño
avenue avenida
to avoid evitar
awake despierto

B

bachelor soltero
back de vuelta
bacon tocino
bad malo (mal)
badly mal
balcony (el) balcón
to bathe bañar
to be estar[viii]; ser[xii]
beach playa
beautiful hermoso
because porque
to become ponerse[x]
bed cama

to go to bed acostarse
    (acuesta-)
before antes
to begin (to) empezar (empieza-)[v]
    (a)
beginning principio
to behave portarse
behaviour conducta
behind detrás
to believe creer[vi]
besides además
best mejor
to bet apostar (apuesta-)
better mejor
between entre
big grande (gran)
bill (el) billete
birthday (el) cumpleaños
black negro
blond rubio
blood (la) sangre
blow (el) golpe
blue azul
body cuerpo
book libro
to bore aburrir
boring aburrido
to bother molestar
bottle botella
boy muchacho, chico
    boy-friend novio
bread (el) pan
to break romper[xiv]
breakfast desayuno
    to have breakfast desayunarse
brief breve
to bring traer[xiii]
brother hermano
to build construir[vi]
building edificio
bus (el) autobús
business negocios
busy ocupado
but pero; sino
to buy comprar

C

to call llamar
candy (los) dulces

capacity (la) capacidad
car (el) coche
   street car tram (el) tranvía
care cuidado
   to take care of (*people*) cuidar;
   (*things*) ocuparse de
to carry llevar
case caso
to celebrate celebrar
cent centavo
center centro
central central
century siglo
certain cierto
certainty (la) seguridad
chance (la) oportunidad
change cambio
to change cambiar
character (el) carácter
characteristic característico
charge: to take charge encargarse
chauffeur (el) chofer
cheap barato
cheese queso
child niño, -ña
Chilean chileno
to choose escoger[vi]
church iglesia
   church service misa
city (la) ciudad
class (la) clase
clean limpio
clear claro
climate (el) clima
to close cerrar (cierra-)
clothes, clothing ropa
coffee (el) café
cold frío
to collect juntar
colour (el) color
to come venir (viene-)[xiii]
   to come back volver (vuelve-)[xiv]
comedy comedia
comfortable cómodo
common común
to communicate comunicarse[iv]
companion compañero, -ra
company compañía
to complain quejarse
complete completo
to complicate complicar[iv]
complication (la) complicación

concerned: to be concerned
   preocuparse
conduct conducta
to confine encerrar (encierra-)
to confuse confundir
to congratulate felicitar
to consent (to) consentir (con-
   siente-) (en)
to construct construir[vi]
contact contacto
to contain contener (contiene-)[xii]
contrary contrario
to convince convencer[v]
cool fresco
corner esquina
correct correcto
to correct corregir (corrige-)[vi]
to cost costar (cuesta-)
to count contar (cuenta-)
country (*not city*) campo; (*nation*)
   (el) país
course: of course claro; desde
   luego
cousin primo, -ma
crazy loco
criticism crítica
to criticize criticar[iv]
to cross cruzar
to cry llorar
cultural cultural
culture cultura
cup taza
curiosity (la) curiosidad
current corriente
custom (la) costumbre
to cut cortar
cute mono

D

Dad papá
to dance bailar
danger peligro
dangerous peligroso
to dare (to) atreverse (a)
dark oscuro
date (*appointment*) cita; (*calen-
   dar*) fecha
daughter hija

day (el) día
deal trato
to deal tratar
dear querido
December (el) diciembre
to decide decidir
to defend defender (defiende-)
to delay tardar
delicate delicado
delicious rico, sabroso
delight encanto
to delight encantar
to deliver entregar[v]
to deny negar (niega-)[v]
description (la) descripción
to deserve merecer[ix]
desire deseo, gana
to desire desear
detail (el) detalle
to detain detener (detiene-)[xii]
dialogue diálogo
to die morir (muere-)[xiv]
difference diferencia
different distinto
difficult difícil
difficulty (la) dificultad
dinner comida
diplomatic diplomático
direct directo
direction (la) dirección
to disappear desaparecer[ix]
to discover descubrir[xiv]
discussion (la) discusión
to displease disgustar
distance distancia
to distinguish distinguir[v]
to divide dividir
to do hacer[viii]
doctor médico
dog perro
door puerta
doubt duda
to doubt dudar
downstairs abajo
to dream soñar (sueña-)
dress vestido
to dress vestir (viste-)
to drink tomar
drive paseo
driver (el) chofer
dry seco
due: to be due deberse
during durante

E

each cada
early temprano
to earn ganar
easy fácil
 to make easy facilitar
to eat comer
effort esfuerzo
egg huevo
eight ocho
eighty ochenta
elegant elegante
eleven once
embrace abrazo
to embrace abrazar
to enclose encerrar (encierra-)
end (el) fin; (el) final; cabo
enemy enemigo, -ga
English inglés, -esa
to enjoy oneself divertirse (divierte-)
enough suficiente
 to be enough bastar
to enter entrar
enthusiasm entusiasmo
entire entero
to entitle titular
equal igual
to escape escaparse
to esteem estimar
even aun; hasta
every cada
exact preciso, exacto
to exaggerate exagerar
example ejemplo
excellent excelente
exchange cambio, intercambio
excursion (la) excursión
to exist existir
to expect esperar
expenses gastos
expensive caro
experience experiencia
to explain explicar[iv]
explanation (la) explicación
to express expresar
expression (la) expresión
eye ojo

F

to facilitate facilitar
fail falta

to fail: not to fail to no dejar de
 fall otoño
to fall caer[vi–vii]
fame fama
family (*adjective*) familiar
 (*noun*) familia
famous famoso
far lejos
fast rápido
father padre
fault culpa
favor (el) favor
fear miedo
to fear temer
February febrero
to feel sentir (siente-)
few pocos
 a few unos cuantos
field campo
fifteen quince
fifty cincuenta
to fight pelearse
figure (el) personaje
to find encontrar (encuentra-)
finger dedo
to finish terminar, acabar
first primero (primer)
to fit entrar
five cinco
 five hundred quinientos
fixed fijo
flavorful sabroso
floor piso
flower (la) flor
to fly volar (vuela-)
to follow seguir (sigue-)[v]
following siguiente
fond: to become fond of aficionarse a
food comida
fool tonto, -ta
foot (el) pie
to forbid prohibir
foreign extranjero
to forget olvidar, olvidarse de
form forma
formal formal
fortune fortuna
forty cuarenta
forward adelante
four cuatro
 four hundred cuatrocientos
fourteen catorce

fourth cuarto
French francés, -esa
frequency frecuencia
Friday (el) viernes
fried frito
friend amigo, -ga
to frighten asustar
full lleno
funny gracioso
furious furioso

G

to gain aumentar
to gather reunirse
gay alegre
general general
gentleman caballero; señor
to get conseguir (consigue-)[v]
 to get on subir
 to get up levantarse
gift regalo
girl chica, muchacha
 girl-friend novia
to give dar[vii]
 to give back devolver (de-
 vuelve-)[xiv]
glad: to be glad alegrarse
glass vaso
to go ir[ix]; andar[vi]
 to go back volver (vuelve-)[xiv]
 to go in entrar
 to go out salir[xii]
 to go up subir
God Dios
gold oro
good bueno (buen)
good-bye adiós
goodness (la) bondad
government gobierno
grammatical gramatical
grandfather, grandmother abuelo,
 -la
grave grave
green verde
to greet saludar
greeting saludo
group grupo
to grow crecer[ix]
to guess adivinar
guide(book) guía
guitar guitarra

H

hair pelo
half (*adjective*) medio
  (*noun*) (la) mitad
ham (el) jamón
hand (la) mano
to happen pasar; suceder
happy contento; feliz
hard difícil; duro
hardly apenas
hat sombrero
to have tener (tiene-)[xii]; haber[viii]
head cabeza
health (la) salud
heap (el) montón
to hear oír[ix]
heat (el) calor
heavy pesado
heel (el) tacón
hello hola
to help (to) ayudar (a)
hemisphere hemisferio
here acá, aquí
high alto
hill colina
to hire alquilar
Hispanic hispano
history historia
to hit pegar
to hold up detener (detiene-)[xii]
horrible horrible
hospital (el) hospital
hot caliente
hotel (el) hotel
hour hora
house casa
how cómo; qué tal
  how many cuántos
  how much cuánto
however sin embargo
humour (el) humor
humorist (el) humorista
hundred ciento (cien)
hunger hambre (*fem.*)
hurry prisa
to hurry apurarse
to hurt doler (duele-); lastimar

I

ice hielo
idea idea
ideal ideal
idiom modismo
if si
ill enfermo
imaginary imaginario
to imagine imaginarse
to imitate imitar
immediately en seguida
impersonal impersonal
importance importancia
important importante
impossible imposible
to impress impresionar
impression (la) impresión
incorrect incorrecto
to increase aumentar
independence independencia
Indian indio
to indicate indicar[iv]
industry industria
information (la) información
ingenious ingenioso
inhabitant (el) habitante
to insist empeñarse; insistir
to inspire inspirar
instead en vez
intelligent inteligente
to intend pensar (piensa-)
interchange intercambio
interest (el) interés
to interest interesar
interesting interesante
to interfere intervenir (interviene-)[xiii]; meterse
international internacional
to interrupt interrumpir
to intervene intervenir (interviene-)[xiii]
intimate íntimo
to introduce presentar
to invent inventar
invitation (la) invitación
to invite (to) invitar (a)
Italian italiano
itinerary itinerario

J

January enero
joke broma; (el) chiste
juice jugo
July julio
June junio

K

kind (*adjective*) amable
  (*noun*) (la) clase
kindness (la) bondad
to kill matar
kilometer kilómetro
to know conocer;[vi] saber[xi]

L

lack falta
lacking: to be lacking faltar
lady señora, dama
  young lady señorita
land tierra
language (el) idioma
large grande (gran)
  larger, largest mayor
last pasado; último
to last durar
late tarde
later luego
Latin latino
to laugh reír (ríe-)[xi]
  to laugh at reírse de
to learn aprender
least menos
to leave dejar; (*go away*) salir[xii]
  to take leave despedirse (despide-)
left izquierda
to lend prestar
less menos
lesson (la) lección
to let dejar
letter carta; letra
library biblioteca
lie mentira
life vida
light (la) luz
like (*preposition*) como
likely probable
line cola
to listen, listen to escuchar
literature literatura
little pequeño; poco
to live vivir
load cuota
long largo
look mirada
to look, look at mirar
  to look for buscar

to lose perder (pierde-)
loud alto
love: to fall in love with enamorarse de
low bajo
luck (la) suerte
lunch almuerzo
  to have lunch almorzar (almuerza-)[v]

M

madam señora
magnificent magnífico
maid criada
main principal
to make hacer[viii]
malted malteado
man hombre
manager (el) gerente
manner manera
mannered: ill-mannered mal educado
many muchos
  how many cuántos
  so many tantos
March marzo
married: to get married (to) casarse (con)
marvel maravilla
mass misa
master dueño
maternal materno
matter asunto
to matter importar
May mayo
meanwhile mientras tanto
measure medida
to meddle meterse
medicine medicina
to meet encontrar (encuentra-); reunirse; (*get to know*) conocer[vii]
  to meet up with tropezarse (tropieza-)[v] con
memory memoria; recuerdo
mention (la) mención
menu lista
merit mérito
merry alegre
message recado
method método
Mexican mexicano
milk (la) leche

million (el) millón
minute minuto
miracle milagro
Miss señorita
to miss extrañar
mistake (el) error; (la) equivocación
mistaken: to be mistaken equivocarse
misunderstanding malentendido
modern moderno
moment momento
Monday (el) lunes
money dinero
monotonous monótono
month (el) mes
mood (el) humor
more más
morning mañana
mosquito mosquito
most más
mother madre; mamá
to move mover (mueve-)
movie película
  movies (el) cine
Mr. señor
Mrs. señora
much mucho
  how much cuánto
  so much tanto
museum museo
music música
mustache (el) bigote
mysterious misterioso

N

name (el) nombre
  last name apellido
near cerca
necessary necesario
necktie corbata
need (la) necesidad
to need necesitar
neighbour vecino, -na
neither tampoco
nervous nervioso
never nunca
new nuevo
news noticias
newspaper periódico
next próximo
nice simpático

night (la) noche
  last night anoche
nine nueve
  nine hundred novecientos
ninety noventa
no no
no (*adjective*) ninguno (ningún)
nobody nadie
noise ruido
none ninguno (ningún)
nonsense tonterías
noon (el) mediodía
no one nadie
nor ni
north (el) norte
  North American norteamericano
not no
to note notar
nothing nada
to notice fijarse en; notar
to notify avisar
November (el) noviembre
now ahora
number número
numerous numeroso

O

to obtain conseguir (consigue-)[v]
to occupy ocupar
to occur ocurrir
ocean (el) mar
October (el) octubre
to offend ofender
to offer ofrecer[ix]
office oficina
old viejo; antiguo
to omit omitir
once: at once en seguida
one uno (un)
only sólo; único
to open abrir[xiv]
opinion (la) opinión
opportunity (la) oportunidad
opposite (*adjective*) opuesto (*adverb*) en frente
or o
orange naranja
order (la) orden
to order mandar; pedir (pide-)
to organize organizar[v]
other otro
  the others los, las demás

P

page página
pain (el) dolor
pair (el) par
paper (el) papel
to pardon perdonar
parrot loro
part (la) parte
party fiesta
to pass pasar
past pasado
paternal paterno
to pay, pay for pagar
peace (la) paz
pen: fountain pen pluma fuente
people (la) gente; pueblo
perfect perfecto
perhaps tal vez
period época
to permit permitir
person persona
personage (el) personaje
Peruvian peruano
pharmacist farmacéutico
pharmacy farmacia
phenomenal fenomenal
photograph fotografía
to pick escoger[vi]
    to pick up recoger[vi]
picture fotografía; película
pie (el) pastel
pile (el) montón
pity lástima
place (el) lugar; (la) parte
to plan pensar (piensa-)
to play (game) jugar (juega-)[ix];
    (music) tocar[iv]
pleasant agradable
to please gustar
pleasure gusto; (el) placer
pocketbook cartera
point punto
to point indicar[iv]
police policía
polite fino
politeness cortesía
poor pobre
port puerto

possible posible
potatoes papas
pound libra
practical práctico
to practice practicar[iv]
to praise alabar
precise preciso
predicament apuro
to prefer preferir (prefiere-)
to prepare preparar
present regalo
to present presentar
to presume suponer[x]
pretty bonito
price precio
primary primario
principal principal
private particular
probable probable
problem (el) problema
to produce producir[x]
professor profesor, -ora
to profit by aprovechar
to prohibit prohibir
to promise prometer
to pronounce pronunciar
to propose proponer[x]
to protect proteger[vi]
provided con tal
psychology psicología
punctuality (la) puntualidad
purpose: on purpose a propósito
to put poner[x]
    to put oneself meterse

Q

quarter cuarto
question (la) cuestión; pregunta
    to be a question of tratarse de
queue cola
quiet tranquilo
    to be quiet callarse
quite bastante
quota cuota

R

raquet raqueta
rain lluvia
to rain llover (llueve-)
rapid rápido
rare raro
rather bastante
reaction (la) reacción

to read leer[iv]
reality (la) realidad
to realize darse cuenta
really de veras
reasonable razonable
to recall recordar (recuerda-)
to receive recibir
red rojo
refreshments refrescos
to regret sentir (siente-)
to relate contar (cuenta-)
relation (la) relación
relative (el) pariente
to remain quedarse
remedy remedio
to remedy remediar
to remember acordarse (acuerda-)
    de; recordar (recuerda-)
to remove quitar
to rent alquilar
to reply contestar
to reprimand regañar
reputation fama
to reserve reservar
to resist resistir
responsibility (la) responsabilidad
rest: the rest los, las demás
to rest descansar
restaurant (el) restaurante
to return volver (vuelve-)[xiv]; de-
    volver (devuelve-)[xiv]
to review repasar
rice (el) arroz
rich rico
right derecha; derecho
rightness (la) razón
to rise levantarse
river río
road camino
role (el) papel
romantic romántico
room sala; cuarto
rule regla
to run correr

S

sad triste
sailor marinero
saint santo, -ta
same mismo
sandwich (el) sándwich
satisfied: to be satisfied contentarse

Saturday sábado
to say decir (dice-)[vii]
to scare asustar
scene escena
scholarship beca
school escuela
to scientific científico
scold regañar
Scotch escocés, -esa
scrambled revuelto
sea (el) mar
season (la) estación
second segundo
secondary secundario
secret secreto
to see ver[xiv]
to seem parecer[ix]
seldom raras veces
to sell vender
to send mandar
sensible razonable
sentence (la) frase
September (el) septiembre
serenade serenata
serious serio; grave
servant servidor, -ora
to serve servir (sirve-)
service servicio
set fijo
seven siete
seven hundred setecientos
seventy setenta
several varios
shame lástima
to shave afeitar
shoe zapato
short corto; breve
to show enseñar
sick enfermo
side lado
sight vista
to sign firmar
silver plata
simple sencillo
to sing cantar
sir señor
sister hermana
to sit down sentarse (sienta-)
situation (la) situación
six seis
sixty sesenta
to sleep dormir (duerme-)
sleepiness sueño

small pequeño
smaller, smallest menor
to smile sonreír (sonríe-)[xi]
snow (la) nieve
so tan; así; conque
so many tantos
so much tanto
social social
socks (los) calcetines
soft blando
some alguno (algún)
somebody, someone alguien
something algo
son hijo
soon pronto
as soon as apenas
sorrow pena
sorry: to be sorry sentir (siente-)
to sound sonar (suena-)
south (el) sur
South American sudamericano
Spanish español, -ola; hispano
to speak hablar
special especial
to specialize especializarse[v]
speech discurso
to spend (*time*) pasar; (*money*) gastar
spite: in spite of a pesar de
spring primavera
to start (to) empezar (empieza-)[v] (a)
station (la) estación
to stay quedarse
step paso; medida
to stop dejar de; parar
store tienda
story cuento
strange raro
street (la) calle
strong fuerte
to study estudiar
subject asunto
to suffice bastar
sufficient suficiente
to suggest proponer[x]
suit (el) traje
to suit caer[vi—vii] bien a
summer verano
sun (el) sol
Sunday domingo
superior superior
to suppose suponer[x]
sure seguro, cierto

sureness (la) seguridad
to surprise extrañar
sweets (los) dulces
to swim nadar
system (el) sistema

T

table mesa
to take tomar; llevar
to take off quitar
to take out sacar[iv]
talk discurso
to talk hablar
to stop talking callarse
tall alto
taste gusto
taxi (el) taxi
to teach (to) enseñar (a)
teacher profesor, -ora
telegram (el) telegrama
telephone teléfono
to tell contar (cuenta-)
ten diez
tennis (el) tenis
term término
terminal (el) terminal
to thank for agradecer[ix]
thanks gracias
that *conjunction or relative* que
that *demonstrative* ese, esa, eso (ése, etc.); aquel, -lla, -llo (aquél, etc.)
the el, la, los, las
then entonces
there allá; allí; ahí
there is, there are hay
thing cosa
to think pensar (piensa-); (*believe*) creer[vi]
third tercero (tercer)
thirst (la) sed
thirteen trece
thirty treinta
this *demonstrative* este, esta, esto (éste, etc.)
thoroughly a fondo
thousand mil
three tres
Thursday (el) jueves
thus así
ticket boleto
time tiempo; (la) vez

from time to time de vez en cuando
to tire cansar
toast tostadas
to toast brindar
today hoy
together juntos
tomorrow mañana
tonight esta noche
too también
too much demasiado
tooth (el) diente
top: on top encima
to toss echar
touch: to get in touch comunicarse
tour (la) excursión
tourist (el) turista
town pueblo
train (el) tren
tranquil tranquilo
to travel viajar
to treat tratar
tree (el) árbol
trip (el) viaje
 to take a trip hacer un viaje
tropics trópico
trouble pena
truly de veras
truth (la) verdad
to try tratar; probar (prueba-)
Tuesday (el) martes
twelve doce
twenty veinte
two dos
 two hundred doscientos

U

ugly feo
uncle tío
under debajo
to understand entender (entiende-)
United States Estados Unidos
unknown desconocido
until hasta

upstairs arriba
usage uso
to use usar
used: to get used to acostumbrarse a
useful útil
useless inútil

V

to vacate desocupar
vacation (las) vacaciones
value (el) valor
various varios
verb verbo
very muy
visit visita
to visit visitar
voice (la) voz

W

to wait, wait for esperar
waiter mozo
to wake up despertar (despierta-)
walk vuelta
 to take a walk dar una vuelta
to walk andar[vi]
to want querer (quiere-)[xi]
war guerra
warm caliente
watch (el) reloj
water agua
waterfront puerto
way manera; modo
 by the way a propósito
weak débil
weakness debilidad
to wear usar
weather tiempo
Wednesday (el) miércoles
week semana
to weep llorar
well bien
what qué

when cuando (cuándo)
where donde (dónde)
which (interrogative) cuál (relative) que
while (conjunction) mientras (noun) rato
white blanco
who, whom (interrogative) quién (relative) que, quien
whole todo; entero
wife señora; esposa
to win ganar
wind viento
window ventana
 show window (el) escaparate
wine vino
winter invierno
wish gana
to wish desear
within dentro
without sin
woman mujer
wonder maravilla
to wonder preguntarse
wonderful magnífico; formidable
word palabra
work trabajo
to work trabajar
world mundo
to worry preocuparse
worse, worst peor
worth: to be worth valer[xiii]
 to be worth while convenir (conviene-)[xiii]
to write escribir[xiv]

Y

year año
yes sí
yesterday ayer
 day before yesterday anteayer
yet todavía
young joven
 young lady señorita

INDEX

TRAVELLERS' VOCABULARY

A

accident (el) accidente
address (la) dirección, (las) señas
air: by air mail por correo aéreo
airport aeropuerto
ambulance ambulancia
arrival llegada
aspirin (las) aspirinas
attendant empleado
avenue avenida

B

bacon tocino
baggage (el) equipaje
  baggage room sala de equipajes
baker panadero
bakery panadería
bank banco
bar (el) bar
barber barbero, peluquero
  barber shop barbería, peluquería
bath baño
to bathe bañarse
  bathing suit (el) traje de baño
  bathing trunks (los) calzones de baño, (el) pantalón de baño
bathroom cuarto de baño
battery batería, pila
bed cama
bedroom alcoba, cuarto de dormir, pieza, recámara
beef (la) carne de vaca
  roast beef asado, (el) rosbif
beer cerveza
  light beer malta, maltina
  dark beer pílsener
belt (el) cinturón
berth (el) camarote
bicycle bicicleta
bill cuenta
blanket cobija, colcha, frazada, manta
block (*city*) cuadra
blotter (el) papel secante, (el) secante
blouse blusa

boarding-house casa de huéspedes, (la) pensión
boat barco, (el) buque, (el) vapor
book libro
bookseller librero, (el) vendedor de libros
bookstore librería
border frontera
bra corpiño, (el) sostén
bracelet pulsera
brake freno
brandy (el) aguardiente, (el) coñac
bread (el) pan
breakfast desayuno
building edificio
bus (el) autobús, (el) ómnibus
  bus stop parada, paradero
butcher carnicero
  butcher shop carnicería
butter manteca, mantequilla
button (el) botón

C

cablegram (el) cable, (el) cablegrama
café (el) café
cake (el) ponqué, (el) queque, torta
camera cámara, (el) kodak, máquina (fotográfica)
candy (los) bombones, (los) caramelos, (los) dulces
  candy store bombonería, confitería
car (*auto*) auto, (el) automóvil, carro, (el) coche
  (*on train*) (el) coche, (el) vagón
care: in care of atención de
carefully con cuidado
to cash (*check, etc.*) cambiar, efectuar
change cambio
  (*money*) moneda, suelto
to change cambiar
  to change trains cambiar de tren
cheap (*inexpensive*) barato
check (el) cheque

baggage check contraseña de equipaje
to check (*baggage, etc.*) dejar en custodia
cheese queso
chicken pollo
chocolate (el) chocolate
cigar cigarro, puro, tabaco
cigarette cigarrillo
  cigarette case cigarrera, cigarrillera
  cigarette lighter (el) encendedor
class: by first class, etc. en primera clase, etc.
cleaner's (*dry*) lavandería en seco, tintorería
clerk dependiente, empleado
closet armario, (el) clóset, ropero
clothes ropa
clothing store tienda de ropa
coat saco
  (*overcoat*) abrigo, sobretodo
coffee (el) café
comb (el) peine, peineta, peinilla
conductor conductor
connection (*train*) (la) combinación, (la) conexión
cotton (el) algodón
cream crema
  cold cream crema de cara
cup taza
curve curva
customs aduana
  customs inspection (la) revisión de equipaje

D

dairy bar bar lácteo
danger peligro
day: per day al día, por día
delivery: general delivery correo general
  special delivery entrega especial, entrega urgente
dentist (el) dentista
deodorant (el) desodorante
department store (el) almacén
departure salida

dessert (el) postre
dining car (el) coche comedor, (el) coche restaurante
dining room (el) comedor
dinner comida
direction (la) dirección
distance distancia
to dock atracar
doctor médico
dress vestido
drinking water agua potable, agua para tomar
to drive guiar, manejar
driver (el) chofer
druggist boticario, farmacéutico
drugstore botica, farmacia

E

egg huevo
electric eléctrico
electricity (la) electricidad
elevator (el) ascensor
emergency emergencia
empty desocupado, vacío
entrance entrada
envelope (el) sobre
excuse me dispénseme
exit salida
expensive caro

F

fare (el) pasaje
to fill llenar
filling station (la) estación de gasolina
film película
fine: to pay a fine pagar una multa
first aid primeros auxilios
first aid station asistencia pública
fish pescado
flashlight linterna
floor: first floor, etc. primer piso, etc.
fork (el) tenedor
forward: please forward sírvase despachar
fried frito
fruit fruta
full lleno

G

galoshes galochas, (los) zapatones
garage (el) garaje
gas(oline) gasolina
gas station (la) estación de gasolina
girdle faja
glass vaso
(material) vidrio
glasses (eye) (los) anteojos, (las) gafas, (los) lentes
glove (el) guante
go (on traffic light) siga
grocer almacenero, tendero
groceries (los) abarrotes
grocery store (el) almacén, tienda de abarrotes

H

hairbrush cepillo de pelo, escobilla de pelo
haircut: to get a haircut cortarse el pelo
ham (el) jamón
handkerchief pañuelo
hardware artículos de ferretería, quincalla
hardware store ferretería, quincallería
hat sombrero
headlight (el) farol, linterna delantera
highway camino, carretera
to hire alquilar, arrendar
to hitch-hike pedir una carrera
hospital (el) hospital
hotel (el) hotel
how far . . . ? ¿ qué distancia . . . ?

I

ice hielo
ice cream helado
information bureau oficina de informaciones
ink tinta
inn fonda, posada
to insure asegurar

J

jacket chaqueta, saco
jewel alhaja, joya

jeweler joyero, platero
jewelry store joyería, platería
judge (el) juez
juice jugo

K

kilometre kilometro
knife cuchillo

L

lace (el) encaje
ladies' room (el) toilet [tualét] de señoras
to land (boat) atracar
(plane) aterrizar
(person) desembarcarse
laundress lavadora, lavandera
laundry lavandería
(dirty clothes) ropa sucia
letter carta
library biblioteca
light (la) luz
limit: speed limit (el) límite de velocidad
linen lienzo, lino
lipstick barrita, (el) làpiz de rouge, (el) lápiz de labio
litre litro
lunch almuerzo

M

mail correo
mail box (el) buzón
to mail echar al buzón, echar al correo, poner en el correo
map (el) mapa
market mercado
match fósforo
meal comida
meat (la) carne
mechanic mecánico
medicine medicina, remedio
men's room (el) toilet [tualét] de hombres
menu lista, (el) menú
mile milla
milk (la) leche
money dinero, plata
money order giro postal
motor (el) motor

motorcycle motocicleta
movies (el) cine

N

nail file lima para las uñas
nail polish (el) esmalte de uñas,
  (el) lustra-uñas
napkin (*table*) servilleta
  (*sanitary*) paño higiénico
necklace (el) collar
necktie corbata
needle aguja

O

occupied ocupado
office despacho, oficina
oil (el) aceite

P

pack (*cigarettes*) cajetilla, cajilla
package (el) paquete
pajamas (el) pijama, (la) piyama
panties (los) calzones
park (el) parque
to **park** estacionar
  no parking estacionamiento pro-
    hibido, prohibido estacionar
passenger pasajero
passport (el) pasaporte
pastry bizcochos, (los) pasteles
  pastry shop bizcochería, paste-
    lería
pen pluma
  fountain pen estilógrafo, pluma
    fuente
pencil (el) lápiz
person: per person por persona
petticoat (la) combinación, fondo,
  refajo
pillow almohada
pilot piloto
pin (el) alfiler
  bobby pin (el) invisible
  safety pin gancho, (el) imper-
    dible
pipe pipa
plane (el) avión
platform plataforma
please por favor

please ... haga el favor de ...,
  tenga la bondad de ..., sírvase ...
police policía
policeman (el) guardia, (el) policía
porter mozo de servicio, portero
postage franqueo, (el) porte
postal postal
postcard tarjeta postal
postman cartero
post office casa de correos, correo,
  oficina de correos
  post-office box apartado, casilla
potatoes papas, patatas
powder (*face*) polvo
price precio
printed matter (los) impresos
private (*car, etc.*) particular
public público
puncture (*tire*) pinchadura, pin-
  chazo

R

radiator (el) radiador
radio (el) radio, (la) radio
radiogram (el) radiograma
railroad (el) ferrocarril
raincoat (el) impermeable
razor navaja
  razor blade hoja de afeitar
receipt recibo
to **register** certificar, registrar
  registered letter carta certifi-
    cada, carta registrada
to **repair** componer, reparar
reservations reserva, (las) reser-
  vaciones
to **reserve** reservar
restaurant (el) restaurán, (el)
  restaurante
rice (el) arroz
road camino, carretera
roast(ed) asado
rolls (*bread*) (los) panecillos, (los)
  panes
room cuarto, pieza, sala, (el) salón
  single room pieza para uno
  double room pieza para dos
rubber caucho, goma
  rubbers zapatos de goma, (los)
    zapatones
to **run** (*well, etc.*) funcionar

S

to **sail** salir
salad ensalada
seat asiento
to **send** (*telegram, etc.*) poner
shampoo (el) champú
to **shave** afeitarse
  shaving cream crema de afeitar
sheet (*bed*) sábana
shirt camisa
shoe zapato
shoemaker zapatero
shop tienda
shower (*bath*) ducha, regadera
sidewalk acera
sign, signal (la) señal
silk seda
sleeping car (el) coche cama
slip (*clothing*) enagua
smoking: no smoking no fumar,
  prohibido fumar
  smoking car (el) coche de
    fumar
soap (el) jabón
socks (los) calcetines, medias to-
  billeras
soup sopa
spoon cuchara
stairs escalera
stamp (*postage*) estampilla
station (la) estación
stationery papelería
  stationery store papelería
steak (el) bisté, (el) bistec, (el)
  bife
stewardess (*plane*) camarera
stockings medias
to **stop** pararse
stop (*on traffic sign*) pare
store tienda, (el) almacén
street: one-way street (la) calle
  de una mano, una vía
string cuerda
suit (*men's*) terno, (el) traje,
  vestido
  (*women's*) estilo sastre, vestido
  sastre
suitcase maleta
sun glasses anteojos de sol, anteojos negros
suspenders (los) tirantes
sweater (el) swéter

T

table mesa
tailor (el) sastre
  tailor shop sastrería
to **take off** (*plane*) despegar
tank (el) tanque
tavern taverna
taxi (el) taxi, taxímetro
tea (el) té
telegram (el) telegrama
to **telegraph** telegrafiar
telephone teléfono
  telephone book directorio telefónico, guía telefónica
to **telephone** telefonear
terminal (el) terminal, (la) terminal
theatre teatro
  movie theater (el) cine
thread hilo
ticket (el) billete, boleta, boleto, (el) pasaje, (el) tiquete
  ticket office boletería, despacho de billetes
  ticket window boletería, taquilla de billetes
  one-way ticket billete de ida, billete sencillo
  round-trip ticket billete de ida y vuelta
tie corbata
timetable horario, itinerario
tip propina
to **tip** dar propina

tire llanta, neumático
  flat (tire) desenflado
toast (las) tostadas
tobacco tabaco
toilet excusado, (el) retrete, (el) toilet [tualét]
  toilet paper (el) papel higiénico
toothbrush cepillo de dientes
tooth paste dentífrico, pasta de dientes
tooth powder dentífrico en polvo, polvos dentales
tour (la) excursión
tourist (el) turista
  tourist bureau oficina de turismo
towel toalla
traffic tráfico
  traffic lights (las) luces de tráfico
train (el) tren
to **travel** viajar
traveler viajero
trousers (el) pantalón
truck (el) camión
trunk (el) baúl
tube (*inner*) cámara
typewriter máquina de escribir

U

umbrella (el) paraguas, sombrilla
underpants (los) calzoncillos
undershirt camiseta

V

vacant desocupado
vegetables (las) legumbres, verduras
violation (*traffic*) (la) infracción
visa, visé visa

W

waiter mozo
waiting room sala de espera
waitress camarera, moza
washbowl (el) lavamanos, lavatorio
watch (el) reloj
  wrist watch (el) reloj pulsera, (el) reloj de pulsera
watchmaker relojero
water agua
  cold water agua fría
  drinking water agua potable, agua para tomar
  hot water agua caliente
  ice water agua helada
  running water agua corriente
welcome: you're welcome de nada, no hay de qué
wheel rueda
  steering wheel (el) volante
wine vino
  red wine vino tinto
  white wine vino blanco
wool lana
to **work** (*well, etc.*) funcionar
writing paper (el) papel de escribir

KEY TO GRAMMATICAL DRILLS AND REVIEW EXERCISES

KEY TO GRAMMATICAL DRILLS

UNIT I
Pages 9–10

1. **the.**

1. el hermano 2. la casa 3. la señorita 4. el profesor 5. la señora 6. las esquinas 7. el hijo 8. las salas 9. el señor 10. el padre 11. los hombres 12. las mujeres 13. el número 14. las hijas 15. los hermanos 16. las señoritas 17. la hija 18. el autobús 19. los mexicanos 20. los hijos 21. el mexicano 22. las señoras 23. los padres 24. las hermanas 25. la mexicana 26. los números 27. la hermana 28. las mexicanas

2. ADJECTIVE ENDINGS.

1. un hijo muy simpático 2. una casa simpática 3. un profesor simpático 4. dos señoritas simpáticas 5. cinco hermanos simpáticos 6. un padre muy simpático 7. un hermano simpático 8. una sala simpática 9. cuatro señoras simpáticas 10. tres mujeres simpáticas 11. dos hombres simpáticos 12. una hija muy simpática

3. BEING: ser.

1. es 2. soy 3. son 4. son 5. es 6. somos 7. somos 8. es

4. BEING: estar.

1. está 2. estoy 3. está 4. está 5. están 6. está 7. están 8. están 9. están 10. estamos 11. está 12. está

5. HAVING: tener.

1. tengo 2. tienen 3. tenemos 4. tiene 5. tiene 6. tengo 7. tiene 8. tienen

UNIT II
Pages 20–21

1. **this** AND **that.**

A

1. este país, estos países 2. esta esquina, estas esquinas 3. este queso, estos quesos 4. estos sombreros, este sombrero 5. esta tienda, estas tiendas 6. este profesor, estos profesores 7. esta sala, estas salas 8. estos hombres, este hombre 9. estas mujeres, esta mujer 10. este hermano, estos hermanos 11. esta señora, estas señoras 12. estas señoritas, esta señorita 13. estos autobuses, este autobús 14. estas hijas, esta hija 15. estos mexicanos, este mexicano 16. estos señores, este señor 17. este padre, estos padres 18. estas hermanas, esta hermana

B

1. ese país, esos países 2. esa esquina, esas esquinas 3. ese queso, esos quesos 4. esos sombreros, ese sombrero 5. esa tienda, esas tiendas 6. ese profesor, esos profesores 7. esa sala, esas salas 8. esos hombres, ese hombre 9. esas mujeres, esa mujer 10. ese hermano, esos hermanos 11. esa señora, esas señoras 12. esas señoritas, esa señorita 13. esos autobuses, ese autobús 14. esas hijas, esa hija 15. esos mexicanos, ese mexicano 16. esos señores, ese señor 17. ese padre, esos padres 18. esas hermanas, esa hermana

C

1. **aquel** país, **aquellos** países 2. **aquella** esquina, **aquellas** esquinas 3. **aquel** queso, **aquellos** quesos 4. **aquellos** sombreros, **aquel** sombrero 5. **aquella** tienda, **aquellas** tiendas 6. **aquel** profesor, **aquellos** profesores 7. **aquella** sala, **aquellas** salas 8. **aquellos** hombres, **aquel** hombre 9. **aquellas** mujeres, **aquella** mujer 10. **aquel** hermano, **aquellos** hermanos 11. **aquella** señora, **aquellas** señoras 12. **aquellas** señoritas, **aquella** señorita 13. **aquellos** autobuses, **aquel** autobús 14. **aquellas** hijas, **aquel** hija 15. **aquellos** mexicanos, **aquel** mexicano 16. **aquellos** señores, **aquel** señor 17. **aquel** padre, **aquellos** padres 18. **aquellas** hermanas, **aquella** hermana

2. ADJECTIVES.

1. **muchos** hermanos, **muchas** hijas, **mucha** sed, **mucho** viento, **mucha** nieve, **muchos** hombres, **mucho** calor, **muchos** profesores, **mucho** frío, **mucha** hambre, **muchos** mexicanos

2. una tienda **grande**, este sombrero **grande**, esas casas **grandes**, dos salas **grandes**, aquellos países **grandes**

3. una señora **española**, los profesores **españoles**, estas mujeres **españolas**, una padre **español**, la sala **española**

4. una señora **inglesa**, los profesores **ingleses**, estas mujeres **inglesas**, un padre **inglés**, la sala **inglesa**

5. un clima **frío**, un clima **hermoso**, un clima **malo**, un clima **fresco**, un clima **seco**, un clima **agradable**, un clima **bueno**

6. esa primavera **fría**, esa primavera **hermosa**, esa primavera **mala**, esa primavera **fresca**, esa primavera **agradable**, esa primavera **buena**

3. BEING.

1. son 2. está 3. es 4. hay 5. hace; tengo 6. están 7. están 8. es 9. tiene 10. es 11. es 12. estoy 13. son 14. es 15. tengo 16. hay 17. es 18. son 19. tiene 20. es 21. es 22. está 23. somos 24. es 25. es 26. hay 27. hace 28. soy 29. tienen 30. tengo

4. NOUN COMPOUNDS.

1. un sombrero de verano 2. la señora del profesor 3. los padres de Pedro 4. la ropa de mi hermana 5. los días del verano 6. un día de primavera 7. este sándwich de queso 8. el sombrero de mi padre 9. el número de la casa 10. el tiempo del invierno 11. el clima de California 12. la casa de mi hermano 13. el calor del verano 14. el número del señor López 15. ropa de primavera 16. aquella tienda de sombreros

UNIT III

Pages 30–31

1. PRESENT TENSE.

1. comen 2. llama 3. aprenden 4. compran 5. descansan 6. ayuda 7. estudiamos 8. imita 9. necesito 10. levanto 11. termina 12. trabaja 13. descanso 14. cree 15. como 16. hacen 17. tomamos 18. gusta 19. saben 20. hablamos

2. COMPLETIVE PHRASES.

1. hemos aprendido 2. han estado 3. he tenido 4. ha sido 5. ha estado 6. hemos terminado 7. ha dado 8. han comprado 9. hemos estado 10. ha tomado 11. ha ayudado 12. ha habido 13. he comido 14. han estudiado

3. PROGRESSIVE PHRASES.

1. están comprando 2. están aprendiendo 3. están descansando 4. está ayudando 5. están comiendo 6. estamos estudiando 7. está trabajando 8. estoy terminando 9. está estudiando 10. estoy hablando 11. están comiendo 12. está haciendo 13. están dando 14. está hablando 15. está trabajando

UNIT IV

Pages 41–42

1. PRESENT-TENSE FORMS OF VERBS WITH ROOT-VOWEL ALTERNATION.

1. quieren 2. entiende 3. puede 4. duermo
5. tienen; empiezan 6. puede 7. duermes
8. quiere 9. podemos 10. pido 11. entiendo
12. sirven 13. piensa 14. podemos 15. prefiero
16. siente 17. piensas 18. prefiere 19. servimos
20. pensamos 21. pide 22. sirven 23. entienden
24. siento 25. entendemos 26. pedimos 27. pueden 28. queremos 29. siente 30. duermo
31. preferimos

2. PRESENT-TENSE FORMS OF **tener, venir, salir, hacer, decir.**

1. tengo; tienes; tiene; tenemos; tienen
2. vengo; vienes; viene; venimos; vienen
3. salgo; sales; sale; salimos; salen 4. hago;
haces; hace; hacemos; hacen 5. digo; dices;
dice; decimos; dicen

UNIT V

Pages 43–52

REVIEW OF UNIT 1: **Writing Spanish.**

1. Buenos días, señora González. 2. ¿ Tiene
usted hermanos? 3. Tenemos casa en Los Ángeles.
4. ¿ Cómo está usted, señor López? — Estoy muy
bien, gracias. 5. Mis padres están en California.
6. ¿ Es simpática Luisa? — ¡ Sí, cómo no!
7. ¿ Dónde estamos ahora? 8. Ricardo Ross es
de Los Ángeles. 9. Yo no soy de San Luis.
10. ¿ De dónde es el señor López? 11. ¿ A dónde
va el señor González? 12. El autobús está en la
esquina. 13. Allá viene la señorita Silvia.
14. Adiós, señora Quiroga. 15. Yo me llamo
Silvia Evans. 16. ¿ Quién es el profesor?
17. ¿ Dónde está la señorita Evans? 18. El
profesor no es muy simpático. 19. Yo no soy la
señorita Ross. 20. Mucho gusto, señor. 21. Ésta
no es la sala número cinco. 22. ¿ Dónde está el
autobús? — Allá viene. 23. ¿ Quién va a la esquina? 24. Tenemos siete hijos: tres hombres y
cuatro mujeres. 25. Los hermanos son muy simpáticos. 26. Yo tengo una hermana y un hermano.
27. ¿ Dónde están Miguel y Ricardo? 28. ¿ Habla
usted español? — ¡ Sí, cómo no! 29. ¿ Cómo se
llama usted? 30. ¿ De dónde es usted? 31. ¿ Es
mexicano usted? — Sí, señora, soy mexicano.
32. Mi padre está en San Luis. 33. Los Ángeles
está en California. 34. ¿ Tiene usted un hermano
o una hermana?

REVIEW OF UNIT 2: **Writing Spanish.**

1. Estos señores son hermanos. 2. ¿ Qué dice
usted, señorita? 3. ¿ Están aquí los hijos del
profesor? 4. Tenemos que aprender eso para
mañana. 5. ¿ Qué va usted a tomar, Ricardo?
6. Yo tengo más hambre que sed. 7. Yo no soy
mexicana, soy española. 8. Los españoles también
hablan español. 9. ¿ Cómo es el clima en California? 10. ¿ Es como el clima de aquí? — Más
o menos. 11. Dicen que no llueve en California.
12. Hace frío en el invierno. 13. Hace calor en el
verano. 14. La primavera es fresca y hermosa.
15. Hace mucho viento aquí. 16. En general el
otoño es seco. 17. No hay tiendas grandes en el
centro. 18. Pedro y Ricardo tienen sueño.
19. Mis padres son españoles. 20. Aquellas dos
señoras son españolas también. 21. No hay nieve
en el verano. 22. Estas lecciones son muy fáciles.
23. Esa señorita no es muy inteligente. 24. Esa
casa es hermosa, y ésta también. 25. El clima de
aquí es muy agradable. 26. ¿ Cómo es el otoño en

este país? 27. Ese queso está seco. 28. Tenemos tres profesores de español. — ¿ Son españoles? 29. No hay teléfono aquí. 30. Quiero comprar algo en aquella tienda. 31. Hace mucho viento en la primavera. 32. ¿ Quién habla inglés aquí? 33. Los hermanos de José son muy simpáticos. 34. El tiempo es hermoso ahora. 35. Éste es el sombrero de mi padre.

Review of Unit 3: **Writing Spanish.**

1. He aprendido la tercera lección. 2. ¿ Ha terminado usted las dos primeras páginas? 3. ¡ Hombre, qué bueno! 4. ¿ Por qué me ayuda? 5. Dicen que esa película es muy buena. 6. Estoy cansado de estas cosas. 7. No he estudiado la lección de hoy. 8. Vamos a dar una vuelta ahora. 9. ¿ Qué película están dando en el centro? 10. Dice que es para hacerme estudiar. 11. Estoy estudiando español porque quiero ser un buen vecino. 12. ¿ Cuánto tiempo tenemos? — Es difícil decirlo. 13. ¿ Cuánto tiempo cree usted que necesitamos? 14. Éste es mi tercer año de español. 15. Ricardo es un muchacho inteligente. 16. ¿ Qué dice el profesor? 17. Es fácil hacer esto. 18. Los niños están aprendiendo el español. 19. Todos imitamos a la profesora. 20. Usted ya ha aprendido mucho. 21. ¿ No están cansados ustedes? 22. Sí, y la profesora también está cansada. 23. Yo creo que el inglés es difícil. 24. ¿ Qué va usted a hacer hoy? 25. ¿ Qué van a hacer ustedes durante el verano? 26. Me levanto para dar una vuelta. 27. Durante las vacaciones voy a ver a unos amigos. 28. ¿ Dónde están los amigos? — Están en Los Ángeles. 29. Todos hablamos inglés. 30. Hace buen tiempo hoy. 31. La película se llama *El Bandido del Río Grande*. 32. Esa cama no es muy buena. 33. Los dos primeros años son fáciles. 34. El tercer año y el cuarto año son difíciles. 35. Gracias a mi hermana, ya he aprendido eso.

Review of Unit 4: **Writing Spanish.**

1. Cada vez que estudio, siento deseos de comer. 2. ¡ Qué hambre tengo ahora! 3. No entiendo eso. 4. ¿ Crees que Jorge es un tonto? 5. Al contrario, es un muchacho muy inteligente. 6. Hago mi trabajo con amigos. 7. ¿ Qué sabe usted de Ricardo Ross? 8. Sólo sé que es de California. 9. ¿ Qué piensas hacer hoy? 10. Yo como desde las seis y media hasta las siete. 11. Vamos a salir. 12. ¿ Cuánto tiempo tarda el autobús? 13. Son las cinco y cuarto. 14. Tienen cita con el profesor. 15. Vamos a ver una película romántica esta vez. 16. No está muy lejos. 17. ¿ A qué hora sale el autobús? 18. Estoy cansado, pero quiero dar una vuelta. 19. ¿ Es difícil el trabajo de mañana? — No, no mucho. 20. Yo creo que Jorge tiene razón. 21. Cuando tengo frío no tengo sed. 22. ¿ Es hermosa su amiga? — Sí, mucho. 23. Yo siento deseos de pedir para Jaime. 24. ¿ Puede usted esperar hasta las tres? 25. Prefiero ir a pie. 26. ¿ Sabe usted dónde puedo comprar corbatas y calcetines? 27. ¿ De quién es ese sombrero azul? No es muy bonito. 28. Es difícil descansar en la clase de español. 29. Los niños mexicanos hablan español. 30. ¿ De quién son esas corbatas? — No son de Jaime. 31. Yo no tengo la culpa. 32. ¿ Qué día es hoy? — ¡ Es sábado, hombre! 33. Vamos a una fiesta esta noche. 34. La ropa de papá no es muy elegante. 35. ¿ Para qué sirven esas cosas? 36. No sé dónde está el restaurante. 37. ¿ Hay tiendas buenas en el centro? 38. Trato de hablar español pero no puedo. 39. Creo que es cuestión de psicología.

UNIT VI

Pages 63–65

1. Present of ir, dar, ver, ser, estar, saber, oír.

1. voy; vas; va; vamos; van 2. doy; das; da; damos; dan 3. veo; ves; ve; vemos; ven 4. soy; eres; es; somos; son 5. estoy; estás; está; estamos; están 6. sé; sabes; sabe; sabemos; saben 7. oigo; oyes; oye; oímos; oyen

2. "do"-COMMANDS.

A

1. habla   2. toma   3. aprende   4. compra
5. descansa   6. ten   7. oye   8. come   9. estudia
10. termina   11. trabaja   12. usa   13. entra
14. olvida   15. empieza   16. ve   17. llega
18. llama   19. di   20. da   21. imita   22. piensa
23. trata   24. vuelve   25. espera   26. ven

B

1. hable   2. tome   3. aprenda   4. compre
5. descanse   6. tenga   7. oiga   8. coma   9. estudie   10. termine   11. trabaje   12. use   13. entre
14. olvide   15. empiece   16. vaya   17. llegue
18. llame   19. diga   20. dé   21. imite   22. piense
23. trate   24. vuelva   25. espere   26. venga

C

1. hablemos; vamos a hablar   2. tomemos; vamos a tomar   3. aprendamos; vamos a aprender
4. compremos; vamos a comprar   5. descansemos; vamos a descansar   6. tengamos; vamos a tener
7. oigamos; vamos a oír   8. comamos; vamos a comer   9. estudiemos; vamos a estudiar   10. terminemos; vamos a terminar   11. trabajemos; vamos a trabajar   12. usemos; vamos a usar
13. entremos; vamos a entrar   14. olvidemos; vamos a olvidar   15. empecemos; vamos a empezar   16. vamos; vamos a ir   17. lleguemos; vamos a llegar   18. llamemos; vamos a llamar
19. digamos; vamos a decir   20. demos; vamos a dar   21. imitemos; vamos a imitar   22. pensemos; vamos a pensar   23. tratemos; vamos a tratar   24. volvamos; vamos a volver   25. esperemos; vamos a esperar   26. vengamos; vamos a venir

3. "don't"-COMMANDS.

A

1. no aprendas   2. no llegues   3. no digas
4. no compres   5. no seas   6. no tomes   7. no descanses   8. no hagas   9. no comas   10. no estudies   11. no termines   12. no trabajes   13. no duermas   14. no empieces   15. no esperes   16. no vayas   17. no pidas   18. no pienses   19. no vengas
20. no uses   21. no entres   22. no olvides   23. no vuelvas   24. no salgas

B

1. no aprenda   2. no llegue   3. no diga   4. no compre   5. no sea   6. no tome   7. no descanse
8. no haga   9. no coma   10. no estudie   11. no termine   12. no trabaje   13. no duerma   14. no empiece   15. no espere   16. no vaya   17. no pida
18. no piense   19. no venga   20. no use   21. no entre   22. no olvide   23. no vuelva   24. no salga

4. TWO-DIGIT NUMBERS.

16	dieciséis
21	veintiuno
38	treinta y ocho
45	cuarenta y cinco
53	cincuenta y tres
64	sesenta y cuatro
79	setenta y nueve
82	ochenta y dos
97	noventa y siete
44	cuarenta y cuatro
71	setenta y uno
36	treinta y seis
69	sesenta y nueve
95	noventa y cinco
23	veintitrés
52	cincuenta y dos
86	ochenta y seis
17	diecisiete
94	noventa y cuatro
77	setenta y siete
68	sesenta y ocho

5. TIME OF DAY.

A

¿ Es la una ? — No, son las dos. ¿ Son las dos ? — No, son las tres. ¿ Son las tres ? — No, son las cuatro. ¿ Son las cuatro ? — No, son las cinco. ¿ Son las cinco ? — No, son las seis. ¿ Son las seis ? — No, son las siete. ¿ Son las siete ? — No, son las ocho. ¿ Son las ocho ? — No, son las nueve.

¿ Son las nueve ? — No, son las diez. ¿ Son las diez ? — No, son las once. ¿ Son las once ? — No, son las doce. ¿ Son las doce ? — No, es la una.

B

1. El autobús sale a las **seis y diez**; a las **tres y cuarto**; a las **nueve y dos**; a la **una y cinco**; a las diez y media; a las **seis menos cuarto**; a las **dos y ocho**; a las **cuatro y cuarto**; a las **diez y diez**.
2. La película empieza a *etc.* 3. Yo como a . . .
4. La cita es a . . . 5. Quiero volver a . . .
6. Pienso llegar a . . . 7. Empiezo a trabajar a . . .

UNIT VII

Pages 75-77

1. PRONOUN POSITION.

1. No **me** han (**te** han, **nos** han) invitado todavía.
2. **Me** están (**Te** están, **Nos** están) esperando unos amigos OR Están esperándo**me** (esperándo**te**, esperándo**nos**) unos amigos. 3. Miguel no **me** quiere (**te** quiere, **nos** quiere) acompañar OR Miguel no quiere acompañar**me** (acompañar**te**, acompañar**nos**). 4. Los señores Quiroga no **me** conocen (**te** conocen, **nos** conocen). 5. ¿ No **me** quiere (**te** quiere, **nos** quiere) esperar Roberto ? OR ¿ No quiere esperar**me** (esperar**te**, esperar**nos**) Roberto ?
6. A veces **me** acompañan (**te** acompañan, **nos** acompañan) unos amigos.

2. PRONOUN VERB-OBJECTS REPLACING NOUNS.

A

1. ¿ Conoce usted aquellos países ? — Sí, **los** conozco. 2. ¿ Conoce usted la casa ? — Sí, **la** conozco. 3. ¿ Conoce usted esas tiendas ? — Sí, **las** conozco. 4. ¿ Conoce usted el coche ? — Sí, **lo** conozco. 5. ¿ Conoce usted a María ? — Sí, **la** conozco. 6. ¿ Conoce usted el centro ? — Sí, **lo** conozco. 7. ¿ Conoce usted a estos señores ? — Sí, **los** conozco. 8. ¿ Conoce usted al profesor Chávez ? — Sí, **lo** conozco.

B

1. ¿ Has visto a mi hermana ? — No **la** he visto.
2. ¿ Has visto mi sombrero ? — No **lo** he visto.
3. ¿ Has visto este reloj ? — No **lo** he visto.
4. ¿ Has visto a esos hombres ? — No **los** he visto.
5. ¿ Has visto la casa de Pedro ? — No **la** he visto.
6. ¿ Has visto los calcetines ? — No **los** he visto.
7. ¿ Has visto las fotografías ? — No **las** he visto.
8. ¿ Has visto al señor Rodríguez ? — No **lo** he visto. 9. ¿ Has visto aquellas tiendas ? — No **las** he visto. 10. ¿ Has visto el coche de mis padres ? — No **lo** he visto. 11. ¿ Has visto a la señorita Fernández ? — No **la** he visto. 12. ¿ Has visto a mis hijos ? — No **los** he visto. 13. ¿ Has visto a la señora ? — No **la** he visto. 14. ¿ Has visto a Juan y a Julio ? — No **los** he visto. 15. ¿ Has visto la nieve ? — No **la** he visto. 16. ¿ Has visto esas cosas ? — No **las** he visto.

C

1. Sí, vamos a comprar**lo**. OR Sí, **lo** vamos a comprar. 2. Sí, vamos a comprar**las**. OR Sí, **las** vamos a comprar. 3. Sí, vamos a comprar**la**. OR Sí, **la** vamos a comprar. 4. Sí, vamos a comprar**lo**. OR Sí, **lo** vamos a comprar. 5. Sí, vamos a comprar**los**. OR Sí, **los** vamos a comprar. 6. Sí, vamos a comprar**la**. OR Sí, **la** vamos a comprar. 7. Sí, vamos a comprar**las**. OR Sí, **las** vamos a comprar. 8. Sí, vamos a comprar**los**. OR Sí, **los** vamos a comprar. 9. Sí, vamos a comprar**las**. OR Sí, **las** vamos a comprar. 10. Sí, vamos a comprar**lo**. OR Sí, **lo** vamos a comprar.

D

1. Sí, **llámalos**. No, **no los llames**. 2. Sí, **cómelo**. No, **no lo comas**. 3. Sí, **cómprala**.

No, **no la compres.** 4. Sí, **tómala.** No, **no la tomes.** 5. Sí, **úsala.** No, **no la uses.**

1. Sí, **cómprelo** (usted). No, **no lo compre** (usted). 2. Sí, **cómprelas** (usted). No, **no las compre** (usted). 3. Sí, **cómprela** (usted). No, **no la compre** (usted). 4. Sí, **cómprelo** (usted). No, **no lo compre** (usted). 5. Sí, **cómprelos** (usted). No, **no los compre** (usted). 6. Sí, **cómprela** (usted). No, **no la compre** (usted). 7. Sí, **cómprelas** (usted). No, **no las compre** (usted). 8. Sí, **cómprelos** (usted). No, **no los compre** (usted). 9. Sí, **cómprelas** (usted). No, **no las compre** (usted). 10. Sí, **cómprelo** (usted). No, **no lo compre** (usted).

3. REFLEXIVE VERBS.

A

1. ¿ A qué hora **se levanta usted?** — **(Yo) me levanto** a las siete, *etc.* 2. ¿ Cuándo **se baña usted?** — **(Yo) me baño** por la mañana, *etc.* 3. ¿ De qué **se está quejando usted?** — **(Yo) me estoy quejando** del calor, *etc.* 4. ¿ Cuándo **va a casarse usted?** — **(Yo) voy a casarme** en agosto, *etc.* 5. ¿ Qué día **piensa irse usted?** — **(Yo) pienso irme** el dos de julio, *etc.*

B

1. ¿ A qué hora **se levanta ella?** — **Se levanta** a las siete, *etc.* ¿ A qué hora **te levantas tú?** — **Me levanto** a las siete, *etc.* ¿ A qué hora **me levanto yo?** — **Te levantas** a las siete, *etc.* ¿ A qué hora **se levantan ustedes?** — **Nos levantamos** a las siete, *etc.* ¿ A qué hora **se levantan ellas?** — **Se levantan** a las siete, *etc.*

2. ¿ Cuándo **se baña ella?** — **Se baña** por la mañana, *etc.* ¿ Cuándo **te bañas tú?** — **Me baño** por la mañana, *etc.* ¿ Cuándo **me baño yo?** — **Te bañas** por la mañana, *etc.* ¿ Cuándo **se bañan ustedes?** — **Nos bañamos** por la mañana, *etc.* ¿ Cuándo **se bañan ellas?** — **Se bañan** por la mañana, *etc.*

3. ¿ De qué **se está quejando ella?** — **Se está quejando** del calor, *etc.* ¿ De qué **te estás quejando tú?** — **Me estoy quejando** del calor, *etc.* ¿ De qué **me estoy quejando yo?** — **Te estás quejando** del calor, *etc.* ¿ De qué **se están quejando ustedes?** — **Nos estamos quejando** del calor, *etc.* ¿ De qué **se están quejando ellas?** — **Se están quejando** del calor, *etc.*

4. ¿ Cuándo **va a casarse ella?** — **Va a casarse** en agosto, *etc.* ¿ Cuándo **vas a casarte tú?** — **Voy a casarme** en agosto, *etc.* ¿ Cuándo **voy a casarme yo?** — **Vas a casarte** en agosto, *etc.* ¿ Cuándo **van a casarse ustedes?** — **Vamos a casarnos** en agosto, *etc.* ¿ Cuándo **van a casarse ellas?** — **Van a casarse** en agosto, *etc.*

5. ¿ Qué día **piensa irse ella?** — **Piensa irse** el dos de julio, *etc.* ¿ Qué día **piensas irte tú?** — **Pienso irme** el dos de julio, *etc.* ¿ Qué día **pienso irme yo?** — **Piensas irte** el dos de julio, *etc.* ¿ Qué día **piensan irse ustedes?** — **Pensamos irnos** el dos de julio, *etc.* ¿ Qué día **piensan irse ellas?** — **Piensan irse** el dos de julio, *etc.*

4. MORE REFLEXIVE VERBS.

A

1. **Yo no me acuerdo** del número. 2. **Yo me levanto** muy temprano. 3. **Yo no me he afeitado** hoy. 4. **Yo pienso casarme** pronto. 5. **Yo me fijo** en las señoritas. 6. **Yo me quejo** de todo. 7. **Yo tengo que apurarme.** 8. **Yo me defiendo** de las mujeres. 9. **Yo me estoy divirtiendo** mucho. 10. **Yo no me he bañado** todavía. 11. **Yo me acuesto** a las diez.

B

1. **Tú no te acuerdas** del número. **Usted no se acuerda** . . . **Mis hermanos y yo no nos acordamos** . . . 2. **Tú te levantas** muy temprano. **Usted se levanta** . . . **Mis hermanos y yo no nos levantamos** . . . 3. **Tú no te has afeitado** hoy. **Usted no se ha** . . . **Mis hermanos y yo no nos hemos** . . . 4. **Tú piensas casarte** pronto. **Usted piensa casarse** . . . **Mis hermanos y yo pensamos casarnos** . . . 5. **Tú te fijas** en las señoritas. **Usted se fija** . . . **Mis hermanos y yo nos fijamos** . . . 6. **Tú te quejas** de todo. **Usted se**

queja . . . **Mis hermanos y yo nos quejamos** . . .
7. **Tú tienes** que **apurarte. Usted** tiene que
apurarse. Mis hermanos y yo tenemos que
apurarnos. 8. **Tú te defiendes** de las mujeres.
Usted se defiende . . . **Mis hermanos y yo nos
defendemos** . . . 9. **Tú te estás** divirtiendo
mucho. **Usted se está** . . . **Mis hermanos y yo
nos estamos** . . . 10. **Tú no te has** bañado
todavía. **Usted no se ha** . . . **Mis hermanos y
yo no nos hemos** . . . 11. **Tú te acuestas** a las
diez. **Usted se acuesta** . . . **Mis hermanos y yo
nos acostamos** . . .

UNIT VIII

Pages 87–89

1. TWO VERB-OBJECT PRONOUNS TOGETHER.

A

1. No, no **me lo** quiere decir. 2. Sí, **me la** está
explicando. 3. Sí, **me las** ha presentado. 4. No,
no **me la** han enseñado. 5. Sí, van a dár**melos.**

B

1. No, no **me lo** quiere decir. 2. Sí, **me la**
está explicando. 3. Sí, **me las** ha presentado.
4. No, no **me la** han enseñado. 5. Sí, van a
dármelos.

C

1. No, no **se lo** quiere decir. 2. Sí, **se la** está
explicando. 3. Sí, **se las** ha presentado. 4. No,
no **se la** han enseñado. 5. Sí, van a dárselos.

D

1. No, no **nos lo** quiere decir. 2. Sí, **nos la**
está explicando. 3. Sí, **nos las** ha presentado.
4. No, no **nos la** han enseñado. 5. Sí, van a
dárnoslos.

E

1. No, no **se lo** quiere decir. 2. Sí, **se la** está
explicando. 3. Sí, **se las** ha presentado. 4. No,
no **se la** han enseñado. 5. Sí, van a dárselos.

2. SUPPLEMENTARY PRONOUNS.

1. mí 2. ti 3. él 4. ella 5. usted 6. nosotros 7. ellos 8. conmigo 9. contigo 10. consigo
11. consigo 12. consigo 13. consigo 14. mí; ti
OR usted; ustedes; él; ella; ellos OR ellas; nosotros
OR nosotras 15. conmigo; contigo OR con usted;
con ustedes; con él; con ella; con ellos OR ellas;
con nosotros OR nosotras 16. mí; ti OR usted;
usted; ustedes; él; ella; ellos OR ellas; nosotros
OR nosotras

3. SUPPLEMENTARY PRONOUNS IN VERBLESS EXPRESSIONS.

1. (a) Yo no. (b) Él no. (c) Ella no. (d) Nosotros no. (e) Ellos no. (f) Jaime no.

2. (a) ¿ Tú también ? (b) Yo también. (c) Ellos
también. (d) Nosotros también. (e) Él también.
(f) Ella también. (g) Yo no. (h) Luis también.

3. (a) ¿ Y usted ? (b) ¿ Usted tampoco ? (c) Ni
yo tampoco. (d) Ni ella tampoco. (e) Ni él
tampoco. (f) Ni nosotros tampoco. (g) Ni ellos
tampoco.

4. (a) Yo no. (b) Yo también. (c) Nosotros
también. (d) Pero tú no. (e) Ellos también.
(f) ¿ Y usted también ?

5. (a) Ni ella tampoco. (b) Pero ellos sí.
(c) Ni ella tampoco. (d) Pero yo sí. (e) Ni ellos
tampoco. (f) Pero ella sí. (g) Ni nosotros tampoco.
(h) Pero el sí. (i) Pero nosotros sí.

4. ASKING: pedir OR preguntar?

1. pregúntales 2. me pregunta 3. a preguntar
4. me pide 5. me piden 6. me preguntan
7. preguntémosle 8. preguntado 9. a pedírselo
10. me preguntes 11. pregunte 12. me pidas

UNIT IX

Pages 100–101

1. POSSESSIVE FORMS.

A

1. mi hermano; nuestro hermano; tu hermano; su hermano 2. mis hijos; nuestros hijos; tus hijos; sus hijos 3. mis padres; nuestros padres; tus padres; sus padres 4. mi país; nuestro país; tu país; su país 5. mi ropa; nuestra ropa; tu ropa; su ropa 6. mis sombreros; nuestros sombreros; tus sombreros; sus sombreros 7. mi tienda; nuestra tienda; tu tienda; su tienda 8. mis amigas; nuestras amigas; tus amigas; sus amigas 9. mi cama; nuestra cama; tu cama; su cama 10. mi clase; nuestra clase; tu clase; su clase. 11. mi lección; nuestra lección; tu lección; su lección 12. mi niño; nuestro niño; tu niño; su niño 13. mis vecinos; nuestros vecinos; tus vecinos; sus vecinos 14. mis hermanas; nuestras hermanas; tus hermanas; sus hermanas 15. mi compañero; nuestro compañero; tu compañero; su compañero 16. mis amigos; nuestros amigos; tus amigos; sus amigos 17. mis calcetines; nuestros calcetines; tus calcetines; sus calcetines 18. mis pies; nuestros pies; tus pies; sus pies 19. mi trabajo; nuestro trabajo; tu trabajo; su trabajo 20. mi papá; nuestro papá; tu papá; su papá 21. mi raqueta; nuestra raqueta; tu raqueta; su raqueta 22. mis abuelos; nuestros abuelos; tus abuelos; sus abuelos 23. mi apetito; nuestro apetito; tu apetito; su apetito 24. mi mamá; nuestra mamá; tu mamá; su mamá 25. mi coche; nuestro coche; tu coche; su coche 26. mi secretos; nuestros secretos; tus secretos; sus secretos 27. mis fotografías; nuestras fotografías; tus fotografías; sus fotografías 28. mi reloj; nuestro reloj; tu reloj; su reloj 29. mi salud; nuestra salud; tu salud; su salud 30. mis cartas; nuestras cartas; tus cartas; sus cartas 31. mi cuarto; nuestro cuarto; tu cuarto; su cuarto 32. mi regalo; nuestro regalo; tu regalo; su regalo 33. mi vida; nuestra vida; tu vida; su vida 34. mi novio; nuestro novio; tu novio; su novio 35. mis zapatos; nuestros zapatos; tus zapatos; sus zapatos 36. mis libros; nuestros libros; tus libros; sus libros 37. mi nombre; nuestro nombre; tu nombre; su nombre 38. mi pluma fuente; nuestra pluma fuente; tu pluma fuente; su pluma fuente 39. mi tierra; nuestra tierra; tu tierra; su tierra 40. mis viajes; nuestros viajes; tus viajes; sus viajes 41. mi cartera; nuestra cartera; tu cartera; su cartera 42. mis consejos; nuestros consejos; tus consejos; sus consejos 43. mis impresiones; nuestras impresiones; tus impresiones; sus impresiones 44. mis vestidos; nuestros vestidos; tus vestidos; sus vestidos 45. mis ojos; nuestros ojos; tus ojos; sus ojos

B

1. un hermano mío; este hermano nuestro; un hermano tuyo; ese hermano suyo 2. estos hijos míos; tres hijos nuestros; esos hijos tuyos; aquellos hijos suyos 3. estos padres míos; esos padres nuestros; esos padres tuyos; esos padres suyos 4. este país mío; este país nuestro; ese país tuyo; aquel país suyo 5. esta ropa mía; esta ropa nuestra; esa ropa tuya; aquella ropa suya 6. dos sombreros míos; estos sombreros nuestros; esos sombreros tuyos; muchos sombreros suyos 7. esta tienda mía; tres tiendas nuestras; esas tiendas tuyas; muchas tiendas suyas 8. unas amigas mías; tres amigos nuestros; muchas amigas tuyas; algunas amigas suyas 9. esta cama mía; esta cama nuestra; esa cama tuya; aquella cama suya 10. una clase mía; esta clase nuestra; alguna clase tuya; esa clase suya 11. esta lección mía; alguna lección nuestra; una lección tuya; otra lección suya 12. este niño mío; un niño nuestro; ese niño tuyo; ese niño suyo 13. unos vecinos míos;

algunos vecinos **nuestros**; tres vecinos **tuyos**; muchos vecinos **suyos** 14. tres hermanas **mías**; estas hermanas **nuestras**; esas hermanas **tuyas**; **cuántas** hermanas **suyas** 15. un compañero mío; un compañero **nuestro**; ese compañero **tuyo**; un compañero **suyo** 16. diez amigos **míos**; unos amigos **nuestros**; **cuántos** amigos **tuyos**; muchos amigos **suyos** 17. estos calcetines **míos**; algunos calcetines **nuestros**; **unos** calcetines **tuyos**; **aquellos** calcetines **suyos** 18. estos pies **míos**; estos pies **nuestros**; esos pies **tuyos**; esos pies **suyos** 19. mucho trabajo **mío**; **este** trabajo **nuestro**; **cuánto** trabajo **tuyo**; mucho trabajo **suyo** 20. ese papá **mío**; **este** papá **nuestro**; ese papá **tuyo**; ese papá **suyo** 21. esa raqueta mía; **esta** raqueta **nuestra**; **una** raqueta **tuya**; **una** raqueta **suya** 22. esos abuelos **míos**; esos abuelos **nuestros**; esos abuelos **tuyos**; esos abuelos **suyos** 23. este apetito **mío**; **este** apetito **nuestro**; ese apetito **tuyo**; ese apetito **suyo** 24. esta mamá **mía**; esa mamá **nuestra**; esa mamá **tuya**; esa mamá **suya** 25. este coche **mío**; un coche **nuestro**; un coche **tuyo**; ese coche **suyo** 26. muchos secretos **míos**; algunos secretos **nuestros**; esos secretos **tuyos**; **cuántos** secretos **suyos** 27. **unas** fotografías **mías**; muchas fotografías **nuestras**; cinco fotografías **tuyas**; esas fotografías **suyas** 28. este reloj **mío**; **este** reloj **nuestro**; ese reloj **tuyo**; un reloj **suyo** 29. esta salud **mía**; **esta** salud **nuestra**; esa salud **tuya**; esa salud **suya** 30. muchas cartas **mías**; algunas cartas **nuestras**; unas cartas **tuyas**; cuatro cartas **suyas** 31. este cuarto **mío**; **este** cuarto **nuestro**; ese cuarto **tuyo**; aquel cuarto **suyo** 32. ese regalo **mío**; un regalo **nuestro**; este regalo **tuyo**; otro regalo **suyo** 33. esta vida **mía**; **esta** vida **nuestra**; esa vida **tuya**; esa vida **suya** 34. este novio **mío**; ese novio **nuestro**; un novio **tuyo**; ese novio **suyo** 35. estos zapatos **míos**; esos zapatos **nuestros**; dos zapatos **tuyos**; **muchos** zapatos **suyos** 36. unos libros **míos**; muchos libros **nuestros**; esos libros **tuyos**; **cuántos** libros **suyos** 37. este nombre **mío**; este nombre **nuestro**; ese nombre **tuyo**; ese nombre **suyo** 38. **una** pluma fuente **mía**; **esta** pluma fuente **nuestra**; **otra** pluma fuente **tuya**; **una** pluma fuente **suya** 39. **esta** tierra **mía**; esa tierra **nuestra**; esa tierra **tuya**; **aquella** tierra **suya** 40. muchos viajes **míos**; algunos viajes **nuestros**; estos viajes **tuyos**; **cuántos** viajes **suyos** 41. una cartera **mía**; esta cartera **nuestra**; una cartera **tuya**; otra cartera **suya** 42. muchos consejos **míos**; algunos consejos **nuestros**; esos consejos **tuyos**; esos consejos **suyos** 43. algunas impresiones **mías**; estas impresiones **nuestras**; esas impresiones **tuyas**; muchas impresiones **suyas** 44. tres vestidos **míos**; estos vestidos **nuestros**; unos vestidos **tuyos**; muchos vestidos **suyos** 45. estos ojos **míos**; estos ojos **nuestros**; esos ojos **tuyos**; esos ojos **suyos**

C

1. mi hermano **y el tuyo**, *etc.* 2. **nuestros** hijos **y los suyos**, *etc.* 3. **tus** padres **o los míos**, *etc.* 4. **su** país **y el nuestro**, *etc.* 5. mi ropa **y la tuya**, *etc.* 6. **sus** sombreros **y los míos**, *etc.* 7. mi tienda **o la suya**, *etc.* 9. mi clase **o la suya**, *etc.* 11. **tu** lección **y la mía**, *etc.* 12. **su** niño **y el nuestro**, *etc.* 13. **nuestros** vecinos **y los tuyos**, *etc.* 14. **tus** hermanas **y las mías**, *etc.* 15. **tu** compañero **o el mío**, *etc.* 16. **nuestros** amigos **y los suyos**, *etc.* 17. **tus** calcetines **y los míos**, *etc.* 18. **mis** pies **y los suyos**, *etc.* 19. **nuestro** trabajo **y el tuyo**, *etc.* 20. **su** papá **o el nuestro**, *etc.* 21. **tu** raqueta **o la suya**, *etc.* 22. **sus** abuelos **y los nuestros**, *etc.* 23. mi apetito **y el tuyo**, *etc.* 24. **tu** mamá **o la nuestra**, *etc.* 25. **su** coche **o el nuestro**, *etc.* 26. **tus** secretos **y los míos**, *etc.* 27. **sus** fotografías **y las tuyas**, *etc.* 28. mi reloj **y el suyo**, *etc.* 29. **tu** salud **y la suya**, *etc.* 30. **nuestras** cartas **y las suyas**, *etc.* 31. mi cuarto **o el tuyo**, *etc.* 32. **tu** regalo **y el mío**, *etc.* 33. **tu** vida **o la mía**, *etc.* 34. mi novio **o el tuyo**, *etc.* 35. **sus** zapatos **y los tuyos**, *etc.* 36. **nuestros** libros **y los suyos**, *etc.* 37. mi nombre **y la suya**, *etc.* 38. **tu** pluma fuente **o la mía**, *etc.* 39. **tu** tierra **y la nuestra**, *etc.* 40. **mis** viajes **y los suyos**, *etc.* 41. **su** cartera **o la mía**, *etc.* 42. **nuestros** consejos **o los suyos**, *etc.* 43. **tus**

impresiones **y las mías,** *etc.* 44. **mis** vestidos **y los suyos,** *etc.* 45. **tus** ojos **y los míos,** *etc.*

2. NON-USE OF POSSESSIVES.

1. Luis no **se** ha puesto **la** corbata. 2. Paquito, no **me** rompas **el** roloj. 3. ¿ Por qué **te** quitas **los** zapatos? 4. ¿ Dónde has puesto **la** pluma?

5. ¿ No puede usted encontrar **el** sombrero? 6. Mis hermanos siempre **me** piden prestada **la** ropa. 7. ¡ No **se** ponga usted **el** sombrero! 8. Ven acá, Juanito; quiero ponerte **los** zapatos nuevos. 9. ¡ **Nos** han quitado **las** fotografías! 10. ¡ Quítate **el** sombrero, hombre! 11. ¿ Por qué no usa Ricardo **la** corbata nueva? 12. Cierra **los** ojos.

UNIT X

Pages 102–109

REVIEW OF UNIT 6: **Writing Spanish.**

1. Vamos a ver al abuelo. 2. Vaya usted a la derecha; no vaya a la izquierda. 3. Ten cuidado, y no seas tonto. 4. Entremos en esa tienda. 5. Vuelva usted acá dentro de cuarenta y cinco minutos. 6. No se vayan, señores. 7. ¡ No hables tan alto! 8. No hablemos de esas cosas serias. 9. Salgamos a celebrar tu cumpleaños. 10. No pongas las fotografías allí. 11. Oye ¿ qué hora es? 12. Por fortuna no tengo reloj. 13. ¿ Tú vas a comer con Gloria? ¡ No hay derecho! 14. Ya hemos aprendido eso. ¿ Qué sigue? 15. No vengas tarde; ven a las cuatro y cuarto. 16. Es mi prima, no olvidemos eso. 17. No te levantes mañana a las once; levántate a las ocho y media. 18. Vamos juntos a la clase. 19. ¿ En qué estás pensando? 20. Estoy pensando en el invierno, el frío, y la nieve. 21. ¿ Vas a conocer a la prima de Jaime esta noche? 22. ¿ Cómo es la prima de Jaime? — Es un encanto. 23. ¿ Usted nunca ha estado en México? 24. ¿ Vive aquí Gloria? — No, sólo está de visita. 25. ¿ Dónde vive entonces, en Búfalo? 26. Quiero presentar a mis amigos de Puerto Rico. 27. Lo siento mucho, señora, pero ya es tarde. 28. ¿ Tiene setenta y cinco años? ¡ No me diga! 29. Hay sesenta minutos en una hora, y veinticuatro horas en un día. 30. ¿ Están bien de salud sus padres? 31. Mi abuela es joven; sólo tiene sesenta y seis años. 32. ¿ Puede usted esperar un cuarto de hora? 33. ¿ Está en casa Mario? — No, está dando una vuelta. 34. Es la

una, ¿ verdad? — No, son las dos y veinte. 35. La casa está a la izquierda, creo.

REVIEW OF UNIT 7: **Writing Spanish.**

1. ¿ Qué le pasa al amigo Carlos? 2. ¿ Para quién es el regalo que vas a comprar? 3. ¿ Es alta y rubia la chica Costales? 4. No me han invitado a la fiesta todavía. 5. ¿ Con quién va a casarse Pablo? — No sé. 6. Poco a poco nos vamos casando todos. 7. ¿ Usted se levanta a las diez? ¡ Qué vida! 8. Pregúntale a Juana a dónde va. 9. Diles dónde vivo yo. 10. Nos acostamos temprano todos los días. 11. ¿ Qué va a pasar el doce de julio? 12. ¿ Qué te pasa? 13. Nada de serio. Me voy a casar el primero de agosto. 14. ¡ Hombre, eso es muy serio! 15. Mañana es día de fiesta, ¿ no te acuerdas? 16. ¿ Por qué tienes que afeitarte primero? 17. A propósito, ¿ los has llamado por teléfono? 18. ¿ Los conoce usted? — Creo que no. 19. ¿ Todavía no ha llegado María? — No, estoy esperándola ahora. 20. Tengo que escribir una carta y no puedo escribirla. 21. ¡ Apúrate, hombre! No puedo esperar todo el día. 22. ¿ No tienes nada que hacer? 23. Sí, pero no quiero hacerlo. 24. ¿ Dónde está Pedro? ¿ Lo ha visto usted? 25. Yo nunca lo veo en estos días. 26. No me gusta pensar en todo el trabajo que tengo que hacer. 27. Entonces ¿ por qué no lo haces? 28. A veces lo hago. ¿ No te has fijado? 29. ¿ De qué se están quejando esos niños? 30. Necesitamos más tiempo para divertirnos.

REVIEW OF UNIT 8: **Writing Spanish.**

1. Para nosotros no hay nada como el clima del sur. 2. Estoy de acuerdo con ustedes. A mí no me gusta la nieve. 3. La primavera y el verano son las estaciones ideales. 4. El invierno también — el invierno de Florida. 5. José dice que no se siente muy fuerte hoy. 6. Jaime es una buena persona, pero siempre habla tonterías. 7. Acuérdese de lo que dice Ricardo. 8. No puedo explicarlo. — Ni yo tampoco. 9. Parece que hacen eso a propósito. 10. ¿ Qué nombre lleva la pluma ? 11. ¿ De qué país son los Carmona ? 12. ¿ Conoces a Pablo Aguilar ? — No tengo el gusto, ni quiero tenerlo. 13. No vuelvo a pedirle el coche. 14. ¿ O'Higgins un nombre chileno ? ¡ No puede ser ! 15. ¿ Hay muchos chilenos en este país ? 16. A mí me parece muy gracioso. 17. ¿ Dónde están las fotografías ? — Búscalas por allí. 18. Los nombres extranjeros parecen raros. 19. ¿ Es lo mismo para usted que para mí ? 20. Vamos a hacer un viaje por el trópico. 21. Está casada con un escocés. 22. Uno de estos días voy a hacer un viaje. 23. A propósito, ¿ son de Irlanda los padres de usted ? 24. ¿ Por qué me pregunta usted eso ? 25. Ésta es la última vez que te lo presto. 26. Dicen que la gente del trópico vive muy feliz. 27. ¿ Usted dice que el trabajo es bueno para la salud ? ¡ Tonterías ! 28. ¿ Por qué te quejas de todo ? 29. Conmigo pasa todo lo contrario. 30. ¿ Por que se queda usted en el sur ? 31. Éste es el último verano que paso aquí. 32. Cada vez que le presto algo, se lo lleva consigo. 33. ¿ Qué quiere decir esto ? — No quiere decir nada. 34. Las fotografías están debajo de unos libros. 35. No se las voy a enseñar.

REVIEW OF UNIT 9: **Writing Spanish.**

1. Se está acercando el invierno. 2. Ya no podemos estudiar al aire libre. 3. Cuando no hace buen tiempo, me encierro con un libro. 4. Entra mucha luz en este cuarto. 5. Primero hago mi trabajo, y después me divierto. 6. Eres admirable. Conmigo pasa todo lo contrario. 7. Cada vez que estudio en este cuarto oscuro, siento deseos de dormir. 8. ¡ Claro ! ¿ Qué más esperas ? 9. Creo que el cuarto de Jaime está en el tercer piso. 10. Su cuarto es pequeño, pero está muy limpio. 11. Hasta cierto punto tú tienes la culpa. 12. Hoy hace sol, gracias a Dios. 13. Las clases empiezan el mes que viene, pero no sé qué día. 14. Yo pienso salir de aquí en seguida. ¿ Y tú ? 15. Yo voy a salir volando. 16. No me voy a quedar ni un minuto más. 17. Aquí todo el mundo usa zapatos blancos, hasta en el invierno. 18. A los extranjeros les parece muy raro. 19. Pienso ir a México a principios del mes que viene. 20. ¿ Has visto que hay tres corbatas tuyas aquí ? 21. No tengo cabeza para pensar en detalles. 22. ¿ De quién es esa raqueta de tenis que está detrás de la puerta ? 23. Debe ser de Enrique. Quitémosla de allí. 24. ¿ Te has fijado en sus ojos ? 25. Es imposible no fijarse en ellos. 26. ¿ Me pongo el vestido negro o el azul ? — Ponte el blanco. 27. Me quito la corbata cuando hace calor. 28. Entonces ¿ por qué no te quitas el sombrero también ? 29. ¿ Con quién salgo ? ¡ Es un gran secreto ! 30. ¿ No quieres hacerle una buena impresión al profesor ? 31. Déme usted un consejo, ¿ quiere ? 32. Siempre me cuesta trabajo desocupar un cuarto. 33. Te los devuelvo mañana. 34. De todos modos no va a ser fácil. 35. Creo que lo mejor es quedarse aquí.

UNIT XI
Pages 122-123

1. PRETERITE PAST TENSE.

A

1. me llamaron 2. fué 3. tomaste 4. nos equivocamos 5. aprendimos 6. compró 7. descansaron 8. me ayudó 9. comieron 10. le dió 11. estudiaste 12. imitamos 13. se levantó 14. terminé 15. conocí 16. durmió 17. dormí 18. empecé 19. entendió 20. te esperamos 21. fueron 22. llegué 23. le pedí 24. trató 25. oyó 26. me acordé 27. volvieron 28. me acompañó 29. olvidaste 30. se afeitó 31. cerró 32. nos divertimos 33. me pidió 34. leyeron 35. se divirtieron 36. escribiste 37. se fijó 38. se quejó 39. busqué 40. explicó 41. me acerqué 42. le devolviste 43. se encerró 44. me vestí 45. prefirió 46. me creyó 47. se vistieron 48. se casaron 49. fueron 50. salimos

B

1. ¿A quién **invitó** usted a la fiesta? — **Invité** a mi novia. 2. ¿A qué hora te **acostaste** anoche? — **Me acosté** a las once y media. 3. ¿Cuándo te **bañaste** la última vez? — **Me bañé** ayer. 4. ¿Dónde **encontró** usted el libro por fin? — **Lo encontré** en mi cuarto. 5. ¿Le **enseñó** usted las fotografías a Luisa? — Sí, **se las enseñé.** 6. ¿Qué te **preguntó** esa señorita? — **Me preguntó** la hora. 7. ¿Qué le **prestó** usted a su amigo? — **Le presté** mi reloj. 8. ¿Cuánto tiempo **se quedaron** ustedes en California? — **Nos quedamos** ocho meses. 9. ¿Quién **se rompió** la cabeza? — No sé quién se rompió la cabeza. 10. ¿Por qué **se enojó** usted? — **Me enojé** porque no me invitaron a la fiesta. 11. ¿Qué clase de corbata **escogiste** tú? — **Escogí** una azul. 12. ¿**Te ofendiste** porque no te llamé por teléfono? — No, no **me ofendí.** 13. ¿**Te quitaste** el sombrero antes de entrar? — No, **me lo quité** después. 14. ¿**Costaron** mucho esos zapatos tuyos? — Sí, **costaron** diez setenta y cinco. 15. ¿En qué parte del país **creció** usted? — Yo **crecí** en el sur. 16. ¿Dónde **compró** usted su coche? — **Lo compré** en Los Ángeles. 17. ¿En qué año **descubrieron** la América? — **La descubrieron** en mil cuatrocientos noventa y dos. 18. ¿Quiénes **se pelearon** y por qué? — **Se pelearon** Luis y Miguel, pero no sé por qué.

2. YEAR-DATES.

1776	mil setecientos setenta y seis
1812	mil ochocientos doce
1238	mil doscientos treinta y ocho
1914	mil novecientos catorce
1866	mil ochocientos sesenta y seis
1085	mil ochenta y cinco
1588	mil quinientos ochenta y ocho
1948	mil novecientos cuarenta y ocho
1620	mil seiscientos veinte
1319	mil trescientos diecinueve
1478	mil cuatrocientos setenta y ocho
1939	mil novecientos treinta y nueve
1193	mil ciento noventa y tres
1850	mil ochocientos cincuenta
1727	mil setecientos veintisiete
1945	mil novecientos cuarenta y cinco

UNIT XII
Pages 131-132

1. PRETERITE PAST TENSE OF ROOT-CHANGING VERBS.

1. dijeron 2. lo supe 3. hicieron 4. trajo 5. estuvieron 6. tuvo 7. quiso 8. estuvo 9. le dijo 10. pudo 11. quiso; lo hizo 12. tuviste 13. pudo 14. vinieron 15. puso 16. me trajiste 17. lo supimos 18. vine 19. estuviste 20. tuvimo

UNIT XIII
Pages 143–144

1. THE IMPERFECT PAST.

A

1. buscaba 2. tenía 3. se llamaba 4. estaba
5. era 6. decía 7. querías 8. me gustaba 9. iba
10. te veía 11. era 12. había

B

1. Antes mi hermano y yo **estudiábamos** juntos.
2. Antes mi hermano y yo **nos levantábamos**
temprano. 3. Antes mi hermano y yo **llegábamos**
a tiempo. 4. Antes mi hermano y yo **entendíamos**
inglés. 5. Antes mi hermano y yo **trabajábamos**
juntos pero ya no. 6. Antes mi hermano y yo
comíamos a las doce. 7. Antes mi hermano y yo
nos acostábamos tarde. 8. Antes mi hermano y
yo **vivíamos** en Búfalo.

C

1. Tú **usabas** ese sombrero todos los días,
¿verdad? 2. Tú **venías** a mi casa, *etc.* 3. Tú
escuchabas el radio, *etc.* 4. Tú lo **olvidabas**, *etc.*
5. Tú **volvías** a casa, *etc.* 6. Tú me **acompañabas**,
etc. 7. Tú nunca **te acordabas** de hacerlo, *etc.*
8. Tú **te afeitabas**, *etc.* 9. Tú **tenías** clase, *etc.*
10. Tú **ibas** a verla, *etc.*

2. IMPERFECT PAST: PROGRESSIVE PHRASES.

1. ¿Qué **estabas mirando** cuando te ví? 2. ¿A
quién **estabas buscando**, *etc.*? 3. ¿Por qué te
estabas peleando, *etc.*? 4. ¿Qué **estabas diciendo**,
etc.? 5. ¿A quién **estabas llamando**, *etc.*? 6. ¿A
quién **estabas siguiendo**, *etc.*? 7. ¿De qué te
estabas riendo, *etc.*? 8. ¿Qué **estabas tratando**
de hacer, *etc.*? 9. ¿Qué **estabas escuchando**,
etc.? 10. ¿A quién **estabas esperando**, *etc.*?
11. ¿Qué **estabas escribiendo**, *etc.*? 12. ¿De qué
te **estabas quejando**, *etc.*?

3. IMPERFECT PAST: COMPLETIVE PHRASES.

1. Yo no **lo había aprendido** todavía. 2. Yo no
la había visto todavía. 3. Yo no **lo había entendido**
todavía. 4. Yo no **se lo había pedido** todavía.
5. Yo no **se lo había preguntado** todavía. 6. Yo no
había oído nada todavía. 7. Yo no **había nadado**
aquí todavía. 8. Yo no **los había comprado**
todavía. 9. Yo no **había hecho** nada todavía.
10. Yo no **había trabajado** allí todavía. 11. Yo no
las había conocido todavía. 12. Yo no **se lo había**
explicado todavía. 13. Yo no **había leído** el libro
todavía. 14. Yo no **había escrito** la carta todavía.

4. IMPERFECT OR PRETERITE PAST?

1. vinieron 2. me aburría 3. me compró
4. éramos 5. llegó 6. fué; era 7. iban 8. me
desperté 9. sabía 10. era; ponía; decía 11. era;
vino 12. vió 13. me lastimaban; eran 14. escuchábamos 15. habíamos; teníamos 16. me perdonó 17. se ofendió 18. se quitó 19. salía
20. estábamos

UNIT XIV
Pages 154–155

1. PASSIVE PHRASES.

1. El libro fué escrito por un autor conocido.
2. Las medicinas son preparadas por el farmacéutico. 3. Los diálogos son pronunciados y
aprendidos fácilmente por los estudiantes. 4. El
hombre fué perdonado después de dos días. 5. El
país va a ser dividido en cuatro partes. 6. La
mujer fué matada por una persona conocida.
7. El trabajo fué empezado hace cinco años.
8. El niño fué encontrado por un vecino. 9. El
trabajo fué terminado en 1947. 10. Todo esto ha
sido traído por mis amigos.

2. REFLEXIVE VERBS.

1. se pronuncia 2. se explican 3. se dice 4. se habla 5. se abre 6. se dice 7. se pueden 8. se puede 9. se venden 10. se encuentran 11. se usan 12. se celebra 13. se hace 14. se sirven 15. se oye

3. DAYS OF THE WEEK.

1. El martes (*etc.*) fuí al centro. 2. Yo no trabajo los miércoles (*etc.*). 3. Mañana es jueves (*etc.*). 4. Llega aquí el viernes (*etc.*) próximo. 5. El sábado (*etc.*) es día de fiesta. 6. El domingo (*etc.*) pasado llovió. 7. Ayer fué lunes (*etc.*). 8. Los vemos todos los martes (*etc.*).

4. NEGATIVE WORDS.

1. **No** hay **nadie** en el cuarto. 2. No, mamá, yo **no** tengo **nada** en el bolsillo. 3. ¿ De dónde vienes tú ? — **No** vengo de **ninguna** parte. 4. ¿ Ese señor **nunca** llegó a tiempo ? 5. No, él **no** llega **nunca** a tiempo. 6. Mi novia **no** me ofreció **ninguna** explicación. 7. **Nadie** vino a la clase esta mañana. 8. ¿ **No** hay **ninguna** diferencia entre las dos palabras ? 9. No, gracias, **no** quiero tomar **nada** ahora. 10. **Ninguna** película me ha gustado tanto como ésa. 11. Roberto **no** quiere ir, **ni** yo **tampoco**. 12. **No** conozco a **nadie** en este pueblo. 13. ¿ **Nunca** ha estado usted en la América Latina ? 14. **No** tengo **ni** hermanos **ni** hermanas. 15. A **nadie** le gusta comer tanto como a Jorge.

UNIT XV

Pages 157–164

REVIEW OF UNIT 11: **Writing Spanish.**

1. ¿ Dónde encontraste a tu amigo ? 2. ¿ Con quién saliste ayer por la tarde ? 3. Creo que me equivoqué ayer. 4. Roberto y Jorge crecieron juntos, ¿ verdad ? 5. Ayer alguien se llevó un libro de mi cuarto. 6. Siempre me equivoco cuando tengo que dar fechas. 7. ¿ Te enojaste cuando ella dijo eso ? 8. Claro que me enojé, y nos peleamos. 9. ¿ En qué año vinieron sus padres a los Estados Unidos ? 10. Paco está de mal humor; tiene dolor de cabeza. 11. Creo que está preocupado por algo. 12. No, él nunca se preocupa por nada. 13. Las muchachas siempre me dicen que están muy ocupadas. 14. ¿ La invitaste a ir a la playa ? 15. Parece que siempre tengo mala suerte. 16. Entró en la casa sin decir nada. 17. Se portó muy bien esta vez. ¿ Lo puedes creer ? 18. No me dieron ninguna explicación. 19. Todavía estoy aprendiendo la lección pasada. 20. ¿ De modo que prefieres aceptar la invitación de otro ? — Pues ¡ acéptala ! 21. Está en el hospital, pero no está muy enfermo. 22. No vuelvo a poner pie en esa casa. 23. ¿ No te gustan mis críticas ? 24. Es mejor no pensar en eso. 25. ¿ Cuántas páginas leíste anoche ? 26. Le doscientas veinticinco páginas. 27. ¿ Qué pasó en mil quinientos cincuenta ? 28. Dicen que ese hombre tiene cien años. 29. ¿ En qué año descubrieron la Florida ? 30. Hay trescientos sesenta y cinco días en un año. 31. Anoche soñé contigo. 32. Pablo cree que va a llover esta tarde. 33. A mí me parece que no. 34. ¡ Te felicito ! Llegaste a tiempo. 35. ¿ Puedo ofrecerle algo ?

REVIEW OF UNIT 12: **Writing Spanish.**

1. Esa palabra no se usa mucho. 2. ¿ De qué se ríe esa gente ? 3. Creo que se ríen de nosotros. 4. ¿ Hay tantos indios aquí como en México ? 5. ¿ Dónde aprendió usted a nadar ? 6. Yo no sé nadar; a mí me parece peligroso. 7. Así parece; pero le aseguro que no es ni peligroso ni difícil. 8. ¿ Son incas los indios del Perú ? 9. Varios países tienen más de cien mil indios. 10. Yo tengo un poco de sangre española. 11. Perdóneme, señor. ¿ De qué país es usted ? 12. Lima está en el Perú, ¿ verdad ? 13. Sólo las mujeres usan esa expresión. 14. Me gusta oírte hablar español; me hace gracia. 15. ¿ Por qué siempre imita usted al profesor en

todo? 16. Lo imito porque quiero aprender las expresiones que usa. 17. El profesor conoce a fondo el idioma inglés. 18. ¿Cómo adivinaste eso? 19. Decidió hacerme algunas preguntas. 20. Tengo interés en saber qué le preguntó. 21. A ver. ¿Cuáles fueron las preguntas? 22. Estuve muy ocupado ayer. 23. Tengo que contestar a las preguntas siguientes. 24. ¿Dónde puse el traje? 25. Ése es un chiste viejo en inglés también. 26. No tuvieron tiempo para comer. 27. ¿Por qué no trajiste a tu hermana? 28. ¿Qué te dijo la señora Rojas? 29. Sólo quedan diez minutos. 30. Sus amigos no quisieron esperar.

REVIEW OF UNIT 13: **Writing Spanish.**

1. No sabía que estabas en casa. 2. ¿A dónde ibas ayer cuando te vimos? 3. Los vieron hace dos semanas. 4. Los niños hacían mucho ruido. 5. ¿Qué estás mirando? 6. No estoy mirando nada. Estoy buscando la biblioteca. 7. Cierra la puerta, ¿quieres? — Ya está cerrada. 8. Entonces hazme el favor de no abrirla. 9. Hay muchas tiendas modernas en la calle principal, ¿verdad? 10. ¿Qué clase de acento tiene usted en español? 11. Tengo el mejor acento posible. 12. No le dejes comprar nada. 13. Se quedaron afuera a mirar a la gente. 14. Eran muy bonitos los vestidos que estaban en el escaparate. 15. ¿No le gustan los zapatos de tacón alto? — Sí, pero no los uso todo el tiempo. 16. No sabía a qué hora salía usted del trabajo. 17. Ayúdame a buscar mi pluma. 18. ¿De qué color eran los sombreros? 19. No me acuerdo de qué color eran. 20. ¿No quiere usted probarse los zapatos para ver si le entran? 21. ¿Qué número de zapato dijo usted que usaba? — Cuatro y medio. 22. ¿No es difícil encontrar zapatos de ese número? — Sí, a veces. 23. ¿En qué calle está la biblioteca? 24. No necesitaba esas cosas que compré. 25. Sin duda no pudiste resistir al precio. 26. Estaba durmiendo, pero mi vecino me despertó. 27. Nunca me había dormido en la clase. 28. ¿Qué decías? No escuchaba. 29. Ten los ojos abiertos, y pon atención a lo que te digo. 30. Estoy aburrido. Vamos a salir. 31. Lo siento, pero no quiero hacer nada ahora. 32. Una voz monótona da sueño, ¿verdad?

REVIEW OF UNIT 14: **Writing Spanish.**

1. No hay nadie tan interesante como él. 2. ¿Qué tiene de interesante? 3. Lo único que hace falta aquí es un periódico. 4. Los sándwiches de jamón me dan sed. 5. Hay una gran diferencia entre el español y el inglés. 6. ¿Cómo se gana la vida esa gente? 7. ¿Le gustan los dulces? — Entonces ponga éstos en el bolsillo. 8. Es inútil explicarle nada. 9. Yo nunca le doy consejos a nadie. 10. ¿Vamos a la playa el sábado por la tarde? 11. ¿Son baratos los libros en su país? 12. ¿Por quién fué escrito ese libro? 13. Siempre estudio mi lección de español en voz alta. 14. Ese pobre hombre habla solo todo el día. 15. ¿Crees que está loco? 16. No se puede negar que esta vida tiene algunas ventajas. 17. Hoy se trata de los días de la semana. 18. No se vende ropa en esa tienda. 19. No podemos verlos antes de mañana por la tarde. 20. ¿Cómo se dice eso en español? 21. ¡Me matan estos zapatos nuevos! 22. ¿De veras? Entonces ¿por qué no te los quitas? 23. En general me quedo en casa los domingos. 24. ¿Qué piensas hacer el martes próximo? 25. Lo mismo que hice el martes pasado: nada. 26. ¿Fuiste a misa el domingo pasado? 27. Anteayer fué miércoles, y ayer fué jueves. 28. De modo que hoy es viernes, ¿verdad? 29. Tienes razón. Me equivoqué. 30. Va a casa cada dos semanas.